boy

One child's fight to survive in
the brutal British care system

NIGEL COOPER

EBURY
PRESS

5 7 9 10 8 6 4

Ebury Press, an imprint of Ebury Publishing
20 Vauxhall Bridge Road
London SW1V 2SA

Ebury Press is part of the Penguin Random House group of companies
whose addresses can be found at global.penguinrandomhouse.com

Copyright © Nigel Cooper 2015

Nigel Cooper has asserted his right to be identified as the author of this
Work in accordance with the Copyright, Designs and Patents Act 1988

First published by Ebury Press in 2015

www.eburypublishing.co.uk

A CIP catalogue record for this book is available from the British Library

ISBN 9781785030789

Printed in Great Britain by Clays Ltd, St Ives plc

Penguin Random House is committed to a sustainable future for our
business, our readers and our planet. This book is made from Forest
Stewardship Council® certified paper.

For Mary – RIP

*'I am not what happened to me, I am what
I choose to become.' Carl Gustav Jung*

*'There is no greater agony than bearing
an untold story inside you.' Maya Angelou*

This book is a work of non-fiction based on the life, experiences and recollections of Nigel Cooper. Some names and descriptions of people, places, dates and sequences of the detail of events have been changed to protect the privacy of others, including staff and pupils.

Contents

1. The Blackbird & The Witch   3

2. The Blue Doll & The Greenhouse Effect   8

3. They're Coming to Take Me Away, Ha-Haaa!   16

4. Electrodes, Tests & Drugs   23

5. The Piano That Never Was   36

6. Under-Age Sex   44

7. Bohemian Rhapsody & My Chair On The Moon   54

8. Outcast   65

9. The Sharp Pencil & Grange-over-Mud   75

10. Regression Therapy   84

11. Rattus Norvegicus   97

12. The Burglary   105

13. Perry, The Liverpool Supporter   113

14. Kleptomania   119

15. The Magistrates   135

16. Near-Death Experience & Runaway Puppy Love   146

17. The Suicide Attempt   158

18. The Peregrine Falcon   169

19. From Code Red to Code Yellow   178

20. Welcome to Dracula's Castle   189

21. Let the (Evil) Games Commence   200

22. London, Here I Come   211

23. Psycho Boy   221

24. Psycho Boy, Part II   230

25. The Evil Boiler Room   241

26. Et Tu, Hugh!   249

27. The Selfish Giant   261

28. Welcome to Hell   273

29. Fight Club   286

30. And So The Bullying Ceased   306

31. Home on Trial   316

32. Goodbye, Sister Moon   320

Acknowledgements   325

Author Biography   326

My parents had to try for 18 months to conceive me, but my father was adamant he wanted one last child. Already I had a brother, Anthony, five years old, and a sister, Lynda, two years old, but my father wanted another boy. After 18 months of trying, my mother eventually conceived and nine months later I was born. My birth was a difficult one.

It was like I was never meant to be in this world.

Chapter 1

The Blackbird & The Witch

I stood next to my older brother and watched as he drew on his catapult, taking aim at an unsuspecting blackbird on the roof of our three-bedroom end-of-terrace council house. He let rip and I quickly turned my head to the left and watched as a small stone whizzed through the air, narrowly missing the startled bird, which flew off, leaving a few loud chirrups in its wake.

After witnessing my brother's failed attempt to kill a bird with his homemade elasticated weapon, I decided that I would try to physically capture one instead. I figured the best way to do this would be to lay a mousetrap, loaded with bread, on the roof of the concrete coal shed adjoining our house. Getting my hands on one was easy – we lived next door to a farm, which meant lots of rodents. I simply took one of the existing mousetraps from inside our coal shed. After grabbing a slice of bread from the kitchen, I climbed up onto the roof, where I carefully pulled back the spring-loaded trap, set it and delicately laid a small piece of bread in the required position. I climbed down from the roof, went to our front garden and waited patiently.

But I didn't have long to wait. After just a few minutes I saw a blackbird land on the roof. What happened next will stay with me for the rest of my life. Although the trap and the bird were not in my direct line of vision due to the height of the roof, the horrific sounds emanating from it told me my plan had worked. The poor blackbird screeched so loudly the noise penetrated my eardrums. Horrified, I stood there, frozen to the spot.

Mortified, I ran inside and screamed for my mum to come and help the bird. Reluctantly, she tore herself away from the kitchen sink and climbed up onto the roof, where the creature was chirruping away frantically. Now that I was on the roof too, the sounds were even more deafening and I could see the full horror of what I had just done. Both the bird's legs were caught under the metal spring-loaded bar of the mousetrap. Its wings thrashed as it tried desperately to free itself. Mum went over and gently pulled back the spring bar to release the bird. To my relief it stopped screeching, hopped a few steps across the roof and then took to the air. As she clambered down from the roof Mum assured me the bird was fine, leaving me to have a long, hard think about the shockingly cruel act that I had just committed.

I was disgusted with myself. The poor bird's deafening screeches still rang in my head; screeches that would never go away, that I would still be hearing more than 40 years later. As I stood there, traumatised, on the roof that day, I told myself two things. First, from that day forth I would become not only a bird lover, but an animal lover too. If it were within my power, I would do whatever I could to see to it that no harm came to them. Instead of putting out traps for birds, I'd put out food and water. Later, I would join what was known back then as the YOC (Young Ornithologists' Club) and would make protecting birds a part of my life. Second, I told myself that I deserved to be punished for the terrible thing I'd just done. And punished I would be, though not quite yet. Little did I know my punishment was on its way, and when it got to me it would arrive with a vengeance. It would take me and engulf me in a dark chasm that I would not be able to climb out of for eight consecutive years. Eight whole years of absolute horror, brutal violence, physical, mental and sexual abuse, and those years would be relentless with no let up, not for a second.

But first, I had another nightmare to contend with, one that would involve a dead female teacher from my primary school up the road.

I have no idea why I started to have this terrifying recurring nightmare but my mum was always convinced that our house in Coniston, in the heart of the Lake District, was haunted. With hindsight, I'm inclined to agree with her. I would have this dream once a week, sometimes twice, and it continued for about three years until I was eventually removed, by force, from my house by a rather large man, of which more later.

I was five years old and in a difficult place in my head. My older sister, Lynda, had died two years earlier from leukaemia at the tender age of five. She was sitting at the kitchen table, quietly drawing, when Mum and her sister, Elizabeth, noticed a large, elongated bruise appear across her forehead. Aunty Elizabeth knew instantly what it was.

According to Mum, my sister's death affected me badly, more than anyone else in the family. As such, my behaviour changed for the worse. They brought Lynda's body home from hospital and she was kept in her little coffin in the spare room on the ground floor. Still too young to pronounce her name properly, I would keep sneaking in and shaking the coffin, shouting, 'Dynda, Dynda, wake up!' Mum tried everything to keep me out of the room, but I was determined to get in. Later, a social worker would say that I had become seriously 'disturbed' because of Lynda's death. Indeed, the loss hit me hard and it would change the course of my life forever. I was nearly three years old at the time. Perhaps this kick-started my recurring nightmare, or maybe Lynda's death made me more receptive to the ghosts and spirits that possessed our house – who knows? All I know is this nightmare was incredibly vivid and absolutely terrifying.

Eventually I'd fall asleep after reading my beloved train magazines (or at least looking at the nice glossy colour photos, after all, they were magazines for train-enthusiast adults) and then at some point during the early hours, the witch would come for me. In my dream I'd wake up, but I hadn't actually woken up. I'd get out of bed and walk over to the bedroom window. From my elevated first-floor vantage point I would look beyond our small front garden to the main road that ran past the front of the house. On the road I'd see a yellow JCB with an elongated trench that it had recently dug. The trench was about 10 x 3 feet wide and 6 feet deep. At the other end of it was a large black lorry, its rear metal roller shutter open. Because of the angle, I could not see into the back of the lorry but there was something quite menacing about it, malevolent even. It gave me the creeps as I stood there, looking through the chink I'd created in the curtains. I don't know if I had hairs on the back of my neck in those days, but I would feel something creep over my spine and neck like a cold, evil spirit.

Then I saw her. My angle of vision would change and now I was having an out-of-body experience as I hovered above the road, looking down into the deep trench. Lying neatly across the bottom of it was a naked woman, around 30 years old. Her skin was pale white, like a porcelain doll. Her eyes were closed and she had jet-black, shoulder-length hair. I don't know how I knew, but something told me that this young woman was a schoolteacher, possibly from my primary school. The image was so vivid, I could see the goose pimples on her breasts. Further down I could see her pubic bone and accompanying bush. The strange thing was, this was the first time I'd seen a naked woman. Prior to my nightmare I'd never seen anybody naked, not on television, nor in a catalogue, not even my own mum. I had no point of reference from which to draw these images, no idea what female body parts looked like. Yet here was a perfectly formed naked young woman, albeit a dead one, in my nightmare.

Then I would be back in my bedroom, peering out through the gap in the curtains again. A large cement mixer lorry had moved into position. Motors sounded as the hydraulics tipped the cement from the cylindrical section of the truck upwards, higher, more vertical, until the cement started to pour, thick and fast, filling the woman's grave in the road.

An invisible rat scurrying up my back would make my spine shiver. I would stand there and shudder involuntarily, shaking it off. Something sinister was lurking, inside and out. I would look across to my left at the black lorry, where a witch in a long, black dress had appeared; she was leaning out the back. She would stare straight at me, our eyes would lock but I could not look away – she'd seen me and she knew exactly where to come to get me. I dared not look away, not even to blink. In her left hand she held a black, leather-bound book. Then, she would slowly lift her right arm, which was thin and pale, and point a long, bony finger towards me. Her mouth opened as she uttered the words to me, but they did not come from down on the street, somehow the witch managed to project them directly into my head telepathically.

To this day, I still cannot bring myself to type the words she spoke to me.

I'd wake up sweating, my breathing erratic. Then I'd scream for my mum, but she never came.

Chapter 2

The Blue Doll &
The Greenhouse Effect

Things were a little different in the early 1970s – more so in the heart of the Lake District in Cumbria, where I lived. Children weren't mollycoddled back then. When I was five years old my mum would tell me to get out of the house and play up on the green so I wasn't under her feet. I especially remember playing with the other kids from the neighbouring streets during the cold nights of November and December. Hide and Seek or Tag were the games of choice for young scallywags from deprived backgrounds, sometimes with a bit of scrumping thrown in.

To say I didn't get much attention as a child would be an understatement. I guess my parents had enough on their plates with my older sister. Lynda was diagnosed with leukaemia when she was two and a half years old, about a year and a half before I was born. By the time I arrived Mum and Dad were spending a lot of time going back and forth between our house in Coniston and the Children's Hospital in Manchester, quite often staying at the hospital overnight. I guess everyone was suffering. Poor Lynda was suffering in hospital, while I was suffering from maternal deprivation, which probably contributed to my waywardness later on.

Lynda was in remission for three years before she died at the age of five. She and I had a very strong bond and, although I don't remember much about it, I certainly feel her absence today. During her remission years, she would look after me. She would insist to Mum that she be allowed to have my cot in her room. Daytimes she would dress up in her little white nurse's uniform and look after me. She would put me in her doll's pram and give me plastic injections. 'Don't worry, pet, this isn't going to hurt,' she'd say. And she would put a little blanket over me and say, 'Are you warm enough, pet?' I guess she had spent so much time in hospital surrounded by nurses that she wanted to be just like them.

Later I would learn from Mum that Lynda died alone in hospital in Barrow-in-Furness. One day, while at home, she suddenly became very ill indeed and my parents feared she was slipping away. When the ambulance arrived, the crew told Mum that, when Lynda died, it would not be pleasant and it would be better if she were not there to see it. To this day I don't know why Mum agreed to this. That very night Lynda passed away and the hospital phoned to give Mum and Dad the sad news. The thought of my beautiful sister dying alone in hospital with just a few strange nurses for company makes my heart ache so much I can scarcely breathe. The only saving grace is that two nights before Lynda died she told Mum about a man who had come to visit her.

'Who came to see you?' asked Mum.

'A man,' said Lynda.

'A man, what man?'

'A sparkly man, he came and sat on my bed.'

'Well, what did he look like?'

'He was all gold and sparkly, and he told me that everything is going to be OK. He made me feel nice,' said Lynda.

My mum broke down in tears right there in front of her.

Over the next two years things got worse – much worse. I guess Lynda's death took its toll. Something like that can make or break a marriage. In my parents' case, it broke it. Mum and Dad separated, and not long afterwards Dad was diagnosed with colon cancer at just 29.

Who knows what emotions were flying around inside my mum's head, or what she was thinking, but she became pregnant as a result of a quick afternoon fling with an Irishman who just happened to be working in the area as a labourer. In her heyday, my mother was a very attractive woman. She liked the attention she got from men and liked to flirt even more. Somehow, she and this man ended up in Bluebell Woods, a picturesque spot on top of a hill close to our house, the ground awash with fragrant bluebells. My younger brother, Jonathan, was the result of 10 minutes rolling around in the grass with a stranger – a stranger who, to this day, is oblivious to the fact that he has a son because he disappeared just as quickly as he came. In my view, a dignified state of celibacy might have been the norm, and it certainly would have led me down a different path in life, but my mother seemed to put her own wants and needs first, with no thought to my dying father.

By now, Dad was out of hospital, colostomy bag attached to his side, and being looked after by his sister, who lived around the corner. He would come to the house to visit us whenever he could. I think it's safe to say my only good childhood memories were those rare moments I got to spend with my dad. He seemed to be a man of few words, but there was a special bond between us.

Whenever Dad left, I felt vulnerable again. I only ever felt truly safe and secure when he was around. When he wasn't there, I'd spend most of my time outside playing in the village, but I was fast changing into a troubled boy. Maternal deprivation didn't do me any good, then Lynda's death hit me really hard, and my dad not being around compounded matters still more. I started getting into trouble. I'd steal things from other people's gardens, the nearby farm and the local shops. I became obsessed with material objects and before too long I had transformed myself into a fully fledged kleptomaniac. I guess I needed some sort of compensatory comfort, which I found in the things I stole. The only trouble was, the gratification of whatever item I'd stolen that day did not last. It kept me going for a few hours, but the following day I would be on the search for my next fix.

Then something happened that would put a stop to my kleptomania: my mum gave me a little dolly. She had long blonde hair and wore a light-blue Mackintosh. Even today, more than 40 years later, I can still smell her plastic coat and synthetic hair – that unique dolly smell. For some unfathomable reason, that 10-inch-high dolly comforted me beyond explanation; she was just the tonic I needed. I took her everywhere and I never let her out of my sight. Now I didn't feel the need to steal things anymore; I had everything I wanted right there in my hand, wrapped in that blue vinyl coat, with her distinct smell. But a few weeks later Lynda would be taken from me for a second time. The dolly had belonged to her and she must have left some sort of vibe on it; I can't think of any other reason why it comforted me so much.

A friend of Mum's persuaded her that it was not a good idea to hang onto all Lynda's things. She advised her to get rid of everything as it was tearing her up inside and this would help her to move on. Little did this interfering woman know that for me her advice would have life-altering consequences.

For a while I had stopped my thievery; I was no longer boisterous and had found some kind of inner peace and content- ment. But Mum took the woman's advice and packed up all Lynda's things, including my little dolly, and got rid of the lot. This happened during one of those rare instances when I'd left the dolly tucked up in my bed while I played outside with my older brother, Anthony, who'd persuaded me to leave her inside. How ironic that this was one of the few times when my older brother let me play with him.

When I returned to my room and saw that she was gone, I was horrified. Panic-stricken, I ran downstairs and asked Mum if she had seen her. This was when she informed me that it was Lynda's dolly and she'd given it away with the rest of her things. I begged and pleaded with her to get it back, but as she stood at the kitchen sink, a cigarette dangling from her mouth, she told me she'd given the doll to a little girl who was visiting our next-door neighbour and that she had since gone home – a long way away – in her parents' car, taking Lynda's dolly with her. At that point my world caved in around me, darkness descended both inside and out. My heart ached, I could scarcely breathe and everything became surreal. That night I cried myself to sleep, only to be woken in the early hours by my recurring nightmare of the pale dead teacher and the malevolent witch.

The next day I was more rebellious than ever. It was as if Pandora's Box had opened up inside me. I stole garden furniture from neighbouring gardens, eggs from the farm next door; I stole anything and everything from the local shops and plums and apples from the orchard. If it wasn't nailed down, I took it. Now my mum got angry with me – she was sick to death of my bringing all these things home and squirrelling them away in my bedroom. As far as I was concerned my emotional tonic – the dolly – was at least 100 miles away, so it had to be replaced by something else. I wasn't getting any support from Mum and my dad was now bed-bound so he couldn't come to see me anymore, and, for some reason unbeknown to me, I was not allowed to go and see him.

It was during this time that I had an accident that should have killed me. Mum had told my older brother, Anthony, to take me out of the house as I was getting under her feet and she was trying to feed my little half-brother, Jonathan. Anthony and I ended up playing on the roof of an old abandoned warehouse. I remember feeling quite scared as we were two floors up. Down one side of the warehouse ran a stream and down the other were two or three glass greenhouses equally decrepit as the warehouse. I noticed that a few of the glass panels were broken and, in about 30 seconds, several more would be broken too.

Anthony had gone back downstairs and headed off somewhere else, leaving me up on the roof, alone. I turned around and noticed that he was no longer there and at that moment I lost my footing and toppled over the edge. I fell two storeys down, smashed straight through the glass and metal roof of one of the greenhouses, taking half the metal structure and several panes of glass out at the same time before my descent was brought to an abrupt halt as I hit the concrete floor.

After the initial shock, I eventually got up as if nothing had happened. It was a hot day and all I was wearing was a pair of white shorts and a white vest, both of which were now sodden in warm blood. I looked as if I'd been the victim of some brutal Chinese torture of a thousand paper cuts, or glass cuts in this case: head to toe in claret from the hundreds of slashes my body had taken as it smashed its way through the greenhouse roof. There were cuts and slashes to my head, shoulders, arms, hands, chest, legs, feet … everywhere. I could feel the blood seeping out of them. By some miracle, or perhaps just extraordinary good luck, I didn't break a single bone in my body and had no bruises, only cuts. I walked back home through the village. Amazingly, nobody stopped me or came to the aid of the little boy who looked as if he'd just done five rounds with half a dozen ravenous Doberman Pinschers.

From the kitchen window Mum saw me coming down the garden path and ran to the front door.

'What the bloody hell happened?' she demanded to know.

I didn't know if she was shocked, horrified or simply upset with me for getting into trouble yet again. Mum didn't call an ambulance – she didn't think it was serious enough and maybe this was just the equivalent of another nosebleed. Instead, she carried me upstairs, stood me in the bath, stripped off my shorts and vest and proceeded to hose me down with the shower attachment until my skin turned from red to something resembling flesh colour again. Then she dried me off with a towel that started off white, but ended up a vibrant red. Now that she'd rinsed away all the blood, she could see where the cuts were. She wrapped bandages around my arms, hands, legs and feet. By the time she'd finished, I looked like a mummified child. I was hoping this near-death experience would cause her to extend me a little love and affection, compassion even, but no. She was too busy directing all her love and affection towards my new little half-brother, Jonathan.

And so I continued to go downhill. Now I stole more than ever and became increasingly boisterous. When talking about me, the locals would use words like 'naughty', 'scallywag' and even 'tearaway' and 'trouble'. Yes, there was no doubting that I'd become a 'sticks and stones' kind of kid. At my primary school the teachers noticed the changes in me and were gravely concerned.

Then my dad died. I'll never forget the day my aunty knocked on the door to break the news. Mum let her into the house and she came into the living room, where I was playing on the floor. Although she whispered the sad news in soft tones in my mum's ear, I heard the message loud and clear.

'He's passed away.'

Mum didn't seem in the least surprised – I think she knew his death was imminent. Later in life, my mum told me that, a few days before he died, Dad had told her that he'd heard Lynda calling for him.

For me that was it: my sister was gone, my dolly had been given away and now my dad had been taken from me too. All I had left was a mother who didn't seem to care, an older brother who did nothing but tease me, pick on me, hit me and never let me play with him or his friends, and a baby half-brother who took all Mum's love and attention. As for Mum, she just told me to 'Get out of the house and play outside!'

It's funny, but I always thought that, when a parent lost a child, they would cherish and protect the ones that were left. However, Mum seemed to pour all her love on Jonathan. It would appear that I was so troublesome she could no longer be bothered with me. By now, Jonathan was about a year and a half old and she was completely smitten. It wasn't as if I was jealous that this new addition to our family had popped out and was now sucking away the love of my mum, but I was angry because it felt like he was drawing 100 per cent of it like a leech, with nothing left for me or anyone else.

I don't completely recall what became of me after that, but it was bad enough for Mum to call in the Social Services. As far as she was concerned she had come to the end of her tether and simply could not cope anymore.

Something had to be done about me, and it must be done now.

Chapter 3

They're Coming to
Take Me Away, Ha-Haaa!

It was early evening on 4 November and all the kids in the neighbourhood were excited about the upcoming Bonfire Night. It was after dark and some of them were parading their Guys, which they'd placed in old prams or just leant up against a wall. 'Penny for the Guy, mister?' they would shout as strangers passed by. Traditionally, kids in those days would make a life-size Guy by stuffing old trousers and jumpers with leaves and anything else they could salvage. Shoes were typically tied to the ends of the stuffed trouser legs and a makeshift head plonked on its shoulders. The money raised was usually spent on sparklers and sweets.

Naturally my older brother would not let me go with him and his friends. Heaven forbid he should have to share any of their takings with his little 'pain in the arse' brother. So, my friend Michael and I decided we would go it alone. We were both so deprived that we didn't have any old clothes to make a Guy with, we were wearing them! But we had concocted a plan: Michael decided that he would be the Guy.

'What do you mean?' I asked.

'Come with me,' he said.

We went up to the village church, whereupon Michael sat down on the pavement and slouched against the wall backing onto the cemetery. His legs were splayed out across the pavement and his arms drooped by his sides; his head was tilted down so that his chin touched his chest. He pulled a woolly hat down over his ears and face to hide his skin and made sure his chunky scarf covered his neck. Thick black mittens ensured his hands could not be seen. He even went so far as to stuff a load of leaves up his jumper and in his sleeves so passers-by could see them poking out. We were ready! I sat on the wall next to my human Guy and waited for our first unsuspecting passer-by. There weren't that many people walking around the village at that time of the evening in the cold but every now and then, some men would tip out of the Crown Inn pub and head further into the village, passing us on their way to the next pub.

'Penny for the Guy, mister,' I said to two young men as they passed by.

No luck, they took one look at our Guy, gave me a dirty look and walked right past. Disheartened, I didn't think our ploy was ever going to work but Michael wanted to try again.

'Penny for the Guy, mister,' I said to a middle-aged man as he strolled by.

He paused, dug deep into his trouser pocket and came out with a handful of change. Sifting the coins around in the palm of his hand, he separated the silver from the copper ones and handed me a weighty pile of coppers. He looked down at the Guy, smiled at me from under the peak of his cap and went on his way. Before he was even 20 paces away, Michael leapt to his feet.

'How much did we get?' he asked excitedly.

He was so loud that I thought the man was going to turn around and notice he'd just been duped. But something told me he already knew, but went along with it anyway. There was 16 pence in the palm of my hand, five two-pence pieces and six pennies.

In 1972 this would buy a goodly portion of sweets for a couple of six-year-olds. We kept at it for another two hours. Just about everyone gave us something and of course they suspected my Guy was in fact a real live person. But they all laughed and gave us some coppers anyway; some even gave us silver ten-pence pieces. It was brilliant, I was in heaven with my friend and the money just kept on coming! Within a few hours our pockets were stuffed with so many coins I thought they would burst at the seams.

November soon turned into December and we arrived at that carol-singing time of year – another opportunity for the kids in the village to make a bit of money. Much to his annoyance, Mum told Anthony to take me with him and his three mates. I had been with my big brother and his friends for about an hour and we had knocked on about 10 doors to sing carols. Each household gave money to the small, unsynchronised and somewhat out-of-tune ensemble that had descended, uninvited, on their doorstep. But the money was always handed to my brother and his friends at the front, while I, small and at the back, was largely ignored. When the door closed, they would get to the end of the path and share out the takings; I was not included in this ritual.

Then I saw my friend Michael leaning against the Donald Campbell memorial on the green. He beckoned me over, so I left my brother and his horrible friends and went to join him instead. Michael suggested that we could do the same: two of us would be enough and we could split any money we made 50:50.

We didn't want to knock on any of the doors where my brother had just been and so we needed to find fresh houses, where no other carol singers had been. A couple of streets away was a combination of terraced and semi-detached properties. On the way we worked out what we were going to sing. Michael knocked on the first door, then looked at me and drew breath as my cue to join him before we both burst into song with 'We Wish You A Merry Christmas'. Hardly original, but it seemed to do the trick. By the time the door opened we had reached the end of the first verse and we didn't know the rest, so we went into repeat mode while they went back inside the house to grab some loose change. I think by now people had realised that kids didn't want figgy pudding anymore. I always hated the stuff anyway, loaded with brandy and other horrible-tasting liquids. For me it was the stuff of adults – good old-fashioned coinage was way better!

Starting at one end, we proceeded to work our way down the street, doing each house in turn. We managed to earn a little money from pretty much every house, at least the ones where folk were home.

At this point everything was perfect, at least as far as I was concerned, though not so for Mum. For months I'd been happily skipping along without a care in the world, but behind the scenes she was making plans.

I'd only been up a short while so I had a bowl of cereal, brushed my teeth and went back to my bedroom. I was in the middle of looking through my train magazines, kindly donated by a neighbour, and pining for Lynda's dolly when my mum entered the room.

'Nigel, there's a man here to see you,' she said.

A strange, middle-aged man in a suit walked in behind her.

'Hello, Nigel. What are you reading there?' he asked.

He sounded friendly enough and he smiled at me, so I answered him.

'My train magazines.'

'Can I see one?' he said, eyeing the small, neat pile next to me.

'Yes,' I said.

The man reached down and picked one up. After briefly flicking through the pages, taking in some of the glossy colour photographs, he placed the magazine back on the pile.

'Well, that's a very nice collection of train magazines, Nigel.'

'Why don't you leave Nigel and I alone to talk for a while?' he told my mum before adding, 'Is that alright with you, Nigel?'

'Yes,' I said.

Well, I just thought he was a friendly man who'd come to see me. I didn't know why. But he was giving me some attention, which I welcomed.

'OK, I'll be downstairs,' said Mum.

The man spent some time looking at my train magazines with me. He asked me why I liked trains. Then he went on to ask me lots of other questions. At first his questions were general, but then he started to talk about my sister and my dad and how I felt now that they were no longer here. He questioned me about my stealing habits and boisterous behaviour and why I could not be a good boy for my mother. Eventually, he went downstairs and talked with Mum. I sneaked down after him and waited just outside the living-room door so I could listen in on their conversation.

'He's been through a lot and he's suffering inside. He's become quite disturbed, and it's not surprising after losing his sister and father so suddenly,' the man explained.

'I know, we've all suffered,' said Mum.

'Nigel's a sensitive boy; it's hit him really hard. He needs professional help and, if he doesn't get it right away, it could have devastating consequences for him in later life,' said the man.

I felt that they were wrapping up the conversation so I sneaked back up to my bedroom. A few minutes later Mum and the man entered.

'Nigel, this man's here to help you,' said Mum, sitting down on the bed next to me.

'What do you mean?' I asked.

'Well, we have to try and fix your behaviour,' she explained.

'But I'll be good from now on, I promise,' I insisted.

Then the man spoke. 'Nigel, your mother's concerned about you, we all are,' he said.

'But I'm OK, there's nothing wrong with me.'

'Well, your mother tells me you've been stealing things,' he said.

'I won't do it again, I'll be good from now on.'

'Oh, Nigel! I'm sorry, but you're going to have to go with this man,' Mum told me.

'No, *please*! I promise I'll be good,' I said.

'Come on, son,' said the man, holding out his hand.

'*No*, I don't want to go! Please, Mum, *please*.'

'It'll only be for a few days, OK?' she said, rubbing my shoulders.

'But I don't want to go. Please, I promise, I won't steal anything anymore.'

'Come on, Nigel. Don't be difficult,' said the man.

It was no use: no matter how much I pleaded and cried, this man was going to take me away. He tried to take my hand, but I pulled it away. The next thing I knew, he'd leant forward, grabbed me under the arms and picked me up. Somehow I ended up over his shoulder as he carried me from my bedroom and down the stairs in a fireman's lift. As I exited the bedroom, I glanced at my bed at the place next to my pillow where I had kept Lynda's dolly. More than anything I wanted her to be there in her blue raincoat, to save me from this man. But she wasn't; she was with another family now and probably missing me as much as I was missing her.

I kicked and screamed and cried as the man proceeded to march through our living room, into the kitchen and out the front door. As he carried me down our garden path I kicked and struggled as hard as I could, but he gripped me all the tighter. I saw my mum standing at the front door as I neared the garden gate. I screamed and cried, arms outstretched, reaching out for my mother, who was not going to help me. She was not coming after me; she was not going to stop this man from putting me in his big car. She just stood there with a blank expression on her face that revealed no emotion whatsoever.

'MUM!' I shouted and cried for her to change her mind, to stop this man from taking me away, but she didn't.

My eyes filled with tears, making the world a blurry and horrible place. As the man put me in the back of his car and slammed the door I realised how much I loved my mum, even if that feeling wasn't necessarily reciprocated.

'If you keep on crying and screaming like that, you'll only feel worse, so settle down,' said the man, starting the engine.

I struggled with the door handle, but it would not open.

'Let go of the door and settle down,' he instructed me, more sternly now.

I put the palms of my hands on the car window and shouted again, 'MUM!' but she turned away and went back into the house. She closed the door and my world crumbled, again.

As the car pulled away, I saw my mum – a spectator from behind the kitchen window. My stomach cramped up and I was reduced to a pathetic, sobbing wretch on the back seat of this stranger's car.

Suddenly I felt sick to the core as the car pulled away from my house and left the village.

Chapter 4

Electrodes, Tests & Drugs

About an hour and a half later the car pulled into the grounds of Lancaster Moor Children's Psychiatric Unit, which was in a lodge on the same grounds as Lancaster Moor Hospital, formerly known as the notorious County Lunatic Asylum and County Mental Hospital. For the next 10 days the Children's Psychiatric Unit would be my home.

The grounds were sparse and, although the children's unit was surrounded by large trees and a huge expanse of well-kept gardens, there was a bleak and eerie feel to it. In the distance I could see what was then the mental hospital. It looked cold and uninviting, kind of evil. The main hospital was built during the early 19th century. It was now 1973 and I suspect the place hadn't improved with age.

The car stopped and the man got out and opened the door for me. As I stumbled out of the vehicle I felt a chilly breeze engulf me. The wind swept across the grounds from the direction of the main hospital. As it hit my face and swept through my hair it carried with it 150 years of unparalleled lunacy, torture, pain, suffering, misery and 'accidental' death. The wretchedness, despair and horror had seeped so deep into the walls it had become part of its very foundations. Pain and suffering that deep can never be scrubbed from the walls, it goes much deeper than erosion. The whole place gave me the creeps.

I ambled along, hesitant and anxious, with my eyes stinging and red, as the man led me towards the children's unit, where the charge nurse, Mr Richardson, was waiting for us.

'Hello, Nigel,' he said, smiling, 'I'm Mr Richardson.'

He seemed pleasant enough and his smile was kind. Children seem to have a special kind of sixth sense when it comes to assessing strangers. Mine, however, was more acute than most. Mr Richardson looked like he was in his early thirties. He was of average height and build and his dark hair was impeccably cut and went well with his short, equally well-groomed beard. With his neatly pressed black trousers and starched white shirt he looked more like an upmarket estate agent than a charge nurse at a small children's psychiatric hospital.

'I'm afraid Nigel's a little upset, he cried throughout the entire journey,' explained the driver.

'Oh dear! Well, come on in, I'll show you around. Let's see if we can make you feel a little better,' he said, placing a firm, but friendly hand on my shoulder.

I can confidently say that Mr Richardson did a lot to try to calm my anxiety.

The man who drove me didn't stick around long. He and Mr Richardson exchanged a few sentences, and then he headed back to his car. Mr Richardson gave me a tour of the children's unit, which was built much later than the main hospital. Downstairs, he showed me the main living room, then along the corridor, past his office, to the compact dining room. Then we went upstairs to the dormitories.

'This is the dorm where you'll be sleeping, and this is your bed,' he said, gesturing with his arm.

I felt sick in my stomach. Scared and anxious, I was also incredibly homesick. There didn't seem to be anybody else around, no other children, though I did notice another man sitting in the downstairs office and a lady wearing a white uniform, looking in a filing cabinet next to him.

'Where is everybody?' I asked.

'The other children are in the school classroom downstairs. They'll be coming out for their lunch soon. Are you hungry?' he said.

'Not really.'

'Well, perhaps you'll feel a little different when you meet the other children. Let's go downstairs and get ready.'

'Mr Richardson, how long am I going to be here?' I asked meekly. Tears welled in my eyes and my bottom lip started to tremble uncontrollably.

'Just a little while, but we'll talk about that a little later, OK? I don't want you to worry about that right now,' he said, putting his hand on my shoulder to comfort me. He could clearly see that I was anxious and upset about my strange new environment.

'Come on, let's go and get something to eat and you can meet the other children,' he added, taking my hand.

As we neared the bottom of the stairs I heard, then saw, several boisterous children rushing along the corridor.

'Quiet down now,' said Mr Richardson.

Most of the children were boys, aged between seven and 11, but there was one slightly older girl called Ghislaine, aged about 13. There were about eight or nine children in total.

'Gelar, where are you going?' Mr Richardson asked one of the boys.

'To the dining room,' he said.

'Have you washed your hands?'

'No, sorry, Mr Richardson,' said the boy, turning on his heels and heading towards the washroom area with the rest of the children.

Gelar looked a little strange to me, kind of Aboriginal; I was intrigued by his complexion. He was one of the oldest kids there, about 11 years old.

'Gelar always wants to be the first in for lunch,' explained Mr Richardson, smiling and leading me into the dining room.

'OK, you have a seat right here,' he added, pulling out a chair for me, 'and I'll be back in a minute.'

I sat down while Mr Richardson headed out of the dining room. Meanwhile, I could hear the children causing a ruckus in the washroom area. I looked around anxiously, twiddling my thumbs under the table while I waited. Then I heard Mr Richardson reprimand the children.

'What's all the noise about? Just wash your hands quietly and make your way to the dining room.'

The children eventually piled into the dining room. There was a loud orchestra of chair legs scraping on the floor as they all took their seats. The bright acoustics didn't help. I winced as the ensemble of metal chair legs screeched on the hard floor, penetrating my eardrums. Although the other children weren't paying me much attention, I desperately wanted Mr Richardson to come back and be with me. I felt alone, vulnerable and scared, and I was aware of my hands shaking under the table.

'OK, everybody settle down,' said Mr Richardson, entering the dining room.

He came over to me and put both his hands on my shoulders.

'I'd like to introduce you all to Nigel, he's going to be staying with us for a while.'

'How long's he going to be staying?' asked one of the other boys.

'We're not sure yet, but I want you all to make Nigel feel welcome and help him settle in.'

Suddenly all eyes were on me and I didn't know where to look. Mr Richardson pulled out a chair and sat at the head of the long table next to me.

Two ladies wheeled in a couple of hot-plate trollies and started to serve up what they liked to call food. There were three stainless steel pots, each containing a slightly different variation of what looked like gruel from the Victorian era. I suspect the food was prepared over at the main hospital, then wheeled across to the children's unit. Still, everybody tucked in, including me. It didn't seem to smell of anything in particular and the taste was bland. I imagine if you mixed up a bucket of flour and water and threw in a large helping of unbranded oatmeal and perhaps half a cup full of wood adhesive, you would end up with something of a similar consistency. It didn't go down well; it clung stubbornly to the walls of my throat as I tried to swallow. My yet-to-be-developed Adam's apple was getting a serious workout. Suddenly I wasn't hungry anymore. Everybody else seemed to be getting stuck in, but in a routine/institutionalised sort of way.

'Are you OK, Nigel?' asked Mr Richardson.

'I'm not really hungry,' I said, putting my spoon into the almost-full bowl of gluey gunge.

'It's OK, you can leave that,' he said, smiling.

'You can leave it this time because you're new, but at dinner time you'll have to eat it all just like the other children,' piped up a thick-set, middle-aged woman with beady eyes.

She didn't smile at me, so I didn't smile back. I didn't know what her position was. Dressed in a white nurse's jacket with dark-blue trousers she looked like some sort of nurse or general help. Whatever she was, I didn't like her; her look was menacing.

I sat and waited while everybody else finished. Plates were cleared and pudding was served. It was jam roly-poly and custard. Although the roly-poly looked a little dense and de-saturated, it was definitely more appetising than what came before. After a couple of spoonfuls, I found it to be reasonably edible, if a little stodgy. Lunch wound up and the other children headed back to the school classroom. Mr Richardson asked me to go with him to his office and explained that there was a nice lady he wanted me to meet.

'Try not to look so worried, everything's going to be OK,' he said, smiling.

I forced a meek smile while he gathered up some papers from his desk. He led me along the corridor and down another corridor and into another office. This office was much larger. There was a lady sitting behind a desk.

'Dr Nolen, this is Nigel,' said Mr Richardson.

'Hello, Nigel,' she said, coming round from her desk to greet me. 'How are you?'

Dr Nolen was the unit's child psychiatrist. I didn't answer – I would later learn that the previous psychiatrist, Dr Lombard, had committed suicide.

'Nigel's still a little upset,' said Mr Richardson.

'I just want to go home,' I explained.

'I'll leave you to it,' said Mr Richardson, handing her a small stack of papers. 'Just bring Nigel back round when you've finished.'

Dr Nolen shot him a knowing nod.

'I'll see you soon, OK?' he added, giving me a friendly rub on the head.

'Why don't you have a seat here?' said Dr Nolen, gesturing to the large chair opposite hers.

'Why am I here?' I asked.

'Well,' she said, looking up at me from her papers, 'we just want to make sure you're OK.'

'But I *am* OK,' I reassured her.

'Look, there's really nothing to worry about. I'm just going to talk to you and do a few simple tests, that's all,' she explained. She laid out various papers on her desk, along with small cards with graphics on them and other strange-looking test charts.

'If I pass the tests, can I go home?' I persisted.

'Well, that's not up to me.'

'Who's it up to?'

'Let's just see how things go, OK?'

She spent the next 30 minutes or so talking to me and asking me lots of questions and writing stuff down. To start with she asked me how I felt and if I knew why I was there. She wanted to know if there was anything that I was upset about. Then she dug deeper and asked me how I felt about losing my sister and if I remembered her at all. With that, I gazed down at my hands and closed up completely. She changed the topic momentarily to something more cheerful in an attempt to get me talking again but within a few minutes she was back to my dead sister and father.

'How about your father, do you miss him?' she asked.

'Yes.'

'Tell me what you miss about him.'

'There are lots of things I miss about him.'

'Can you tell me some of them?'

'I felt safe with my dad.'

'Don't you feel safe now?'

'No.'

'Why don't you feel safe, Nigel?'

'Because he's not here to protect me anymore.'

'Did he make you feel secure?'

'Yes, but I don't feel secure anymore.'

'How do you feel now?'

'Alone.'

'But you still have your mum and two brothers.'

'I don't think my mum wants me anymore.'

'Why do you say that?'

'Because she had a man take me away in a car and bring me here.'

'Nigel, your mum *does* want you, she's just concerned about you. We all are.'

Dr Nolen continued asking me questions. Then she moved on and wanted to know how I felt about my brothers, especially my younger brother, Jonathan. Eventually, she picked up a stack of white cards with images and shapes on them and explained that we were going to do some simple tests, like a game. She held up cards, one at a time, and asked me what I saw or what the image/shape meant to me. After about eight cards I interrupted her sequence.

'I don't think I'm getting many of them right,' I said.

'It's not really that sort of test, there are no right or wrong answers,' she told me.

'But every time I tell you what I think the picture is you write loads of stuff down.'

'Don't worry about that, it's all just part of the test. You're doing really well.'

But I could see through her forced smile.

There was a knock at the door.

'Come in,' she said.

'So, how are we getting on?' said Mr Richardson, entering.

'Well … Nigel's by far and away the most enigmatic young boy I've ever seen.'

'Is that good?' I wanted to know.

They both laughed. 'It just makes you a very interesting little boy,' she said light-heartedly.

'I can walk Nigel back if you're finished?' Mr Richardson offered.

'Yes, we're finished now,' she said.

Mr Richardson and I talked in his office briefly, then he took me to see another lady, in a different office. Mrs Young was the resident occupational therapist.

'Hello, Nigel. I'm very pleased to meet you,' she said with a smile.

Mrs Young was a little younger than Dr Nolen, and was more smiley and less serious. I spent about an hour or so with her. Like Dr Nolen, she asked me lots of questions, but they were more general, at least to start with. Although I was still upset, tearful and lonely, at least I was starting to come out of my traumatised state. The rest of the afternoon didn't really drag, but it didn't fly by either. Mrs Young and I talked quite a lot and played some games too. In hindsight, I suspect she was more concerned with my social skills than anything else. Since my sister and father had died, I'd become not only an unruly, boisterous child, I'd also been something of a closed book. I'd become a social recluse, shutting everybody and everything out. I kept myself to myself and lived in my own dream world. Essentially I'd shut down and gone into 'survival mode'.

At the end of the session Mrs Young escorted me to the washroom area so I could wash my hands before dinner. I was a little anxious about that because of the seed the beady-eyed lady had planted during lunch; that I'd have to eat 'all' my dinner. During the walk along the corridors I prayed mentally they were not serving gruel again – all the crying and mental exhaustion had made me hungry. Luckily it was sausage, mash and baked beans. It resembled a typical school dinner, but right then, I'd happily take it. As before, I sat next to Mr Richardson. I felt comforted by his presence and bonded with him almost instantly. I wolfed down the sausages and beans, but the mash left a lot to be desired – it was gruel-like, with no taste and a thick, gluey consistency.

'Remember what I told you at lunchtime, Nigel?' said the beady-eyed lady, as she observed me playing with the mash.

I looked up at her. 'Yes,' I said.

'Good, because boys who don't eat all their dinner don't get any pudding and they go on regression.'

But I didn't know what 'regression' was and I was too scared to ask. Wary of this threat, I forced down every last bit of the stodgy white mash.

After an apple crumble and custard pudding, there was another ritual, one that didn't happen during lunch. A nurse wheeled in a white trolley like a pharmacy on wheels; it was crammed with small beakers and an assortment of pills and other medication. The nurse called out the children's names, one at a time. When it was their turn, each child went over to the trolley and the nurse would pop a pill on the child's tongue and they were given a beaker of water to wash it down. She then ordered them to open their mouths so she could be sure they had swallowed it.

'Nigel Cooper!' shouted the nurse.

My heart leapt, a lump formed in my throat and I had a mild panic attack right there at the table. I glanced at Mr Richardson for help.

'It's OK, Nigel, it will make you feel better,' he explained.

'But there's nothing wrong with me,' I pleaded, tears forming in my eyes.

'Come on, Nigel, it'll help you settle in,' said Mr Richardson, patting me on the shoulder.

I reluctantly got up and went over to the nurse and her trolley.

'Open,' she said, with zero emotion.

'What is it?' I asked.

'That's none of your concern, young man. Now, are you going to give me any trouble?'

'No.'

'Good, now open wide.'

I did so, reluctantly.

She placed a pill onto my tongue. 'Swallow it with this,' she said, handing me a small beaker of water. I did as she asked.

'Open.' She grabbed my head with both her hands and pulled and squeezed as she jerked my head up and down and right to left.

'Lift your tongue,' she said, still gripping my head hard with her talon-like hands.

'Good,' she said, releasing her vice-like grip. 'Now, I'm not going to have any trouble from you again tomorrow, am I?'

'No.'

'Good, now go and sit down.'

'Good lad,' said Mr Richardson, smiling at me.

The children cleared out of the dining room and went to the TV room. Mr Richardson left me in the hands of two female care staff and the other children. I sat in the corner and kept to myself, preferring not to socialise. Instead, I thought about my mum and why she had sent me away and why I was there. Suddenly I felt anxious, confused, abandoned and lonely, all at the same time. The evening passed slowly as I sat alone, stewing in my own misery, the tears welling and then drying up. Eventually we were all taken upstairs to the dormitories, where, one at a time, we were bathed and prepared for bed. Next to my bed was a small suitcase containing my clothes and some personal items. Somebody must have brought them there from my house in Coniston.

My emotional state in tatters, I had a restless night of broken sleep. No Lynda dolly, no Lynda, no dad, and a mother who didn't want me at home, yet I longed for her, just to be with her.

The next morning, we all had breakfast then the other children went to class, while I was instructed to stay behind. I had to see somebody else today, a man. Mr Richardson escorted me along the corridor and around the corner, then along another corridor, much further this time. He led me into a large living room filled with medical equipment. A man was waiting there for us.

'Good morning, Doctor. This is Nigel,' said Mr Richardson.

'Ah, hello, young man,' he said.

'I'll see you shortly, OK?' said Mr Richardson, patting me on the shoulder before leaving.

'Why don't you come over here and have a seat?' said the man.

I sat down and gazed out of the window into the car park beyond, and the driveway beyond that. My thoughts turned to home and I wondered how long it would take me to walk back, or if I could even find the way.

'So, how are you settling in?' he asked.

But I wasn't settling in at all and I didn't know what to say so I just watched him as he made some adjustments to his equipment.

'Don't look so worried, this isn't going to hurt, I promise you won't feel a thing,' he told me, picking up a strange, Space-Age-looking cap. 'Now, keep still, I'm just going to pop this on your head.'

He proceeded to tug, pull and adjust the rather tight-fitting cap to my head until he was happy with its position. Then he attached lots of wires to various parts of it; the other ends of the wires were connected to his strange-looking machine.

'Sitting comfortably?' he asked.

I didn't answer.

'You don't talk much, do you?' he said, turning dials on the machine and pushing buttons on a keyboard. 'OK, try and relax. I just have to take some readings.'

'What do you mean?' I said.

'Well, it's quite simple, really. This machine has been designed to take electronic readings from your brain.'

'Will I feel it?'

'No, not a thing, it's like magic.'

'What's it for?'

'It's just going to tell me if your brain's working as it should,' he explained, smiling. 'There's nothing to worry about, I'm sure you're fine. It's just something we do with all the new children here.'

The whole procedure took about 15 minutes as he adjusted settings on his machine, punched buttons on his keyboard, viewed the monitor and adjusted the wires coming from my head. I don't know what he was doing, and I didn't really care. It didn't hurt at all and the truth was that this man was giving me some much needed personal attention that I so craved.

In the afternoon Mr Richardson took me out in his car to see yet another person, this time away from the children's unit. The occupational therapist, Mrs Young, had suggested I see a speech therapist to try to get rid of my slight lisp. I had a lazy tongue and could not pronounce the letter 'S' properly; I would slur any words beginning with 'S'. Mr Richardson waited outside while I went into the speech therapist's office.

He was a nice enough man, who soon told me what the problem was.

'You have a lazy tongue, it droops at the edges. You'll need to retrain it, but don't worry, I'm confident I can help you get rid of your lisp,' he explained.

'Thank you,' I said.

'OK, I want you to try and make a hissing sound, like a snake,' he said.

I duly obliged.

'Now, can you hear how that sounds?'

'Yes.'

'You have to make that sound every time you say a word that begins with the letter "S",' he told me. He went on to ask me to repeat back several words beginning with 'S', adding that if a little bit of a whistle came out while I was doing snake impersonations, that was OK. Eventually, it would all settle into a natural sound.

I was supposed to go back to see this man on a regular basis until my speech impediment was totally cured, but due to my short stay, it didn't happen. My speech impediment would be cured, but not until later in life, when I was 29 years old.

Over the next nine days I went through more of the same, sometimes joining the other children in the classroom for an odd afternoon or morning. But most of my time was spent with the child psychiatrist, the occupational therapist and various other doctors and strange people, who proceeded to carry out every type of psychiatric test imaginable.

On the tenth day, Dr Nolen discharged me, much to my relief. A social worker came to pick me up and took me home.

I was ecstatic; I was going back home to my mum.

Chapter 5

The Piano That Never Was

'Come on, boys! Get up, my allowance has arrived, we're going to Ulverston,' Mum bellowed up the stairs with an enthusiasm that suggested she'd won the pools.

Oh yes, those shopping trips to Ulverston, how could I ever forget? This fortnightly routine had been going on since my dad died. Mum didn't waste any time claiming her widow's allowance. While my dad's brother, Bill (along with Dad's side of the family), was busy arranging the funeral, my mother was filling out social security forms to claim whatever pittance the government saw fit to give her every two weeks. Her priorities seemed all wrong.

My mother was at the very bottom of the working-class ladder. Whenever she did work it was only ever part-time and typically involved cleaning or some sort of general dogsbody kitchen work in a local pub, B&B or mid-market hotel. Therefore to Mum, the widow's allowance must have seemed like her personal fortnightly pot of gold.

'Come on, Nigel! Get up, we're going to Ulverston,' she said, bursting into my bedroom.

'I don't feel well,' I said.

In fact, I was seriously ill. My stomach churned, I felt like I was going to vomit, my skin was grey, the sheet beneath me soaking wet and the walls were moving in a strange, surreal way.

'Oh dear! Never mind, you can stay at home then. But don't worry, I'll buy you something nice,' she said.

This was not the first time it had happened. I'd been left at home a few times due to typical childhood illnesses, while my mum and two brothers went off shopping.

'I'll bring you a bucket in case you want to be sick,' she added.

Within half an hour she and my brothers were heading out of the house and up the road to the bus stop.

So, I lay in my damp, hot bed with the room spinning; seven years old, all alone in the house. The morning went slowly, I'd thrown up a couple of times into the bucket by my bed. Having a clock next to the bed was no help at all as I kept looking at it every five minutes, wishing the day away. Come 12 o'clock, I didn't feel like eating the sandwich that Mum had prepared for me before she went out. She'd also made sure my favourite train magazines were within easy reach but I didn't feel like looking at them at all. The afternoon dragged like a snail trying to journey across a thin slick of treacle.

Eventually, I heard the front door open.

'Yoo-hoo, we're back!' shouted Mum.

Although I was glad she was home, my enthusiasm was not on the same level as hers. I could hear her unpacking the government-bought shopping – she had to get her priorities right. Ten minutes later she came up to my room.

''Ello, Nigel, how ya feeling?' she said, putting her palm across my forehead. 'Oh dear, you're still a little hot! I'll go and fetch you a cold drink. Ay, I've got you something nice,' she added before exiting the room.

Crayons, I thought.

Yup, a few minutes later my mum came back with a glass of pop in one hand and a brown paper bag shaped suspiciously like a small pack of crayons in the other.

''Ere you go, love. I'll be back to check on you soon,' she said, heading back downstairs to indulge in whatever goodies she'd bought in Ulverston.

I struggled to sit up to drink some of the pop and then I picked up the brown paper bag that Mum had plopped onto my stomach. Yup, just as I suspected: bloody crayons again! She always bought me a pack of crayons. It wasn't fair. I would ask for felt-tip pens, way cooler than boring old crayons, but I never got them. My older brother, Anthony, always got felt-tip pens, while I was given cheap, horrible crayons from the market. Of course, once Anthony had exhausted every last drop of damp colour out of them, my mother would give me his cast-offs. No matter how much I licked at the nibs or dipped them in water, all I ever got was a hint of colour that never made it past a two-inch stroke across the paper. To add insult to injury, the paper was usually the reverse side of some of Anthony's reject drawings.

The months rolled by and things went from bad to worse in the family, with me the sore sticking point. My thievery was getting worse and now I was manipulating the neighbourhood kids into either giving me their possessions, or at least swapping them, making sure I got the better end of the bargain. The other parents in the village were sick to death of me stealing things out of their gardens and doing crap deals with their children over their toys.

My own mother was sick of it too. She'd called our social worker on numerous occasions and had even taken me to Barrow-in-Furness to see Dr Nolen, the child psychiatrist that I'd seen at Lancaster Moor Children's Psychiatric Unit. As well as spending odd mornings and afternoons in Lancaster, Dr Nolen had her own private office in Barrow. Dr Nolen had tried hard to get me back on the straight and narrow but she had now come to the conclusion that the death of Lynda and my dad had left me deeply disturbed. She said my kleptomania was some kind of emotional substitute. Even I could not explain why I did it.

My whole life I'd suffered maternal deprivation, been emotionally deprived and starved of love as I was passed from pillar to post. I missed my sister and had no dad; my mother didn't have the time of day for me. Despised by the adults in our village, I was disliked by most of the children too. My emotions were in tatters, my mind an emotional junkyard. What was I supposed to do?

But the straw that broke the camel's back came on my eighth birthday. My mum had scraped some pennies together (including those vacuumed up by mistake or found down the back of the couch) and bought me a few presents, the best of which was a soap-on-a-rope car.

'I thought you'd like that. You can play with it later,' she said, as I observed the light-blue scented automobile.

And play with it I did. I spent the morning alone in the spare downstairs room, where Lynda's coffin had previously been kept. This room had a hard, dark-brown tiled floor, which made an ideal play area for my new soap car. It was brilliant and for a while I was in heaven. The soap car had four protruding wheels that left perfect soap tracks across the dark floor. I pushed the car along the floor, making broooom, brooooooooom noises as I did so and sketching out my own personal Brands Hatch race circuit right there. Again and again I went over it. It looked amazing! I was so proud of my floor art that I went to get my mum.

'What the bloody hell have you done? I only cleaned that floor yesterday!' she screamed.

'But, Mum—'

'Just get out, and give me that!' she screeched, snatching the car out of my hands.

I headed outside to play in the street.

'Bloody hell, I'll have to get the mop and bucket out again and clean all this mess up!' I heard her annoyed voice say as I reached the front door.

This was not the response I was hoping for.

A nice man from across the road saw me hanging around in the immediate vicinity of his front garden. His door was open and he caught my eye. He could see that I was curious about his big house and its contents in the large room beyond the front door.

'Hello, Nigel. What are you up to then?' he said.

'Nothing much,' I told him.

I was kind of bored and had been hanging out on the street for a while with nothing to do and nobody to play with.

'Come with me, I'd like to show you something,' he said, inviting me inside his house. Back then, there was less concern about kids going off with strangers, especially in the north of England.

As soon as I set foot inside the door I was awestruck at the sight of the beautiful musical instruments. I'd never seen anything like them.

'Have you ever played an instrument before?' he asked.

'No.'

'Well, perhaps you should learn. This one right here is a piano,' he said, gesturing towards it. 'And this one is a harpsichord. They both make slightly different sounds,' he explained.

I was all-ears. Not only because for the first time in my life somebody (other than my dad) was giving me some much-needed attention, but I was fascinated by these huge musical instruments.

'With the piano, you can play the note so softly you can hardly hear it,' he added. He lightly pressed one of the white keys very gently; it did not make a sound. 'But with the harpsichord, no matter how hard or soft you press a key, it will always make a sound.' He pressed one of the keys on the harpsichord and it made the most delightful sound as the key triggered the plucking mechanism across the string.

'Wow, that sounds great!' I said.

'Would you like to try?'

'Yes, please,' I said, on an enthusiastic high.

'OK, press one of the white keys … gently,' he said, pointing to the piano.

I pressed one of the keys in the middle. The sound was so beautiful. I looked up at him, with a great beaming smile on my face.

'Can I press another one?'

'Of course, but be gentle.'

So I pressed one white key, then another, and another.

'Why don't you try the harpsichord now?' he said, putting his hand on my shoulder and guiding me to the magnificent instrument.

When I pressed the first key and felt the clicking sensation under my finger, followed by the mellow twang and a sustained note as the sound reverberated across the soundboard, I was transported into another world, a world I did not want to leave. I pressed three or four more keys and wanted that moment to freeze forever.

It was my introduction to music and I was hungry for more, but that hunger for the piano would not be satisfied for another 17 years, at least not seriously. Sure, my mother could not afford a piano, but when I ran back into my house, shouting and screaming enthusiastically about my musical experience, she made absolutely no effort whatsoever to try to find a way for me to play the piano, or even have lessons. If she had, perhaps my life would have turned out very differently indeed.

'That's nice, Nigel. Now get out of the way, I'm trying to mop the floor,' was all she could say.

I skulked off up to my bedroom and fantasised about playing the piano but my fantasy was rudely interrupted by a visit from our new social worker, Mrs Clements. She was with another man. He was very tall and spoke with a broad Glaswegian accent.

'Hello, Nigel,' said Mrs Clements.

'Hello,' I said nervously.

What are they doing here?

'Nigel, this is Mr MacGregor,' she said.

'Nigel, how would you like to go for a little ride in the car?' asked Mr MacGregor.

'I don't want to.'

Mrs Clements looked at my mum with a sad expression on her face.

'Come on, love, you've got to go,' said Mum.

'But, Mum, I don't want to. I want to stay here with you.'

'I know, love, but it's just not working,' she told me.

With that, I went into full-on panic and burst into tears, which soon turned into gulping great sobs, then full steam ahead screaming as I pleaded and begged for her not to send me away. The tall man took my hand.

'Come on, Nigel, it'll be alright,' he said, pulling me up.

'Mum, I don't want to go, please, *please*! I promise I'll be good, *please* don't let them take me away, *please* …'

But it was no good; my screaming, crying, begging and pleading carried no weight whatsoever. Like the first time, I was manhandled down the stairs by Mr MacGregor, with Mrs Clements and my mum in tow. Resistance was totally useless, so I gave in as Mrs Clements and Mr MacGregor marched me down the garden path to their car. As Mr MacGregor put me in the back of the car I was filled with dread. Sheer panic hit me as I suspected that I was not going to be back home in 10 days' time as before.

Why me? I hadn't done anything wrong. Why couldn't they take

Anthony away, why did I have to go?

Later in life my mother told me a story about when she went to see my dad in hospital in Barrow-in-Furness a few days before he died. It was the last time she saw him and one of the last things he said to her was, 'I've fucking had it, love. Please, promise me you'll do the best you can for the kids.' But it felt like my mother's needs always came first. Getting rid of the awkward/naughty child would free up time for her shopping trips and relationships with anyone who showed an interest. It felt like, rather than fulfil my dad's dying wish, she tossed me out like the garbage.

My mother's idea of my being difficult was my drawing tracks on the tiled flooring with my soap-on-a-rope car, or my coming home with cuts and bruises on both knees or with dirt in my hair and face, or my getting under her feet while she was trying to mop the kitchen floor. In other words I was a typical boy. It wasn't that I was beyond parental control, more that my mother was beyond parenting capabilities. For some reason, my older brother's misbehaving and bad behaviour seemed to go unnoticed or unpunished, possibly because he was the man of the house now and my mum relied on him.

'Don't forget this!' shouted Mum.

Mrs Clements went back up the garden path to the door to collect a suitcase with all my things in it. The ignition started up and the man put the car into gear, motion was imminent. Mrs Clements put my suitcase in the boot, and then got into the front passenger seat.

I placed the palms of my hands up at the window. '*MUUUUUUM!*' I shouted, tears streaming down my face. But she just waved goodbye as the car pulled away.

Chapter 6

Under-Age Sex

I sat in the back of Mrs Clements' red Ford Cortina Mark III, crying uncontrollably. My throat was closing up and I could scarcely breathe. Full-scale panic set in as I was taken away for a second time.

'Aw, you'll be alright, wee man. We're taking you to a lovely place,' said Mr MacGregor, the other social worker.

'I don't want to go, I want to go back home,' I protested through my sobs.

'Nigel, you can't go back home. You have to go away for a little while,' said Mrs Clements.

'But I don't want to, why can't I just go home? I want to go home.'

I cried my eyes out throughout the entire 24-mile journey as we headed south to Ulverston, taking the same route as the Ribble bus, then beyond to Barrow-in-Furness. By the time the car pulled into Lesh Lane, a little over 35 minutes later, my eyes were swollen and puffy and stung like hell. It felt as if someone had scrubbed the lining of my throat with a Brillo pad from all the choking and sobbing.

'OK, Nigel, we're here,' said Mrs Clements, as we pulled into the car park at Newbarns House Observation & Assessment

Centre, where I would remain for the next three months. Though what I was being assessed for eluded me. Mr MacGregor got my case out of the boot while Mrs Clements opened the car door for me.

'Are you ready?' she said.

'No, I want to go home,' I pleaded.

I was all cried out and had no more tears. Already I'd been through so much trauma and emotional turmoil in my life. All I wanted was for somebody to love me – anybody. Mrs Clements was concerned about my welfare, but what I really craved was love and a little bit of attention.

I stood next to the car, looking at the building, while Mr MacGregor closed the boot. The place was about the size of a five-bedroom detached house, only more purpose-built for the purpose of assessing dysfunctional problem children. Not that I was one of those. It wasn't particularly cold, but I could feel my whole body shivering and shaking and I thought I was going to lose control of my bladder. I was so scared and all alone again. They took me inside, where we were greeted by a suited man in his forties. I stood in the large hallway and became very aware that there were several children whispering and looking around the door at me from the TV room.

'OK, everybody, settle down,' said a female voice from inside the room.

'Why don't I take Nigel into the living room so he can meet the others?' suggested the man.

'I think that's a good idea. What do you say, Nigel?' said Mrs Clements.

I didn't say anything – I just wanted to make a run for the door.

'Come on, I'm sure you'll like everyone,' said the man, placing the palm of his hand between my shoulder blades to encourage me along.

'Everyone, this is Nigel. He's going to be staying with us,' he said.

'Hello, Nigel,' said a lady sitting close to the door. 'Everybody, say hello to Nigel.'

'Hello, Nigel,' came an unsynchronised ensemble of voices.

I scanned the room. There were about six boys and five girls. The boys were all around my age, some a little older, while the girls were all older, aged 14 to 16, I thought.

'This isn't too bad, is it?' said Mrs Clements in an attempt to cheer me up.

But I didn't want to be there, surrounded by strangers.

'Can you look after Nigel for a while?' said the man.

'Of course,' said the lady in the TV room. 'Why don't you come over here and sit next to me?' she said, patting the seat.

'We'll come and say goodbye before we go, OK?' said Mrs Clements.

My two social workers and the man went to his office, leaving me in the large TV room, with 11 pairs of eyes sneaking peeks at me. I struggled to hold back the tears; my lower lip was starting to tremble again. In an attempt to stop it I gritted my teeth and forced back the tears that threatened to make their journey down my face. I didn't want to cry in such a public place with all these strangers looking at me, so I focused instead on the TV screen mounted high up on the wall. But I had absolutely no idea what was showing; I was looking, I wasn't watching. All I could think about was my mother and how much I longed to be with her and how I desperately wanted her to want me and love me.

And so I retreated into my own personal cave and stayed there for the remainder of the evening. Dinner came and went. Somehow I got through it on autopilot, with no recollection of what I ate or drank, if anything. Most of the staff seemed to be women. There were just a few men, who spent most of their time in the office, smoking cigarettes. Some of the women tried to talk to me after dinner, but I was not receptive to their efforts; I remained unreachable.

I got up to leave the TV room and one of the two female staff members asked me where I was going.

'To the toilet,' I said.

'We have a rule here. When you want to leave the room, you have to ask one of the staff first.'

'Oh, can I go to the toilet, please?'

'Yes, but come right back, you understand?'

'I will.'

I didn't really need the toilet, but I was severely homesick and wanted to cry, just not in front of everybody else. Once there I sobbed and thought about my mum and longed to be with her at home. *Mum*, I sobbed to myself. I'd been sitting in one of the cubicles for about three minutes when one of the women came looking for me.

'Nigel, are you OK in there?' she asked, knocking on the door.

'Yes.'

'Are you ready to come back and join us in the TV room?'

When I came out, the woman must have been able to see clearly that I'd been crying, but she didn't seem overly concerned. She led me back to the TV room. I sat in the corner nearest the door, as far away from everybody else as I could get, then closed off again until bedtime.

I was placed in a large dormitory with the six boys, who all enjoyed pillow fighting and general messing around once the staff had closed the door and gone back downstairs.

'Nigel, you wanna play with us?' asked one of the boys.

'No, thank you,' I said, hoping he wouldn't insist.

But he just turned his attention back to the others and continued swinging his pillow at them. As they engaged in general tussling around on their beds, I lay staring up at the ceiling, thinking about my mum and my home in Coniston. Quietly, I cried myself to sleep.

The next morning, a woman came up to the dorm to wake us up. We washed our hands and faces, got dressed and went downstairs for breakfast. It was all very routine and regimented. Apart from the questionable and occasional schooling that was held in a designated classroom at the far end of the building, I spent quite a lot of time with my psychiatrist, Dr Nolen, who would come in to see me two or three times per week, and an occupational therapist (a different one to Mrs Young from Lancaster). The new one shared the same ideas as Mrs Young and followed a similar structure regarding her psychological occupational therapy techniques.

Later that evening in the TV room I witnessed something most unusual. Eight-year-old David came rushing into the room in what was his typically energetic way and proceeded to hop, skip and jump from girl to girl, kissing and groping them all in turn. There were about 15 individual armchairs arranged around the outer walls. David leapt onto the lap of one of the older girls and kissed her while fondling her breasts. It was all very theatrical, with lots of energy and movement. He'd continue for about 30 seconds before getting down and moving clockwise onto the next girl. Sometimes he kissed them while touching their breasts and other times he kissed them while groping between their legs over their skirts or trousers. All the girls seemed to love this little boy doing this, and to my utter amazement, the female staff appeared to find it amusing too. David never got up to any sexual antics with them – at least not there in the TV room.

About two weeks had passed when I received an unexpected visit from my mum. After breakfast one of the male staff told me that she was coming to visit me early that afternoon. I was so happy, and it must have showed.

'Oh, well, that's cheered you up a bit, hasn't it?' he said.

I smiled at him and for the rest of the morning I was on a high. It was a 'free' morning when the children would entertain themselves in either the TV room or the playroom. I spent most of the morning flitting from the TV room to the playroom and the dormitory. Every 10 or 15 minutes I'd go out into the hallway to check the large white clock on the wall. I think the hands on it must have been incredibly lethargic that morning – they certainly didn't seem to have any get-up-and-go! I must have walked a good few miles as I paced from room to room, waiting for the arrival of my mum.

As soon as lunch was over (which I could hardly eat as I was too excited) I waited in the large open hallway for Mum to arrive. I paced up and down, looking out onto the car park in anticipation. Eventually, at around 1.15 p.m., I saw her strutting across the car park towards the main door. I could hardly contain myself, I wanted to burst through the doors and run out to meet her, but children were given strict instructions never to leave the house unaccompanied. Mum pushed the door open.

''Ello, love,' she said, as I embraced her.

One of the men came out of the office to greet her before showing us to a large visiting room, where we could have some privacy.

She'd brought me some presents: packets of sweets, chocolate, biscuits and some cans of pop. I was so happy to see her, but I soon ruined the moment by asking her when I could go home.

'Not yet,' was all she could say.

I pestered her and tried to get her to be a little more specific, but she dodged the question every time I asked. She tried to dissuade me by asking about the place: had I made any friends? Was I enjoying the classes? I think she must have stayed with me for about 90 minutes, but the time seemed to fly past. When it came for her to leave, the tears flowed (at least on my part) and an overwhelming wretchedness kicked in. At the front door I hugged and squeezed her, refusing to let go.

'Come on, son. I'll come back and see you again,' she said.

'When, Mum, *when*?' I asked.

'Soon, OK?'

'Tomorrow?' I pleaded.

'No, not tomorrow, but soon, I promise.'

'When, *when*, Mum?' I persisted. I figured if she at least gave me a date – next week, two weeks – at least I'd have something to look forward to.

Reluctantly, the staff allowed me to walk across the car park with her to the taxi, something they soon regretted for I grabbed hold of her and refused to let go. With all my might I clung on, crying and pleading with her to take me with her in the taxi. It took two men to drag me off her. They manhandled me back across the car park, kicking and screaming and crying, '*MUUUUUUUM*!!!'

Back inside there was hell to pay for my unforgivable outburst.

'Now listen to me, boy, and listen carefully,' said one of the men, 'if you ever behave like that again you won't be allowed any visits, not from your mother or your social worker. Do you understand me?'

'Yes,' I said, through tear-filled eyes.

'Right, I'm going to keep these in the office and I'll dish them out to you, one at a time, but only if you behave. Understood?' he added, taking my carrier bag of goodies.

'Yes.'

'Yes, what?'

'Yes, Mr Blakely.'

'Good, now go up to the dormitory and get cleaned up.'

And so I obeyed him and stayed in the dorm, crying, until one of the staff came to get me for dinner. I sat there with the staff and the other children, but only managed a few forkfuls of food. I had no appetite and felt like I was going to be sick. The sadness and homesickness ran so deep it was making me feel physically ill. Everybody was looking at me and there were a few tuts and headshakes from the male members of staff. I guess nobody liked a pathetic, miserable child who didn't interact with the others.

After dinner, David, seeing how upset I was, came out into the hall where I was loitering and gave me his tartan Bay City Rollers scarf. A huge fan of the Scottish pop band, he had a pair of white, ankle-showing bell-bottoms with tartan around the hems and a matching white denim jacket with tartan trim to prove it. Fascinated by the band myself, having seen them on *Top Of The Pops*, I loved their attire. I did not expect David to ever part with any of his beloved gear, so I was over the moon when he presented me with the scarf.

'To keep?' I said.

'Yeah,' he smiled.

'For ever?'

'Yes,' he said, hugging me. 'Come on, you'll be alright.'

And for a brief time, I was. I had a friend at last, but something bothered me about David – or rather what he got up to during the night.

Us boys had to go to bed an hour earlier than the girls because we were younger. But once the girls came up to bed and were settled in their dorm, further down the corridor, David would creep out of our dorm and tiptoe down the corridor to the girls. I would fall asleep before he came back, but he was always in his bed when I woke up in the morning. One night when he did this, curiosity got the better of me and I quietly slipped out of bed and followed him. Slowly, I opened our dormitory door and peeked around the corner just in time to see David disappear into the girls' dorm. I looked up and down the corridor; all was quiet. Tiptoeing down the corridor to the girls' dorm, I stopped outside. I put my ear close to the door, but dared not open it. From inside I could hear sniggering, whispering and some sort of muted commotion going on.

'Me first,' said one of the girls.

'Hey, that's not fair! I wanted to go first tonight,' said another.

Not exactly sure what David was up to, I opened the door a

few inches and looked in. It was quite dark, but there were small night-lights on. Judging by the silhouettes of spread legs and the various moans of pleasure coming from the girls, they were thoroughly enjoying whatever it was he was doing.

'Hey, it's my turn now! You've had him long enough,' said another girl.

I was worried that one of the staff would come and see me standing in the corridor so I sneaked back to my dorm and got back into bed, where I lay and thought about what David was doing.

The next morning I asked him what he did when he went off to the girls' dorm in the night.

'I finger-fuck them,' he said.

I didn't ask him to elaborate and I was shocked that he knew such a sexual term, but I assumed he'd got that from the older girls.

Looking back, I doubt David was having full-on sex with those girls, but they were definitely using him as their personal masturbatory slave, an undertaking he was more than happy to perform. After a while I became convinced that the staff knew what was going on; I even got the impression (from listening to gossip among the girls) that one of the female staff was involved on a casual basis during her night shift. The fact that seriously under-age sex was going on under the noses of the staff was quite shocking.

My three-month stay at Newbarns House was a cloudy amalgamation of emotional anguish, mental and physical torment and mind-boggling shock at what I'd witnessed with little David, all wrapped in a surreal state of boyhood confusion.

As the weeks rolled painfully forward, the other boys not only distanced themselves from me, but seemed to take a positive dislike to me too. You see, I'd hardly made an effort to fit in. Instead, I preferred to encapsulate myself in my own dream world. As for the girls, well, they never really took a shine to me anyway. After a while, even David didn't want anything to do with me either.

'Nigel, I'm sorry, but I can't be your friend anymore,' he announced one day.

'Why?'

'I just can't. The others are starting to tease me about it,' he said, looking over his shoulder in the direction of the TV room, where some of them were watching him.

'But I thought we—'

'Please, just don't talk to me anymore, OK?'

Then he was gone. I was distraught; David was the closest thing to an emotional attachment I had, and now he didn't want to be my friend anymore. Although devastated, I understood his predicament so I respected his wishes and spent the remainder of my time at Newbarns House in the solitary confinement of my mind, sticking to unoccupied areas of the building where I would not be teased or bullied by the other boys.

Alienating myself led to my becoming the number one target of bullying, whispered jeers and ugly looks from the others as they passed me in the hallways and corridors. The TV room was a no-go area for me now. Instead, I'd sit in the dormitory and re-read the letters my mum and social worker, Mrs Clements, had sent me.

Once I came across David with some of his friends in the hallway while I was wearing the tartan scarf he gave me. Noticing he had clocked it as they all walked past, I was convinced he was going to reach out and grab it to take it back, but he didn't. Instead, he just looked into my eyes and I could clearly make out a knowing smile in them. He'll never know how grateful I was. It was the one kind act that kept me going in there. That tartan scarf was a source of comfort during some of my darkest hours because of the kindness and friendship that it represented.

I continued to get those knowing looks from David whenever we passed in the hallways or glimpsed each other in the dormitory. He was still my friend; he knew it, and I knew it. But from then on until the day I got out of that place, ours was to remain an unspoken friendship.

Chapter 7

Bohemian Rhapsody & My Chair On The Moon

Suddenly I was on the move again without any warning. After breakfast one of the male members of staff told me that I would be leaving that day and I was to go up to the dormitory and pack all my things up in my suitcase, which he'd brought to his office from the storeroom.

'Am I going home?' I asked, full of excitement.

'No, you're being transferred somewhere else,' he told me.

'But—'

'No buts, take this and go and pack,' he said, sliding the suitcase across the floor to me.

'But where am I going?'

'Somewhere else, where you'll be much happier. Now go and pack, your social worker will be here in about an hour.'

I wasn't going home, but at least I was getting out of that depressing place. As I packed up my clothes, including the tartan scarf and other belongings, I was in a heightened state of apprehension, anxiety and excitement all at the same time, with the ever-present feeling of homesickness and a longing for my mum. When Mrs Clements and Mr MacGregor arrived, I was waiting in the office with my suitcase. I didn't get a chance to say goodbye to David, and as for the others, I didn't care to say goodbye, preferring to slip out unnoticed.

'Hello, Nigel,' said Mrs Clements, smiling.

'Hello,' I said, happy to see her.

Mrs Clements had been to visit me more than my own mother and with my built-in sixth sense I knew that she genuinely cared for my wellbeing. I could sense her sadness for me, as well as seeing it in her eyes; I enjoyed the times we spent together too. Whenever she came to visit me, we would talk about all sorts of things and she would show an interest in my life – what I liked, what I didn't, how I felt. Sometimes she would take me out of the building to a nearby park or café, where we would sit and talk. She always brought things for me: sweets, felt-tip pens, drawing pads and comics. But for all her efforts, she could never fill the massive void; the parental love every child craves, the birthright no child should ever be deprived.

'OK, are you ready?' she said.

'Yes. Where are we going?' I asked.

'We'll talk about it on the way,' she told me.

Mrs Clements pulled the Cortina out of the car park, with Mr MacGregor in the front passenger seat and me in the back. Mr MacGregor leaned around and explained that I was being moved to another place where they felt I might fit in better and have a greater chance of settling down.

'Where is it?' I asked.

'In a town called Grange-over-Sands. It's a quiet little seaside town – I think you'll like it,' he said.

'What about the actual place where I'll be living?' I said.

'It's called Crag Bank. It's a little smaller than Newbarns and it's a proper children's home so it has more of a family feel about it.'

Crag Bank, now that doesn't have a very nice ring to it at all.

The journey wasn't very far, about 25 miles in total. We drove north, passing Ulverston, but we did not continue north to where my house was in Coniston. Instead, the car headed east, doing a sling-shot up and over Greenodd and the Lady Syke waters at the head of the Ulverston channel, then back down to the coastal town of Grange-over-Sands.

About 45 minutes later the car pulled off Grange Fell Road and down the steep drive to the house that was Crag Bank. It looked like a short, private row of early 1960s terraces but most of the internal parts of the building were connected via corridors. Inside it was fairly deserted, with no sign of any children, just an older woman and an older man, whom I later learned was her husband. He was a man of few words.

'Hello, this is Nigel,' said Mrs Clements, introducing me.

'Hello, Nigel, I'm Aunty Eileen, but you can just call me "Aunty" like the other children do,' the woman said. Her husband gave me a brief grin, then disappeared into his office.

Aunty, I thought. *Strange, she is not my aunty.* But I would soon learn that all the children referred to the female staff as 'Aunty' and the male staff as 'Uncle'.

'All the other children are out at school, so it's nice and quiet. Let me show you around,' explained Aunty as we entered the building. 'This is the dining room,' she said, gesturing. The dining room was the first room I noticed as it was directly off the main hallway. It was large and airy, with a huge bay window. Aunty then showed us the living room, an elongated affair with a TV at one end and about eight comfy armchairs arranged in an L-shape around the room. The entire length of one wall was an enormous expanse of floor-to-ceiling, double-glazed windows that looked out onto a large, downward-sloping rear garden. At the back of the living room behind the arrangement of chairs sat a small table and a floor area, where children could sit and entertain themselves.

Along the short corridor I noticed the main office, then the stairs that went up to the various rooms. There was a dormitory with four single beds in it, and three or four small single rooms.

'This is your room here,' said Aunty, opening the door to one of the single rooms. It was furnished with a single bed, chest of drawers, wardrobe and a little table.

'This is nice, isn't it?' said Mrs Clements, smiling.

I had to admit this would be better than sharing a dorm with several other boisterous boys, but my heart still ached as all I wanted was to go home to my mum.

'How long do I have to stay here?' I asked.

'I think it's a little early to be talking like that, Nigel, you've only just got here,' Aunty warned.

'Give it a chance, Nigel. It's very nice here,' said Mrs Clements.

Mrs Clements and Mr MacGregor didn't stay long. But before she left, Mrs Clements promised she'd come and see me soon to see how I was settling in. Then, I was left alone with Aunty Eileen.

'Why don't you unpack your clothes and put them away in your room, then come back down and join me in the living room?' she suggested.

'OK.'

So I took my case upstairs, unpacked, then sat down on my new bed and pondered on things. I thought about my mum and my house in Coniston and suddenly I felt very alone and afraid, again. My lower lip started to tremble as I sat in this lonely place, miles from home. I had to get out of this little claustrophobic room, so I headed back downstairs to join Aunty in the living room.

'All done?' she said.

'Yes.'

'Good, have a seat – the other children will be coming in from school soon.'

Aunty Eileen was quite old; she must have been in her late sixties, maybe even 70. She chain-smoked and had a terrible wheezy death rattle. Her hair was bunched up on top of her head and she wore a large theatrical brooch on her lapel. The other man who was there was her husband, also in his sixties, but he didn't spend much time with the children. He was either in the office, or in the private living quarters of the building where they both lived permanently.

Shortly afterwards the other children started coming in from school. Crag Bank, unlike the other places I'd been in, didn't have a schoolroom. Instead, the children went out to the local state school. They were all told to change out of their school uniforms promptly, have a wash, and then come back to the living room to wait until dinner was ready. Soon the living room had filled up with all the children who found themselves residents of this 'special' children's home. The first two boys to arrive were brothers, Nick and Billy, aged 15 and nine respectively. I would quickly learn that the Mason brothers were two extremely nasty pieces of work from a rough part of Leeds. Then in came Martin and Phoebe, who were brother and sister. Martin was 10 and his sister was 12. Oliver was the oldest; he was nearly 16 and Elvis Presley's number one fan. Colin was 13 and Craig was eight.

'Hello, Aunty,' they all said, respectfully, upon arrival back from school. I would soon discover that Aunty was quite strict: she believed in manners, discipline and decorum, she did not tolerate rowdiness or boisterous children. To her, little boys and girls should be seen and not heard.

During dinner I could hardly eat. Again, I found myself sitting with seven strange children, and Aunty. Nobody really said much, but their eyes constantly glanced over towards the new boy, me. My sixth sense kicked in and I didn't pick up a very friendly vibe from the other children, especially the Mason brothers. Now terribly homesick, I felt nauseous and I didn't want to be there. I stared out of the large dining-room window at the steep drive and the road beyond it and fantasised about sneaking out the door and running away. *Maybe I don't have to stay here, maybe I really can run away.* This fantasy gave me a glimmer of hope.

After dinner the children either went upstairs to their rooms, or into the TV room. I opted for the TV room, where at least I could be close to (and protected by) Aunty and away from most of the other boys. The only other children in the TV room (apart from Aunty, who was sitting in her chair, smoking a cigarette) were the brother and sister, Martin and Phoebe. They were Pakistani children and their complexions fascinated me – I'd never seen anybody from South Asia in real life. They stuck together quite a lot, but they welcomed me into their circle of two pretty fast. It soon became obvious that they got bullied a lot and took a lot of stick from the other boys; my becoming friends with them made me a target too. But I would soon become a target anyway as I preferred to keep myself to myself. The other boys took this as some sort of primitive insult and often punched and kicked me when there were no staff members around. The main perpetrator of my random bruises was the elder of the Mason brothers, Nick, a very unpleasant boy.

The first evening dragged. I sat in the TV room with Martin, Phoebe and Aunty, watching whatever game show Aunty had decided to watch. Some of the other boys wandered in and out throughout the evening, eyeing me as they left. As most of them were upstairs in the dorm, I didn't want to go up to my room and put myself in the line of fire for whatever treatment they felt the need to put the new boy through. Bedtime eventually came and after washing and brushing my teeth I found myself alone in bed with just my miserable thoughts for company. Petrified, I felt vulnerable as I'd heard Nick and Billy whispering my name a few times earlier in the evening while watching me. As I listened out, I expected to hear footsteps outside the door, followed by the Mason brothers entering my room, uninvited, to beat me up. But anxiety had got the better of me and, although the beating didn't come, it was in the post. I fretted most of the night and only managed a few hours' broken sleep.

The next morning everybody got up, had breakfast and went off to school apart from me. I stayed behind with Aunty and Uncle (her husband) for I would start school on the Monday. This gave me the chance to get to know my surroundings without the other children being around. Most of the time I sat in the TV room either reading comics that Mrs Clements had brought in for me, drawing, playing or watching TV. Every now and then Aunty would come and check on me. She let me go outside to play in the large garden for half an hour, but there wasn't much to do apart from kick a football around by myself, which quickly grew tiresome.

Soon enough the afternoon came and went, the others came in from school and we all sat down with Aunty and Uncle to have dinner. The only other staff members I'd seen were two women in the kitchen through the serving hatch to the left. It was during dinner that I landed myself in big trouble for the smallest of misdemeanours. We were having a salad-based dinner, part of which was hard-boiled eggs. It was the first time I'd ever had a whole de-shelled, hard-boiled egg all to myself. In the past my mum had cut them up into quarters and shared them out, with me typically getting two quarters of an egg, at most. With all I was going through, my brain was not engaged at that precise moment. Happy to have an entire egg to myself, I stuffed it into my mouth in one go.

'Did you just put a whole egg in your mouth?' said Nick.

I said nothing; I simply chewed, my cheeks bulging like a greedy mouse.

'Aunty, he just put a whole egg in his mouth,' he continued.

With a look that could kill, Aunty turned to me in disgust. Her glare caused me to change into a quivering wreck right there in my seat. But I just kept on chewing, while looking down into my lap to avoid the nasty gaze of Aunty and the other children. She said nothing, but I could feel her glare. I felt sick and I wanted to run away, to be with my mum at home rather than here with these horrible people.

After dinner I thought I'd got away with my egg-eating antics. We were sitting in the TV room watching *Top Of The Pops*. Queen's 'Bohemian Rhapsody' had just come on and I remember thinking how fitting and poignant those opening few paragraphs of the song were as Freddie Mercury sang them out with perfect clarity.

You see, at that time my life and Freddie's opening lyrics were uncannily similar. I'd created a fantasy life for myself where, in my head, I'd go to the moon and sit there on a large comfy chair, alone and in peace. Generally, I lived in my own little world, which often seemed surreal to me, not knowing what was real and what was fantasy. I could not escape my predicament. Up in the sky was the moon, 'my' moon, where I, the poor boy who got no sympathy, would go on vacation on a regular basis. On the whole, whatever happened nothing really mattered to me anymore. I was most certainly a poor boy from a penniless, lower-working-class family and nobody loved me. And nobody spared me my life from the monstrosity I found myself in.

The song was not even a minute in. Freddie had just started to play the piano in his theatrical silver shiny ensemble and just as I was admiring his attire and the dangly flaps at the ends of those silver sleeves my concentration was broken.

'What do you think you're doing?' said Aunty, in a rather angry voice behind me.

At first I didn't know that she was talking to me. Everybody turned around, including me, and then I saw her, those sharp, spiteful eyes boring right into mine.

'You can't watch TV, young man, not after what you did during dinner. Come on, come with me right now,' she said.

Oh no, I thought. *What punishment could she possibly have in mind for my attempting to eat a whole egg at once?*

I got out into the corridor, the other children sniggering as I left the room, and saw Aunty standing a little way past the office, her hand on an open cupboard door.

'Inside,' she ordered.

As I approached her I looked into the little room, which was in fact a tiny broom cupboard.

'But I won't fit,' I protested.

'Yes, you will. Now get inside!' she said, scowling.

Her voice was cutting, like shards of glass being jabbed into my eardrums. I almost wet myself with fear. Aunty was only a frail little thing, but she scared the living daylights out of me. I was only halfway into the small cupboard when she put the palm of her hand between my shoulder blades and gave me a good shove with a strength belied by her physique. As I fell forward, I hit my forehead against the wall inside. She closed the door and I heard a bolt clang on the other side.

I struggled to manoeuvre myself into a more comfortable position, as comfortable as one could get in a tiny broom cupboard. But there was no room and the floor was stacked up with cleaning products so I could not sit. Yet I could not stand properly either as it had a slanted ceiling due to being directly under the stairs. So I stood, crouching like an eight-year-old version of the Hunchback of Notre Dame, my neck twisted and my head forced down at an uncomfortable and painful angle. It was pitch dark in there and my hearing had intensified. I could hear Freddie and crew still belting out 'Bohemian Rhapsody'. Then another song started, then another, and so on and so forth. I don't know exactly how long I was locked inside. All I know is that *Top Of The Pops* came and went, and so did the following programme as I heard the end credit music play out to both.

It was during my visit to the broom cupboard that I discovered a large, comfy reclining chair on the moon; it was to become my vacation, somewhere I could go when things got tough, right there on the surface of the moon, in the deepest, most private place in my mind. Beautiful! I'd appear there and see a large, comfy reclining chair looking all inviting, just waiting for me. I'd walk over to it, the moon's surface warm, fine and soft beneath my bare feet. It felt as if I was walking on warm, tropical sands, only it didn't feel really grainy like sand, more like toasty warm baking flour.

Although my spot on the moon was in relative darkness, I didn't mind – it made viewing the bright-blue earth easier in the same way viewing a large cinema screen is easier when the house lights are dimmed right down. I'd reach my chair and sit back, adjust the recliner and relax back into it with my feet on the padded foldout footrest. Though sometimes I'd fold the footrest in and place my feet flat on the warm, comforting surface of the moon. Other times I'd have my dolly, Lynda's dolly, with me. I'd hold her safe and we'd watch the earth rotate together, bright and blue, imagining all those millions of people down there going about their lives, but none of them could touch me up here. I was safe, I was in my own private heaven and nobody else could hurt me – for a while, anyway. Even though I was almost 238,000 miles away, I could still hear Freddie singing and playing the piano, ever so faintly, in a very distant background that I'd momentarily left behind.

When I started school, things went from bad to worse. It didn't take long for the other boys to realise that not only was I from the 'home' in Grange Fell Road, but I was the new boy there too. You see, the boys from Crag Bank stood out like sore thumbs due to the fact that we were the only kids wearing short uniform trousers.

Talk about making things worse! Aunty was not only strict, she was old-fashioned too and believed children should wear short trousers, right up to the age of 14. Having to walk up that steep hill to school with the rain lashing down against my bare legs or cold snow turning them numb, just to spend the rest of the day being bullied, teased, kicked and punched by the older boys gave a whole new meaning to the phrase 'adding insult to injury'.

Naturally, all this teasing and bullying hindered my education. I'd stay at my desk at the back of the class and keep my mouth shut, knowing if I answered a question wrong then the other children would laugh at me. By now, my brain was fully engaged in what I later learned was 'survival mode', which didn't really allow much of it to absorb the valuable education I was supposed to be receiving. As an adult, I would learn of the effects that my tortured upbringing could have on a child. The hostile and uncaring environments in which I found myself would force my brain to go into what is known as 'survival mode'. Absorbing new information is not high on the list of priorities for the brain when in survival mode. Instead, the vital parts of it tend to lean towards survival and staying alive, physically, mentally and emotionally.

Then of course I still had the bullying to come from Nick when I got back to the children's home. My life was terrible. I hated those itchy grey polyester short trousers, I hated the school and everybody in it, and I hated Crag Bank, Aunty and Uncle and most of the boys who lived there. All I had to look forward to were the occasional visits from Mrs Clements and, rarer still, visits from my mother, whom I desperately loved and longed for and cried over. An unloved, unwanted child in an uncaring world, imprisoned in my own personal nightmare, I wanted the whole miserable world to burn while I watched from the comfort of my chair on the moon. And I myself wanted to die.

Chapter 8

Outcast

My social worker, Mrs Clements, came to visit me out of the blue. I didn't get any advance warning, not even on the day itself. We'd finished dinner and I was sitting at the small table, alone, at the back of the TV room, away from the others. I felt Mrs Clements' presence momentarily before I actually saw her. When I looked up, there she was, a huge great beaming smile running across her face.

'Hello, Nigel,' she said.

'Hello,' I said, excited, but a little confused.

'Why don't you use the office?' said Aunty.

'That's a good idea, thank you,' said Mrs Clements.

'Come on, young man,' said Aunty.

At this I practically ran across the room to be with my social worker.

Children were not usually allowed into the office, it felt strange.

'Nigel, I've got some news for you. Your mum's moving house.'

'Where to?'

I was now filled with apprehension and an uncomfortable feeling of anxiety engulfed me. Was my mother moving far away? Was that what Mrs Clements had come to tell me?

'Don't look so worried,' she said, leaning forward and squeezing my knee. 'She's moving to Ulverston, so not very far.'

'Oh,' I said.

'And I've got some very good news for you,' she said, her big smile returning. The suspense was killing me, but she didn't keep me waiting long. 'Because it's a new start for your mum and brothers, in a new town, everyone's agreed it would be a good idea if you made that new start with them.'

'You mean I can go home?'

'Yes, you can.'

Oh my God, it was like all my Christmases and birthdays had come at once! Unable to contain myself, I leapt forward and hugged Mrs Clements, who in turn patted and rubbed my back. As I held her, joy, love and warmth began coursing through my veins again after seven months in exile.

'When?' I said. 'When can I go home?'

'Your mum's moving to Ulverston on Saturday. She'll need a week to get settled in, then you can join them.'

'But why can't I go straight away?'

'There are still a few things we need to arrange, such as your new school, but it won't be long, OK?'

'How long?'

'About two weeks.'

'Brilliant!'

Two weeks wasn't that long. After 196 days of relentless belittling, bullying, verbal and physical abuse and general hatred, both at Crag Bank and at the local school, I knew I could handle two more weeks. For me those 14 days couldn't pass quickly enough, and they didn't: it was like the world had gone into slow-motion mode, just for me. I was convinced the earth's rotation had slowed down, like it was stuck in treacle. And there was nothing I could do about it, not even from my chair on the moon. But the earth continued to turn, one slow rotation followed by another.

A week later I learned from Aunty that Mrs Clements was to come and collect me the following Friday after I got back to Crag

Bank from school. I did not recall a single word the teacher said that final Friday afternoon at the end of a tediously long fortnight; I'd spent most of it looking at the second hand ticking round on the large clock on the wall. And when I was not looking at the clock, I was daydreaming about being back home with my mum. I had my books, pens and pencils packed away five minutes before the end of the final class and, the second the bell went, I was up like an Olympic 100-metre sprinter, out of the classroom, out of the school and sprinting off down the hill towards Crag Bank. When I arrived back, huffing and puffing and out of breath, I saw Mrs Clements' familiar red Ford Cortina parked on the drive. Oh, how my heart lifted with joy! She and her colleague, Mr MacGregor, were waiting for me inside.

'Hello, Nigel,' said Mrs Clements.

'Hello,' I said, breathless and excited.

'How you doing, wee man, looking forward to going home?' asked Mr MacGregor.

'Yes.'

'Well, you'd better run along and get changed out of your uniform,' said Aunty. 'You can have your dinner before the others get here so's not to delay Mrs Clements and Mr MacGregor,' she told me.

Suits me, I thought.

I ran upstairs and was changed in 30 seconds flat. Out of those itchy polyester short trousers for the last time. I'd packed my suitcase and all my things two days earlier and had my change of clothes ready and waiting on my bed; that horrible, uncomfortable bed! I brought my suitcase down with me, put it in the hall and then sat down to eat my dinner, which was waiting in my usual place at the large dining table. I didn't want to eat; I just wanted to get the hell out of there before anybody could change their mind. It only took me marginally longer to eat my dinner than it did for me to get changed out of my school uniform – I must have practically inhaled my food without chewing.

'Ready,' I said, after downing orange squash in one go, slamming the empty glass down on the table and wiping my mouth with the back of my hand.

Mrs Clements and Mr MacGregor smiled. She said, 'Come on then, let's make a move.' Oh how those words resonated in my ears!

'Do you have everything?' said Aunty.

'Yes, Aunty,' I replied, aware of the other children coming in from school. Only Martin, Phoebe and Colin said goodbye, while Nick and Billy gave me evil looks from the end of the hallway. But I didn't care; I was never going to see them or that terrible place again. Good!

The car pulled up the drive and paused momentarily, indicator clicking, waiting for another vehicle to pass on the main road.

'Are you ready?' said Mrs Clements, turning round to look at me in the back.

'Yes,' I murmured.

I'd never been more ready for anything in my entire life. At that moment, I knew how a prisoner felt on his release.

During the 25-mile journey from Grange-over-Sands to Ulverston, I sat in the back of that car glowing, inside and out. It was the happiest day of my life; in about 50 minutes I would be back home with my mum. Relief washed over me.

It was not a dream, it was really happening.

Later in life I would learn, via relatives on my father's side, the truth behind my mother's reasoning for moving from Coniston to Ulverston. Mum was born and raised in Heywood, Greater Manchester, and had a grim upbringing herself. Ten years old when her father bought a small end-of-terrace house in Torver, in the Lake District, she went to school in the village of Coniston, a few miles away. When she was 13 years old the Local Education

Authority picked two girls from several local schools to attend Camp School for a year. Her father agreed to this, maybe because he would not have to feed her for a year. During her time at Camp School she lived in military-style barracks and, although classes and regular education continued, a lot of time was spent participating in outdoor activities.

It was during her stay at this Camp School that she formed a deep friendship with another girl called Lynda. Mum was to name her own daughter after this good friend. When she returned home a year later her own mum was in bed, dying of lung cancer. At 14 years old she started a live-in job at Heathwaite Farm, a farm/guesthouse in Coniston. Her duties included collecting the hens' eggs, helping to milk the cows and serving breakfast to the guests. However, a year later she had to leave as the owners of the farm were retiring. During this period of working at the farm, her mother died. Then she spent a few months working as a live-in help for an elderly lady (until her employer passed away) before moving back home to live with her dad.

After a few months, he went to a marriage bureau in Leeds and met his new wife-to-be, Mary, who already had three children of her own. Mary took an instant dislike to my mum, so Mum moved out and went to stay with her friend, Betty, for a while. She then took another live-in job near Kendal before eventually moving to another live-in job at the picturesque Waterhead Hotel in Coniston.

Soon after starting work at the Waterhead Hotel, Mum met my dad, Joe, at a dance at the Coniston Institute. She was 17 years old and Dad was 21. At the time, Mum was already seeing a nice young lad called Ernie from the nearby town, Ambleside. She claims that my dad muscled in as he had designs on her and also that they never had sex until after they were married.

Within a year of meeting, they were married, which was typical in those days. My dad already lived in Coniston with his parents, so, after they married, Mum simply moved in with the family. After a short while they found their own place to live in the village of Torver. Mum fell pregnant with my older brother, Anthony, almost immediately, then two years later she gave birth to my sister, Lynda. My dad was insistent that he wanted another boy, and that boy would end up being me. But it wasn't easy; they tried for nearly 18 months before my mother finally conceived. Back in the mid-1960s you wouldn't have thought getting pregnant would be quite so difficult, and with my older brother and sister, it wasn't. But when it came to me … well, it was almost as if I was never meant for this world, a thought I often find myself pondering on.

But then, on 8 March 1966, I was born, reluctantly. The midwife struggled to get me out, complaining above my mother's screams about my broad shoulders.

A few months after I was born, Lynda was diagnosed with leukaemia. After this devastating news Dad wanted to be closer to his family in Coniston for extra support. As luck would have it, the council had a vacant property on the same street as my dad's family, including his brother, Bill. Various friends and relatives would look after me while my parents spent a considerable amount of time at Manchester Children's Hospital with Lynda. After she died, Mum and Dad split up and my dad moved in with one of his friends. But soon afterwards he was diagnosed with colon cancer and started to go downhill pretty fast.

This is where the crux of Mum's reason for moving from Coniston comes into play. While my father was dying of cancer, she was busy getting pregnant with my younger half-brother, Jonathan, right under the noses of Dad's family, who were nursing him on his deathbed (my mother did not keep what could be called a dignified silence while my father was dying). After the funeral (where Mum sat at the back on her own during the service), Dad's family didn't speak to her anymore. My dad had a sizeable number of relatives who lived in Coniston, and with it being a small village with small village gossip, Mum found the hatred towards her too much to bear, so she got a council exchange to the town of Ulverston, 15 miles away.

By the time I arrived back home at our new house in Ulverston in Mrs Clements' car, my mum and brothers had already been there more than a week. At first, things went swimmingly. We were all excited about living in Ulverston; I was welcomed back into the family and started school locally. But then things started to go horribly wrong. The emotional damage had already been done earlier in my life and it was all too deeply rooted.

I hated my new school – I didn't like the teachers and I hated the other children so I started to play truant. The thing is, during those delicate, early years, young children need to go through a process, one I did not have the privilege of going through. I've since learned (as an adult) that during childhood a child will go through various stages of development but, if he or she misses out, there is a psychological therapy that they can go through later in life to compensate for the lack of nurturing, love and guidance, allowing them to get back on track.

From an early age I was always the lone kid hanging around street corners in the village for my mother never wanted me in the house. Then, when I was first sent away, I experienced animosity from the other children, so I didn't mix with them. I soon started to dislike (even positively hate) my peers and so I alienated myself more and more. And I started to view other children as the enemy. I didn't mix with them during my stay at Lancaster Moor Children's Psychiatric Unit, Newbarns House Observation & Assessment Centre or Crag Bank, and things were not going to change any time soon.

It was because of this that I found it so hard settling into my new school in Ulverston. I'd lost trust in both children and adults. Nobody could understand why I just couldn't be 'normal'. Always

I was the odd one out, I didn't belong and I felt increasingly anxious and vulnerable.

During my truanting days I'd wander aimlessly through the streets of Ulverston, or I'd hang out in the town library or in the local pet shop. I spent so much time in that pet shop that the black mynah bird got to know me by name and, whenever I came in, the shopkeeper would say, 'Hello, Nigel,' then the mynah bird would repeat it, chirruping, 'Hello, Nigel.' Some mynah birds are regarded as talking birds because of their unique ability to reproduce sounds, including human speech, when in captivity. My mynah bird had the added luxury of lots of practice upon hearing the shop owner say my name so many times! I typically hung out in the pet shop during the school lunch hour, so the owner never really suspected that I was bunking off. Then it was on to the library before more walking through town until it got to the end of the school day.

Of course, my mother always found out about my truanting when the letters and/or phone calls came, enquiring why I had not been to school on any given day, or days. My mother would go ballistic and I'd usually end up getting a clout. The thing is I just didn't want to be in school with the other children, I preferred to live in my own private dream world. Sometimes, when I was in the library, I'd close my eyes and go to the moon to get away from it all.

Things were not much better at home either. Jonathan, my younger brother, was always number one, which I resented with a vengeance, while my older brother, Anthony, was hardly an ally. Well, what self-respecting 15-year-old would want his foolish, delinquent 10-year-old kid brother hanging around? He made this clear to me by hitting me if I ever tried to involve myself in any of his or his friends' projects or activities.

An outcast in my own family, my kleptomania soon returned as I sought some kind of materialistic substitute for the much-needed love and attention I was not getting at home. My stealing was not done out of any sort of maliciousness or naughtiness or even for financial gain. My psychiatrist, Dr Nolen, stated in one of her reports that I did it out of sheer need; it was some sort of emotional fix. I myself didn't regard it as stealing, it was a momentary feel-good factor that lasted a few hours, a day at most, which is why I gave away, or swapped most of my swag the following day. Not that this makes it right. Although Dr Nolen knew my stealing was a substitute, she and her team never really had a plan of action to cure me. Eventually, my kleptomania would land me in hot water with the police, several times.

My truanting, thievery and general bad behaviour as I rebelled against my mum and brothers quickly snowballed out of control. I was full of resentment at having been sent away. Mum called Mrs Clements almost daily and pretty soon she seemed to be visiting our house on a weekly basis. I could sense the hammer would fall any day now. And it did for I heard my mother say during a phone conversation with Mrs Clements, 'I've had enough of him, he'll have to go back into care.'

Although I pleaded with Mum all evening not to send me away again, she was adamant that I could not stay at home any longer. It was all planned behind my back in meetings. Within a week Mrs Clements had told me that I had to go back to Crag Bank in Grange-over-Sands. I could spend the weekend with my so-called 'family', but first thing Monday morning she would be back in the car to collect me.

I cried and pleaded with both Mum and Mrs Clements, but it was useless: my fate had already been decided. Upon hearing this Anthony responded with an uncaring and taunting look on his face.

'You fucking bastard, I hate you!' I cried.

'Nigel's going away again, Nigel's going away again …' he sang, taunting me still more.

I'll never forget the smirk on his face as he sang this torment. I wanted to smash my fist through his nose, and if he hadn't been five years older and so much bigger than me, I surely would have.

'Anthony, go upstairs and leave him alone,' said Mum.

And he did, but not before sticking his tongue out and smiling at me as he disappeared round the corner.

So there was nothing I could do. I could not beat Anthony up as he was much bigger than me, and it seemed there was nothing I could do to prevent myself from being returned to Crag Bank on Monday morning, where I would be welcomed back with open fists by the evil Mason brothers, Nick and Billy, along with the other bullyboys at Crag Bank and the local school. I could see it now: constant belittling on a daily basis, cruel torments, regular beatings from the bigger boys, periodical incarcerations in tiny, dark broom cupboards and other cruel and unusual punishments for the most inconsequential misdemeanour or trivial act on my part, which Aunty and Uncle deemed punishable offences.

My life was shit and I wanted to die.

Chapter 9

The Sharp Pencil
& Grange-over-Mud

I'd only been back at Crag Bank five minutes before the bullying started. I said goodbye to Mrs Clements and Mr MacGregor and watched them walk up the drive to the car through my teary, sore eyes and then headed upstairs to my bedroom, the same little single room I was in the last time. As I passed Nick on the stairs he turned and punched me really hard on the back of my head. His knuckles struck my skull with such force I felt the most excruciating pain ever. The back of my head was on fire and throbbed so hard I could hear it pounding inside my head. I screamed and squealed in pain as I collapsed on the stairs, crying. Nick ran for cover just as Aunty came out of the TV room to see what all the fuss was about.

'What is it? What's going on out here?' she wanted to know.

'Nick hit me,' I said, holding my head with both hands as I sat in a tight ball on the stairs.

'Nick!' she shouted.

'What?' he said, appearing from round the corner.

'What's going on? Why did you hit Nigel?'

'What? I never touched him.' He shot me a look that suggested he would kill me if I said another word. But I didn't care.

'Yes, you did! You punched me on the head.'

'Aunty, I don't know what he's talking about.'

'Get up to your room right now and stay there,' Aunty ordered Nick.

As he passed me on the stairs he jabbed his knee into my shoulder and said, 'I'm gonna kill you.'

'If anyone's going to kill anyone, I'll be killing *you*! Now go to your room and don't come out until I say,' said Aunty, before turning her attention to me.

'Come on, let's have a look,' she said, leaning closer to me. I tilted my head forward and Aunty felt across the back of it. 'Oh dear, that's a big bump!' she noted. But I didn't need her to tell me that – already I could feel how big the throbbing bump was, sticking out the back of my head.

'Come with me,' she murmured, heading for the kitchen. There, she grabbed a large packet of frozen peas, sat me down on a dining-room chair, wrapped the bag in a tea towel and placed it against the back of my head. 'Hold that there for 10 minutes,' she instructed me, then headed back to the TV room, took her cigarette from the ashtray next to her chair and continued watching the screen in her own personal aura of cigarette smoke.

So I sat there, feeling sorry for myself. I looked out of the large bay window at the drive and fantasised about Mrs Clements coming back to get me, to take me home to live with her. I knew this was a ridiculous idea, but I needed something to hang onto and I couldn't spend all my time sitting in my comfy chair on the moon.

Nick kept his promise and beat me harder and with increasing regularity. Sometimes some of the other older boys, or his brother, helped him, not that he needed any assistance, being older and much bigger than me. At school, things were just as bad, with the compulsory short trousers making me stick out like a delinquent all over again.

I'd only been back at Crag Bank a few months when something quite unusual and out of the ordinary took place, though I would not learn the full extent of just what happened that day until I read my very thick file from Cumbria Children's Services, 38 years later.

It was the weekend and a couple in their late thirties called Mr and Mrs Jenkins visited Crag Bank. Who exactly they had come to visit I didn't know. They arrived under the pretence that they were visiting all the children, but it soon became apparent that they were showing a particular interest in me as they watched and spoke to me more than the other kids. When they were not spending time with me, they were talking to Aunty and Uncle, while glancing in my direction, smiling. I didn't really know who they were, but I felt their warmth and love and wanted nothing more than for them to take me home with them. At the time I did not know that I was being studied as a potential foster child and how close I came to going to live with them.

Thirty-eight years later I read in great detail that Mr and Mrs Jenkins were at Crag Bank for the sole purpose of checking out a potential child to adopt into their family, a little boy who had become available: a 10-year-old boy called Nigel Cooper. Unfortunately for me, it didn't quite happen. The reason was that the Jenkins had recently let go a 16-year-old boy whom they were fostering. This boy had developed an unhealthy relationship with their four-year-old daughter. When the boy left, the little girl started having nightmares and wetting the bed. Mrs Clements had told the Jenkins in a meeting that I had previously teased my younger brother, which I had out of resentment, but nothing malicious. Although the Jenkins really liked me and even sympathised, they decided not to take me as they felt that their own child needed a little more time to re-adjust after the experience with her foster brother. A few months later, they took on another foster child.

When I read this in my file as an adult while researching this book, I sat on the couch and cried. You see, all I ever wanted was a sister to love and protect (as my own sister had loved and protected me) for I missed Lynda so much. Living with the Jenkins and their four-year-old daughter would have been the absolute cure to all my issues. At the time, nobody really knew or understood this.

Meanwhile, Mrs Clements and her team continued to try to find foster parents for me. My own mother had given them permission to do so, which says it all. Unfortunately, there were no foster parents available to take me. And back then, finding foster parents for an older child was notoriously more difficult.

Then, something else happened that would momentarily change the course of events at Crag Bank: Aunty Eileen passed away. She'd gone home to her own house, where she and her husband lived when they were not living in at Crag Bank and carrying out their duties as carers. Relief staff had come in at short notice to run things while Aunty Eileen was off sick, but she never recovered (I suspect she might have died from lung cancer).

The relief staff ended up taking the post permanently. Margaret, or 'Aunty', as we called her, was younger (in her early forties) and had a compassionate, caring quality about her. Her husband was also a nice man, although he seemed to spend most of his time in the office.

Margaret had her own ideas about how Crag Bank should be run so it was out with the old, in with the new. One of the first things she did was to take us younger boys down into the town of Grange to the school uniform shop to kit us out with long trousers. I couldn't believe it; no longer would I have to wear those itchy short trousers. No more frostbitten or rain-lashed red legs! Margaret bought me two pairs of trousers so I had a spare pair and they were made of a softer material and felt nice to wear.

The first day of school arrived and, as I walked up the hill, I felt 10 feet tall in my flash new attire. Why I thought my new long trousers would make me fit in and provide some relief from all the bullying and abuse I don't know. All the others at the school already knew that I was from the 'home' so the cruel teasing, bullying, punching and kicking continued. Then, one day, it all came to a head when I beat the crap out of this kid with the help of a very sharp pencil.

His name was Philip and he sat next to me in class. We were only ever half-friends, something he felt obliged to be due to us sharing the same desk. A new kid called Travis had just started at the school. Travis came from London and had a strong cockney accent, like nothing we'd ever heard before. At first, some of the other boys teased him about it, until he punched one of them and made his nose bleed. After that, everybody instantly became his friend. A few weeks later he had the prettiest girl in the class as his girlfriend. When Travis took a dislike to me, my desk mate, Philip, stepped up his disapproval of me, too, for Travis's benefit. Travis had threatened to beat me up, but had not yet had the opportunity to get around to it. For him that opportunity would never come.

Philip had spent the entire week calling me names and chanting disgusting things about me. Also, the previous day he'd sneaked up behind me in the playground and got me in a headlock. He squeezed so hard I thought my neck was going to break. Eventually he loosened his grip, allowing me to drop to the floor. While I lay on the cold concrete playground, struggling for breath as my windpipe reopened, he kicked me in the ribs, then leaned down and spat in my face. I remember his saliva running into the corner of my open mouth while I tried to gulp in air. When I got to my feet and wiped my mouth, I saw Philip laughing with Travis.

Back in the classroom Philip continued his verbal abuse and threats. 'You wait until we get back out onto the playground at break time,' he said, extra-loud so Travis, at the next desk, could hear him.

Philip was desperate to impress Travis, and, to do so, he continued to prod, dig and provoke me until, finally (like an otherwise friendly dog who'd been poked and prodded one time too many by an annoying child), I snapped. Philip lifted the heavy wooden lid on his side of the desk and had his head deep inside while he pretended to get a book so he could snigger and call me names. I jumped to my feet, lifted the lid of his desk and slammed it down as hard as I could, smashing it into the back of his head. He screamed out in pain and started to cry, but that did not stop me: there were months of built-up anger from all the bullying and tormenting inside of me, and it needed to come out. I slammed the lid down again, grabbed my freshly sharpened pencil with my right hand, drove my knee into Philip's ribs, then grabbed his hair with my left hand and dragged his bleeding head out of his desk. My hand turned claret with his blood as I dragged him to the floor.

I noticed the teacher stand up behind his desk at the front of the class to get a better view. He shouted something, but what it was I don't know for I was hell-bent on hurting Philip as much as I could. As he was dazed and in pain I ended up on top of him and overpowered him easily. Holding his head down by his hair, I drove my sharpened pencil into his cheek with such force I felt the pencil point hit the bone in his gum beneath the skin just above his top lip. Then I pulled it out, stretching the skin of his cheek away from his face as I did so. I proceeded to stab his face over and over again, lifting my arm high in the air and driving it down into his face with all my might, while he screamed and thrashed about to try to prevent my pounding stabs.

He managed to get both his hands in front of his cheeks and eyes, so I drove the pencil down into his forehead instead. The tip of it broke off against the hard bone of his head. In a few short seconds the teacher ran from his end of the classroom to my desk and pulled me off him, grabbing my pencil and shoving me away into the corner. He observed the bleeding, screaming Philip and was at a loss as to what to do next. The whole class was in a state of shock and some of the girls were screaming.

'Jennifer, go and get the headmaster, now!' he instructed one of the pupils. 'Philip, take your hands away from your face, I need to see,' he said.

But Philip was too traumatised. Like a badly wounded animal he was squealing and writhing around the floor. There was blood all over his hands and it was running down his neck. Everyone was in a state of shock. I stayed on the floor in the corner, adrenaline in overdrive and my heart pounding hard.

'Still want to beat me up?' I said, giving Travis my best evil look.

'No,' he said, cowering into his chair and gazing down into his lap.

The headmaster took me to his office, away from the bloody scene, and called an ambulance before giving me the cane. Philip was taken away to have the numerous puncture wounds to his face patched up while I was sent home to Crag Bank, where Uncle was waiting to beat me senseless after getting a telephone call from the school explaining why I was being sent home.

After this incident I was invincible; nobody at school taunted me anymore. Indeed, they all gave me a wide berth and wouldn't speak to me. That suited me fine – I didn't want anything to do with them anyway. Philip came back to school the next day with a large, bald patch and bandage on the back of his head and several bulging Band-Aids on his face. He proudly told the class that he had had to have eight stiches to the back of his head, a butterfly stitch on his forehead and a general patching up of the punctures on his left cheek.

Not only did the teacher separate Philip and me, but I also had to sit at a desk on my own at the back of the class. At least nobody called me names or bullied me anymore, possibly because I always kept a freshly sharpened pencil in my top shirt pocket for all to see.

But my reign of terror didn't last. My violent outburst had already got back to Crag Bank and in turn to my social worker, Mrs Clements, who then came to the school for a meeting with the head and my teacher. Mrs Clements came to see me at Crag Bank afterwards. She asked me why I had done such a horrific thing and tried to explain that violence was wrong. When I showed no remorse and explained that I had wanted to stab his eyes out, she was visibly shocked. I told her that I wanted to kill him and that I wanted to die myself; I wanted to go to the moon and never come back. She must have seen something in my eyes that she had never seen before and she looked positively alarmed.

Unfortunately, my violent attack on Philip had not been witnessed by any of the boys at Crag Bank, who continued to intimidate and bully me. But I wasn't about to start stabbing people in the face with a pencil there – already I'd taken all my pent-up aggression out on poor Philip. I was done, for now. As the bullying and cruel torments continued, I closed up, vanished into my own dream world and became more depressed to the point where I didn't want to live anymore.

One day I didn't go to school. Instead of turning left up the hill, I turned right and headed down to the seafront. I climbed over a wall, crossed the railway tracks and walked out onto the muddy sand while the tide was out. Then I sat down, hoping I'd sink into the muddy sand and disappear forever, but I did not. Instead, I dug my fingers into the sloppy, sandy mud and smeared it thickly onto my face, into my hair and around my neck and shoulders until I looked like a clay man. A member of the public had brought the scene to the attention of a policeman, who came out onto the sand to see what I was doing.

'Shouldn't you be at school, young man?' he said, as he approached.

I turned around and looked up to face him.

'What in God's name are you doing?' he asked.

But I just sat there in silence; I didn't say anything and I didn't move.

'Come on, let's get you cleaned up,' he said.

'I don't want to get cleaned up, I want to stay like this forever,' I murmured.

He paused for a moment, adjusted his footing to avoid his black shoes sinking into the mud, then said, 'Well, let's at least get you off this mud and back home. Where do you live?'

'Crag Bank.'

'Is that the place on Grange Fell Road?'

'Yes.'

I didn't know if the policeman had a car, or just didn't want Clay Boy muddying his back seat, but he walked me all the way back up the hill to Crag Bank, where Aunty was waiting. The policeman hung around just long enough to wipe the mud from his shoes and trouser bottoms with a wet tea-towel that Aunty had given him.

'Nigel, what happened, why are you all covered in mud? Look, it's all in your hair!' she said.

'I wanted to look on the outside how I feel on the inside,' I explained.

'Oh, my poor love! Come on, let's get you out of those muddy clothes and bathed.'

Aunty was clearly concerned by my actions and while I was in the bath she called Mrs Clements to tell her what had happened.

My mud-mask antics, coupled with puncturing Philip's face multiple times with a pencil, were of grave concern to Mrs Clements and my psychiatrist, Dr Nolen. It was recommended that I be taken away from Crag Bank and placed back under the care and supervision of the professional psychiatric doctors and staff at Lancaster Moor Children's Psychiatric Unit.

Chapter 10

Regression Therapy

When I arrived back at Lancaster Moor Children's Psychiatric Unit, the staff had a slightly different attitude towards me. They'd obviously been given the heads-up on my violent outburst and Clay Man antics on the muddy sands of Grange, though it was the former that concerned them most. Now they thought I was capable of injuring others and possibly myself, so Dr Nolen prescribed medication to help – I suspect some sort of sedative anti-depressant. But pretty much every child in the place was on something.

Most of the children I recognised from the last time I was there; only two had left, with two new arrivals. So, there were still eight or nine children aged between seven and 10, except Ghislaine, who was now about 13 and the only girl. All sorts of medication was flying around the unit: Amitriptyline, Nitrazepam, Largactil, Dothiepin, Barbiturate, Valium, Thioridazine. Acuphase injections were also administered with frightening regularity whenever a child was especially naughty, got too far out of line, or simply didn't conform. This procedure was known as 'the jab' among the staff and children in the unit. The injections left you in a lobotomised state with 10-inch drool hanging from your mouth, unable to take in your immediate surroundings. It was all very surreal and dream-like, and usually lasted around 48 hours.

Within a few days a specialist doctor wired my head back up to a machine to carry out further tests to my brain. It all seemed rather barbaric and unnecessary to me as I felt there was nothing wrong. I also spent a considerable amount of time with the child psychiatrist and the resident occupational therapist, Mrs Young. Dr Nolen probed deeper than ever during our marathon sessions as she tried desperately to get to the root of my issues. Mrs Young also worked much harder with me. I took more psychological tests than I care to remember. Even back then I thought they were all missing the point and looking for something that simply was not there. I was just a little boy who desperately craved the love and attention he'd never had – it was that simple.

I didn't like the fact that I had to take medication twice a day, at dinner time and again before bed, especially as they made me feel groggy, sick and nauseous, so I started to rebel and refused to take it. But that didn't work. They would simply crush the tablets up into a gritty powder on a spoon and then two strong members of staff would hold me down while another forced the powder down my throat. Then, while I was still on my back on the floor, the beady-eyed Matron would wedge a beaker of water to my mouth and make me drink. It was a cruel way of forcing children to take their medication when they didn't want to. I remember one time feeling as if I was going to drown as water started to go down the wrong way. During a struggle I inhaled for breath and took water into my lungs. I started to choke and splutter.

'OK, get him on his side,' said the charge nurse, Mr Richardson.

Beady-eyes then proceeded to slam the palm of her hand into my back with such force I thought she was going to break my spine. I coughed up the water and I remember her examining it to make sure there were no traces of my medication mixed in. Thank God there wasn't, otherwise I would have had to go through the whole barbaric procedure all over again.

'Now, you don't want us to give you your medication like that every day, do you?'

'No,' I said, still spluttering and trying to clear out the last dregs of water from my lungs.

'Good, now let that be a lesson to you,' she said.

'But I don't want to have medication, I don't need it,' I protested.

'That's not for you to decide, young man. We'll tell you what you need and you'll bloody well do as you're told!' she instructed me.

'I don't like it here, I want to go home,' I said. My bottom lip started to quiver and I began to sob.

'The only place you're going is up to your dorm, and you can stop that crying because it won't get you any sympathy around here. Now get up to your dorm and wipe that snotty face!'

'No,' I said, rebelling.

'Right, you want to play it that way,' she said, grabbing me by the hair and pulling me to my feet. Seizing the back of my neck, she marched me out of the dining room, her fingers digging into my skin hard. She took me to the 'naughty boys' room, opened the door and shoved me inside.

'Now, you can stay here and have a long, hard think about your behaviour,' she said, slamming the door and turning the key in the lock.

The misery soon crept back, staking its claim on me. It was a small bare room with no furniture and nothing on the walls. Kind of like a padded cell, only without the padding. I found myself in this room on more than one occasion, sometimes just for an hour, sometimes an entire morning, afternoon or evening for three or four hours at a time. While locked in the naughty boys' room I'd spend my time dreaming of home, though that dream was getting fainter and more distant with each passing month, crying, or watching the earth from my prime position on the moon. High up in the sky I'd picture the UK, surrounded by the sea and imagine it sinking. During this fantasy, all the horrible people (including Beady-eyes) drowned, while the good ones managed to swim to the coast of France. I'd imagine flying back down to earth and living in another country where it was warm and everybody was nice to you.

It was during this second stay at Lancaster that I learned what going on 'regression therapy' involved. The worst case of regression therapy meant you got an Acuphase injection and were locked in the naughty boys' room for the whole day. My worst regression punishment came one Saturday afternoon when I lashed out at a male member of staff, Jack Donavon. He was a large, well-built man who got his kicks from bullying and torturing the children in his own sick, perverted ways. One of his favourite things was to drive really fast in his car to scare his young passengers in the back. Sometimes some of us were taken out to town if we needed new clothes and sometimes, if we were good, we were taken to the cinema in Lancaster. Sometimes there would be two supervising members of staff, and sometimes it was just Mr Donavon. I remember one time he had taken me and two other children to a nearby park for the morning. During the drive back along narrow, winding country roads, he suddenly sped up really fast. Me and the other two boys grew worried as we sat in the back of his powerful Ford Granada. We didn't have seatbelts.

'Mr Donavon, you're driving fast,' said one of the other boys, sounding quite anxious.

'What's the matter, don't you like it when I drive fast?' he said.

'No, it scares us.'

'Well, you'd better get used to it because I'm going to drive even faster now,' he murmured.

He shifted the car into a lower gear and pushed the accelerator pedal all the way to the floor. The engine screamed and our bodies were forced back into the seat under the car's acceleration.

'Please, Mr Donavon, slow down!' I shouted.

'Why, you're not afraid to die, are you?' he said.

I remember his evil laugh as he raced dangerously around those country roads.

'*Please*,' we pleaded.

But he did not stop; he just enjoyed the thrill of driving like a maniac and scaring the living daylights out of us.

'Please, *please*, stop!' said one boy.

'Don't tell me what to do,' he said.

'Please, Mr Donavon, slow down,' I said.

'Do you want to die? Do you want me to crash the car?' he shouted.

'*No!*' we shouted in unison.

'Well, fucking shut up then!'

And so we sat, squeezing each other's hands, sweating and wincing as the scenery whizzed by at an insanely high speed. Tears ran down our faces as our bodies were thrown from side to side across the rear bench seat as Mr Donavon took one hair-pin bend after another, often moving across onto the other side of the road, tyres screeching.

When we got back, I vomited in the back seat of his car, partly from carsickness but also after seeing my life flash before my eyes.

Mr Donavon also got off on getting the children in headlocks, squeezing so tight around your neck that your windpipe would close up and you could not breathe. He did this to me that afternoon after he had to clean my vomit off the back seat of his car. But sometimes he didn't need a reason. I was sitting in the TV room, still shaking and feeling ill, trying to physically recover from my ordeal in the car when he entered. There were three other kids in the room at the time.

'What are you doing?' he said, aiming his question at me.

'Nothing,' I said.

'Come over here,' he told me.

I didn't know what he wanted, though I suspected it wasn't going to be good. But I got up and ambled over to him, head down and still feeling queasy, like a nervous dog who knows a beating is imminent. I was about a yard away from him when he reached out, grabbed my hair and pulled me close. He got me in a headlock and squeezed hard. Immediately, I could not breathe. I thought he would let go after a few seconds, but he did not; he held his vice-like grip on me. His powerful arm gripped my neck like a python squeezing the life out of a rabbit. More seconds passed and I started to feel faint, but he continued to hold me.

'What are you lot staring at?' he said to the other three children, who were looking seriously concerned. 'Nigel and I are just tussling around. Now turn your heads and get back to watching TV.'

I could only just make out his words, as one ear was pressed hard against his side and the other against his thick arm. More seconds passed, and more. Everything started to go fuzzy, like a television that badly needed tuning in. The fuzzy picture started to get darker, like a slow fade-to-black at the end of a horror movie – in this instance, a sick movie with a psychopathic male nurse playing the lead role. Darker and darker it got as I sank deeper and deeper into a black bottomless well. I felt my body go limp just before I passed out.

I don't know how long I'd been out when I came round on the TV-room floor, hearing a faint voice.

'Now, you're not going to be sick in my car again, are you?' said Mr Donavon.

I opened my eyes and looked up at him feebly.

'Say, "No, Mr Donavon".'

'No, Mr Donavon,' I said, still feeling sick and a little surreal – it took me a moment to figure out where I was.

'Good, and if you tell anyone about this, you'll go on regression,' he said, leaving the room.

I hated him, not just for this but also for all his other petty torments and the cruel and unusual punishments he so enjoyed. My emotions running high, I started to cry, but I was also full of anger and hatred for him. Everything I'd been subjected to since arriving back here had taken its toll. Mr Donavon's latest antics were the straw that broke the camel's back.

I shouldn't even be here, I just want to go home, I thought.

My blood was boiling but I didn't know what to do to release my inner hatred and anger. So, I grabbed the glass jar of pencils off the table in the corner, ran out into the corridor after Mr Donavon, ran up behind him, screaming and shouting, 'I hate you, I *hate* you!' and threw the glass jar as hard as I could in the direction of his head. Just as he turned, the jar whizzed past, missing him by a few inches before smashing to pieces on the wall behind. I ran up to him and punched him in the chest. As I drew my fist back to hit him again, he grabbed me and wrestled me to the floor.

'What the bloody hell do you think you're doing?' said Mr Donavon.

I cried in pain as he dug his knee hard into my spine and twisted my arm up my back. It hurt so much I thought my arm was going to break. I squealed in agony.

Mr Richardson came rushing out of his office to see what all the commotion was about.

'What's going on?' he said, seeing Mr Donavon on top of me and shattered glass and pencils all over the corridor floor.

'I don't know, he just ran out here and threw a glass at my head and hit me in the chest.'

'Matron!' shouted Mr Richardson.

'Let go of me,' I said, trying my hardest to wriggle free, but it was useless. I started to scream.

Mr Richardson didn't say anything to Matron, but with one side of my face squashed hard into the cold floor, I saw him give her a knowing look.

'*No!*' I shouted, knowing what was coming next.

A minute later, Matron returned with a large syringe. She pulled my pants down and stabbed me in the right buttock. It hurt like hell and after a short while my legs started to feel numb. I wasn't sure if this was because of the injection, or Mr Donavon's weight on my body. My cheek was pressed into a pool of my own drool on the floor.

'OK, he's done,' said Matron.

Mr Donavon and Mr Richardson took me away to the naughty boys' room and locked me in there for the rest of the afternoon. As I collapsed onto the cold floor, I started to feel faint all over again as the medication made its way through my system. I was seriously drugged up to the eyeballs and the world went into slow motion, becoming surreal and nondescript. My heavy eyelids closed and I became engulfed in a strange dark world as the medication took me down.

I don't know how long I was out before I was woken by Matron shaking my shoulder.

'Wake up, wake up!' she said.

'Huh?' I mumbled.

'Wake up, here's your dinner,' she said, before leaving me and locking the door again.

I tried to turn over, but found it hard to move, my limbs refusing to obey the messages my brain was trying to send them. The side of my body that had been on the hard floor was now cold and numb from being in the same position for too long. Although I struggled to shift into a more comfortable position, the effort was all too much. I slumped back down again and drifted into a deep sleep.

'Wake up, wake up!' came Matron's voice again. She shook me harder. I stirred, but could hardly open my heavy eyelids or lift my head off the floor. 'You haven't eaten your dinner,' she admonished me. 'You know what happens to naughty boys who don't eat their dinner. You're in enough trouble as it is for attacking poor Mr Donavon. Now when I come back I expect that plate to be empty.'

I heard the key turn in the lock just before I drifted down into a deep, dark place again.

When I woke up I was no longer on the cold, hard floor of the naughty boys' room, I was in my bed in my dorm with the other children. I don't know how I got there. It was dark outside, the little night-lights were on and most of the other kids were asleep, except one or two, whom I could hear sobbing themselves to sleep. I was aware that I was naked; somebody must have undressed me. My right buttock throbbed like hell and my legs were still dead. It took all my effort just to shift my weight onto the other side. I tried to sit up, but my body was too tired and heavy so I slumped back down, my head hit the pillow and I was out again.

I was trapped, not only in this place, but also inside my own body. I was at the mercy of these cruel people who were supposed to be caring for me. Scared and vulnerable, I lay there, trying desperately not to slip into a deep sleep again. But just waking up for those few moments was enough to exhaust me; within a minute I was out again.

I stirred again, some time later, aware of something moving under my sheet. It was moving around my penis between my legs. Worried it was a rat, I tried desperately to pull myself out of my dazed and dreamy drugged state so I could rid myself of whatever it was. I moaned and struggled to move.

'Oh, you're awake then?' said a man's voice.

Whatever it was between my legs crawled over my thigh and out from under the sheet. I could just about make out the silhouette of a person sitting on a stool next to my bed. It was one of the night staff, but they usually sat in a large comfy chair out in the hallway.

'They asked me to keep a special eye on you,' said the man. 'You seem to be OK, so I'm going to go back to my chair,' he added.

My eyes started to close again as he made his way back to the landing to once more take up his post.

'Come on, you've got to get up,' said a man.

My eyes opened, it was daytime.

'If you get up, you can come downstairs and have something to eat,' he added.

I turned my head to the right and noticed all the other beds were empty. The other children must have got up and gone to class already.

'What time is it?' I said.

'It's time you got up, young man. You've been asleep all day. You have to get up because you need to eat, to get your strength up,' he said.

It was surreal; it felt like a strange dream. I was exhausted from whatever it was they stuck in my backside the day before.

'Where are my clothes?'

'Don't worry about your clothes, just put your pyjamas and slippers on and come down to the dining room. Don't be long.'

It seemed so much effort just to swing my legs over the side of my bed, but somehow I managed it. I sat there for a few minutes, heavy head in hands, planning my next move and how I was going to manage to get into my pyjamas. My brain wasn't really engaging and I was ambling like a zombie across the dormitory floor.

'You're ready then, it took you long enough,' the man observed. He was one of the day staff, who typically spent a lot of time in the office. I didn't know his name and right now it wasn't important.

'Come on, chop, chop!' said one of the dinner ladies. 'The table and chair won't come to you.'

But I just stood there in the doorway, ready to collapse. It felt like it took me at least five minutes to drag my feet, slowly, one in front of the other to the table.

'There, now just sit quietly and wait for the others, they'll be out of class in a minute,' she told me.

I glanced up at the clock and could not believe the time. She was right – the children had about three minutes of school day left before coming into the dining room for their dinner. I was given the jab in my backside just before lunch at about 12 o'clock the day before. I'd been out all yesterday afternoon and evening in the naughty boys' room and at some point stripped of my clothes and put into bed later in the evening. I'd then slept all night and all day, until I was woken some time after 3 p.m. And I felt like I was about to collapse and fall asleep again, right there at the table. My head felt like a ton of bricks. It was as if I could hardly balance it on my shoulders and it took all my might and inner willpower to prevent it from flopping forward and smashing onto the table.

I heard the children washing their hands after class, and then they all came into the dining room to join me. They were so noisy. My head hurt so much and their shrill voices and the chair legs scraping across the floor grated. It was as if my brain had become a blackboard and there were several little elves inside my head scraping it with scissors and knives. Then the beady-eyed matron came in, louder than ever.

'OK, pipe down and take your seats,' she ordered. Then she turned her attention to me. 'Oh, here he is! You've missed a good few meals, young man, so I hope you're going to eat this one.'

I ignored her.

'Well, *are* you?'

'Yes.'

'Good, because we all know what happens to children who misbehave and don't eat their dinner, don't we?'

How I hated her. She actually enjoyed being cruel to the children and now she had singled me out for special treatment. I hated her so much, I hated this place and, even in my surreal, drugged-up state, I could not understand how I'd ended up in such a terrible institution or what I was doing there to begin with. The staff often threatened the kids with a visit over to the main mental hospital.

But I wasn't the only one to endure such punishments, abuse and general cruelty; the other children got it too, some worse than me. One kid, Terry, was a seriously boisterous boy, what the staff called 'a troublemaker'. Once I remember two of the male staff dragging him, kicking and screaming, over to the main hospital, where they gave him electric shock therapy and loaded him up with drugs. Terry was just nine years old. When they brought him back, he looked as though he'd been lobotomised. It was nearly a week later before he started to resemble something normal.

So I did eat my dinner, every last morsel. I have no idea what it was, but my body demanded it, with a vengeance. In fact I was so hungry I could have eaten *three* dinners. I ate all my pudding and drank three times more water and orange squash than I would do normally. Mr Richardson was aware of my hunger and after I had scraped every last drop out of my pudding bowl, he said, 'Do you want another pudding?'

Music to my ears!

'Yes, please.'

He took my bowl, went over to the trolley and filled it again, then ladled lashings of custard on top. My mouth was watering.

'There you go,' he said, smiling and putting it in front of me.

I managed a meek smile for him.

'Don't worry, you'll feel better tomorrow,' he said, putting his hand on my shoulder.

At this I nearly cried. He was the only person in the place to show me any compassion, and when he did, my emotions usually got the better of me.

After dinner, I sat in the TV room but soon fell asleep again. I was woken up at bedtime so I could walk up the stairs and get ready for bed. Already in my pyjamas, all I had to do was wash and brush my teeth, which required a lot of effort.

'Come on now, let's be having you,' said the night duty man. 'It doesn't take that long to wash your faces and brush your teeth!'

I made my way over to my bed, noticing the same small wooden stool next to it, which wasn't there when I got up that afternoon. Comforted by the fact that I was wearing pyjamas, I climbed in bed and collapsed, exhausted. Within a few minutes of my head hitting the pillow I fell asleep to the faint sound of one of the other boys sobbing in his bed at the far end of the dorm.

Chapter 11

Rattus Norvegicus

I'd been at the children's unit for about three months. My mum had been to see me once whereas Mrs Clements had visited me three times. I was showing signs of improvement and was well behaved so Mrs Clements and Mr Richardson had arranged for me to go home for the weekend. Although I was doing better and behaving myself, some of the staff still enjoyed their petty torments and punishments. One of the more sadistic members of staff thought it was amusing to lock me in one of the smaller wooden outbuildings with a wild fox that had managed to get trapped in there while scavenging for food. The fox was going frantic and didn't like my company any more than I liked his. I was terrified, screaming for the man to let me out, but he found my terror hysterical and made me stay in there for what seemed like an age. When he did eventually let me out, the fox bolting out before me, he mumbled something about being a little fucking faggot who can't even deal with a fox.

Mrs Clements picked me up in her car and we arrived at my house in Ulverston late Friday afternoon. Well, I say 'my' house, but I felt more like a visitor than a family member. My older brother ignored me while my younger half-brother entertained himself. As for my mum, she continued to treat me in an offhand sort of way.

It was now 1977. I'd had my 11th birthday, an uneventful affair, while in the children's unit at Lancaster, the highlight being Mrs Clements visiting me with some presents. The weekend at home was strange. I felt like a stranger, like I didn't belong. I spent the whole weekend wandering around aimlessly with my thoughts. My older brother was still being as horrible as ever towards me – not letting me go out with him and his friends, not sharing any of his things or letting me watch anything I liked on TV. On the rare occasions when I was home I always wanted to watch *Planet Of The Apes*, but Anthony preferred *Colditz* on the other channel. Luckily for me, there was a nice couple living just over the back from us and they used to let me go into their house to watch it. They were about 50 years old and were very kind to me. She would always bring me a glass of something to drink and a plate of biscuits. They didn't have any children (unless they had grown up and left home) and I fantasised about what it would be like to live with them. I really can't imagine it was much fun for them watching Roddy McDowall and Ron Harper being chased around by men dressed as apes, but they did it for me and they gave me some attention.

Something else happened over that weekend. The Stranglers had recently released their debut studio album, *Rattus Norvegicus*. I remember seeing it in the window of the small independent record shop in Ulverston town centre. The band's name fascinated me, as did the rather odd-looking band members on the cover. Inside the shop I found the vinyl LP and took it out of the rack. The front cover intrigued me, but the back grabbed my attention even more: the image of a rat running across a fallen log with the yellow sun silhouetting it against a red sky was incredible. Mesmerised by that image, I had to have it. Mrs Clements had seen to it that I had some pocket money for the weekend and I spent it all in one go on the album then went straight home to play it.

My mum had one of those all-in-one system record players that were popular during the seventies. It had a built-in amp and radio tuner across the front and two separate, teak-effect speakers. My older brother was out with his friends so I was left in peace. After carefully removing the album from its sleeve I placed it on the record player, then sat down to look at the pictures and read the track titles on the inner sleeve and back cover. The first song on side A, 'Sometimes', started. Nothing remarkable to begin with; Jet Black laid down a minimalistic beat on the drums, Jean-Jacques 'JJ' Burnel's bass farted along in time, while Dave Greenfield gave his right hand an arpeggio workout. Then it happened: Hugh Cornwell started singing, with purpose and a strong hint of aggression. Whatever he was singing about, he meant it, every single word. It was the most amazing combination of sounds I'd ever heard; I was instantly addicted. The next song, 'Goodbye Toulouse', was equally brilliant; the same unique flavour, just a different song. That album had so many great songs: 'London Lady', 'Hanging Around', 'Grip', 'Ugly', 'Down In The Sewer', and not forgetting the amazing single 'Peaches'. Pure utopia to my ears, I was in musical heaven. Hugh Cornwell fast became my hero, life coach and casual Latin teacher via his lyrics and album titles.

I knew I was going to have to go back to Lancaster on the Sunday evening, but for now, I wasn't bothered as I knew they had a record player in one of the other rooms and we were allowed to use it, not that any of the kids ever did as none of them had records. Now I had two forms of escapism: the moon and The Stranglers.

When I arrived back at the unit, Mr Richardson was thrilled to see that I was smiling. It was the first time I'd returned from one of my rare weekends home without a big fuss and lots of tears.

'You look happy,' he said.

'Yes, I am. I've bought a really great record,' I told him.

'Let's have a look at it then,' he said.

I had the record in a carrier bag in my hand, as I didn't want it getting warped in my case with my clothes. I took it out and handed it to him.

'The Stranglers,' he said, observing the cover. 'OK, take your things up to the dorm; you can play this on the record player later on.'

He smiled and handed me my record back. I was so pleased – for a moment I'd been worried that he would not approve, but Mr Richardson was quite young and open-minded.

Mrs Clements said goodbye and she too looked so pleased to see me smiling – lord knows, it was the first time in ages.

Mr Richardson was as good as his promise and let me play my record in a quiet room. In fact, I played both sides twice each! My friend, Gelar, was with me and he loved the album too. In fact, he liked the track 'Peaches' so much he wanted to know if it was possible to somehow physically cut that one track from the 12-inch album with a knife so he could have it. He was serious, but there was no way I would entertain such a thing.

Rattus Norvegicus was now my most prized possession and Hugh Cornwell was helping to 'get me through'. He was doing more for me than any psychiatrist had ever done. I understood him via his sharp, witty and intelligent lyrics and I knew that he understood me too. My favourite track on the album was 'Down In The Sewer' – it was so hypnotic. That track almost sent me into a trance every time I heard it. All my anxiety dispersed and I was more relaxed than I'd ever been. The 50 minutes it took to play both sides of the album proved by far the best therapy session I'd ever had, and Hugh Cornwell was happy to see me once a day on a one-to-one basis: just me and him in a quiet room while the record player's platter spun at 33⅓.

For the first time in my life, I was at one with myself. Even Dr Nolen noticed an improvement. Finally the doctors and staff could see a glimmer of light in my eyes, though they did have reservations about my all-new dress sense as I emulated The Stranglers with my charity-shop attire: black Doc Martens, jeans, black T-shirt and a black leather jacket, complete with a few random safety pins.

Things started to look up and, every now and then (usually when I was in one of my therapy sessions with Hugh), I actually experienced an internal feel-good factor. However, I still suffered mental and physical abuse from some of the staff and the regular night duty man continued to try to touch me up and do things to me while I was in bed asleep, more so if I was drowsy, due to my medication for anxiety and depression. But he was part-time and generally on night duty just at the weekend, so I only had to fight him off once or twice a week. He would try to talk me into having some 'fun' with him and, whenever I refused, he would get annoyed and typically slapped me around the head; sometimes worse, and he would always threaten me with horrible and violent things if I ever told my mum or social worker, or anyone else for that matter. Then he'd move onto his next victim, usually a kid much younger, more vulnerable and therefore easier to overpower. Any child who was doped up to his eyeballs would be first choice. Of course, his victims were threatened with regression therapy, should they tell anyone.

Sometimes, if I was heavily sedated and could not physically retaliate, I'd go to the moon and block out those bad things while they were happening to me. At other times Hugh would just tell me, 'Nigel, you're better than any of those fuckers! You're smarter, more intelligent and you shouldn't even be here. Stick with me and we'll beat the bastards together.' The first time Hugh 'spoke' to me, I knew right then that I'd never become institutionalised, unlike most of the others.

Encouraged by my newfound passion for The Stranglers, Mr Richardson wanted to build on that and so he introduced me to bird watching and wildlife. Although bird watching was a little incongruous with The Stranglers, Mr Richardson probably figured that, if I could be that enthusiastic about one thing, then perhaps I could be just as enthusiastic about another – he was right. The grounds surrounding the unit were quite beautiful; neatly kept gardens, big trees, several of which had bird houses nailed to them, and a large bird table in the middle of the green expanse down from the dormitory window. It was an area rife with birds. I really got into bird watching and, before I knew it, Mr Richardson and I had filled out the forms for me to become a member of the YOC (Young Ornithologists Club). Having paid my subscription, two weeks later I had my membership card, iron-on badge and complementary magazine. Mr Richardson arranged to get me a book on British birds and some binoculars too so I could identify the birds that landed on the bird table outside the dorm window.

Then I remembered the despicable thing that I'd done to that poor blackbird, back at our house in Coniston when I was six; also the promise I'd made to myself about protecting birds and wildlife. In the YOC magazine I received there was a recipe for making bird cake, which (if my memory serves me correctly) involved melting down a pack of lard in a pan and adding various seeds, nuts, brown bread and other goodies that birds enjoyed and needed to get them through the harsh winter months. After stirring it all up under Mr Richardson's supervision I would tip it out onto a baking tray and leave it to set. Once set and cold I'd take it out and break it up into small chunks then put it out on the various bird tables around the unit and put fresh water in the birdbaths.

The birds loved my special bird cake. I'd make it every week, enough for seven days, and every day I'd put out more and change the water again. More and more birds started to appear and I'd watch and identify them with my binoculars from the upstairs dorm window. When winter came, they appreciated it even more.

In the meantime, Hugh Cornwell and The Stranglers brought out their second studio album, *No More Heroes*, which was every bit as good as the first. The cover was superb: a wreath of red flowers placed on a coffin with some visible rats' tails around the outside (rats were a Stranglers trademark). They even continued the rat theme on the inner cover, which sported the same wreath image, only with a rat poking its head up out of the centre. Now I had more material for my therapy sessions with Hugh. He had new things to tell me via songs: 'Bitching', 'Dagenham Dave', 'No More Heroes', 'English Towns' and 'School Mam', for example.

After two or three therapy sessions with Hugh and his latest album, I thought it was even better than *Rattus*. Oh yes, Hugh let rip this time, no holding back! *No More Heroes* was faster, nastier and even more intelligent, musically and lyrically, than the first album. After nearly four years of physical and mental abuse, I needed to rebel, and Hugh and The Stranglers were just the vehicle.

Perhaps because of my new improved mood, Dr Nolen changed and reduced my medication. Now I was on only two pills per day for anxiety and depression. Though I was not happy about taking them, as I didn't feel that I needed them, I was not going to be half-drowned or jabbed in the arse again so I took them and kept my mouth shut. Then one day I overheard a conversation between Dr Nolen and Mr Richardson. I'd just had a therapy session with her; she'd walked me back round to the TV room before heading into his office. As I got up to go and play *No More Heroes* in the record-player room, which was just past Mr Richardson's office, I paused when I heard my name mentioned.

'Nigel really shouldn't be here,' said Dr Nolen. 'There's really nothing mentally wrong with him. He's unhappy and emotionally disturbed, deeply disturbed, but who wouldn't be after what the poor boy's been through? Half his family died and he's seen his world crumble and now he's finding it impossible to adjust and function in life. He's not psychotic and he doesn't have any serious behavioural problems. The boy just needs a loving home.'

'I'm inclined to agree with you,' said Mr Richardson, sighing.

As they wrapped up the conversation, I crept back to the TV room and waited until the coast was clear. By the time the last track on side A, 'Something Better Change', had started, I was wondering if Dr Nolen's conversation with Mr Richardson meant that I'd be able to leave the children's unit at last and return home.

As Hugh sang 'Something Better Change', I got the distinct impression that for me something was about to change. Maybe Hugh was sending me a personal message here. Things were about to change and I would be leaving the children's unit after all.

But they were not sending me home – far from it.

Chapter 12

The Burglary

A few short weeks later, I was back at Crag Bank in Grange-over-Sands. Talk about out of the frying pan and back into the fire! I'd asked Mrs Clements why, if I was OK, I had to go back to Crag Bank and not back home to be with my mum. She just said the time wasn't right; I took that to be my mother not wanting me.

None of the residents at Crag Bank had changed – it was the same seven children and, to my utter dismay, prime bullyboys, Nick and Billy, were still there. Colin looked the same as he ever did. Martin and Phoebe were still getting stick for being of Pakistani origin, while Oliver was still listening to Elvis records at every opportunity, or trying hopelessly to play them on his acoustic guitar. Although listening to Elvis had never bothered me before, I was now concerned because I had my two Stranglers LPs and something told me that Oliver would not let me near the record player. Although it was the house record player, he had somehow adopted it and only his records got played on it.

'What's this rubbish?' he wanted to know, holding my two Stranglers albums as if they were soiled babies' nappies. 'You're not playing these on my record player,' he said, slamming the albums into my chest.

I didn't say anything; I knew it would be useless. Just as well I'd played both albums about a hundred times and had all the tracks firmly committed to memory, lyrics and all. Hugh would still be with me, just without the aid of electronics to amplify his point, but his messages remained in my mind.

Within a few days the bullying started up again, right where it left off, with Nick at the helm. Now that I was back, his unjust bullying and beatings were worse than ever. He hated me and blamed me just for being there.

'What are you doing back here? We don't want you back here,' he said, as if I had a choice in the matter.

'I don't want to be here either, but what can I do?' I said.

'Well, you'd better do something because if you're still here next week I'm gonna beat you up worse than ever.'

Great, I thought. *What did he expect me to do? Perhaps he just expected me to run away. Maybe it was because I'd only been back a few days.*

The week passed and I was convinced he'd forgotten his threat. Sure he'd punched and kicked me and made me cry a few times in passing, nothing new there. Then, one night, when everyone had gone to bed, me in my own small single room, Nick struck. Without warning, he stormed into my room, jumped on my bed and proceeded to punch me over and over again in the face. I could not pull my arms free to block his punches or defend myself. His knees were pinning the heavy blanket tightly around my body, pinning my arms to my sides. It was quite dark and I could not see his blows coming so I didn't know which way to move my head to try to avoid them. One of his punches caught me square on the nose, sending an agonising sting right up between my eyes. My eyes watered and my nose bled. I screamed for Aunty to come to my aid. My shouting, crying and screaming was loud enough to send Nick running back to his dorm.

Aunty and Uncle hadn't gone to bed yet and heard my screams for help from the TV room.

'Oh my good God!' said Aunty. 'What happened?'

'It was Nick,' I told them, through the blood and tears.

While Aunty studied my battered and bloody face, Uncle stormed out of the room and marched straight to Nick's dormitory.

'Get out of that bloody bed right now!' he yelled.

'What? I ain't done nothing,' I heard Nick say.

'I'll bloody give you nothing!' said Uncle.

The next thing I knew, he had dragged Nick by the hair to my room.

'You call that nothing, boy!'

'What, I didn't do that,' he protested.

'Yes, you did!' I shouted, angry as well as hurt.

Nick showed me his gritted teeth and clenched fist. Unfortunately for him, Uncle saw this threatening gesture too. He slapped Nick so hard across the side of his head it knocked him out of my room and onto the outside corridor floor.

'Get down them bloody stairs before I knock your block off!' he said.

'Are you OK, love?' asked Aunty.

'No, I hate it here and I want to go home!' I said, sobbing, as Aunty wrung a flannel out in the little sink next to my bed and proceeded to wipe away the blood.

I could hear Uncle shouting at Nick downstairs and I could not help but think there would be hell to pay for my telling on him. Aunty could see I was scared and visibly trembling.

'Don't worry, love. I'm going to lock your door tonight, OK?' she said.

Once she'd cleaned me up and was sure my nose had stopped bleeding she said good night and left. I heard the mortise lock clunk as she turned the key from the outside. Now I was more of a prisoner than ever and in the event of a fire I'd have to leap from the first-floor window onto the grass below, possibly breaking bones. But I didn't care; I was safe behind my locked bedroom door, where the big, bad Nick could not get to me ... for now.

The next morning I saw the effects of Nick's punches when I glanced in the mirror to wash my face. Both my eyes were extremely swollen and varying shades of purple, blue and yellow. My top lip was fatter than the bottom one, my nose stung like hell. Unfortunately, my social worker and my mother would not see the state of my face as I had no weekend leave lined up and, back then, documented photographic evidence and written reports simply did not happen.

I don't know what Uncle had said or done to Nick, but he didn't hit or kick me over the next few days, although he still glared at me during breakfast. But something else happened: Nick changed his bullying technique a little and explained to me that he would stop beating me up if I stole a pair of fishing waders for him. He was into a few things – fishing (when he went home for the odd weekend) and bikes, as in pedal cycles.

What Nick was essentially offering me was an odd kind of protection racket. He would prevent my face from being smashed to a pulp if I stole things for him. I had still not come out of my kleptomania phase, something I was desperately working on, but that particular project would have to be put on hold for now. Nick's suggestion actually appealed to me, though my agreeing to steal for him was more out of fear of the older boy. And so he set me to work and gave me a well-laid plan. When I say 'well-laid', it would end up more of an improvisation, though.

'There's a cobblers in town that sells waders. You can break in when the shop's closed and get me a pair, size nine,' said Nick.

Although a cobbler would not typically sell shoes, let alone waders, there was a big fishing community in Grange-over-Sands (the sea might have had something to do with it) and the local cobbler had spotted a chance to make some extra money.

After school, Nick took me down the hill into town and showed me the shop. Aunty and Uncle often let some of the kids go out for a walk after school, or go down the hill into town at the weekend to spend our pocket money. The cobblers shop was a small side-street affair. Nick showed me the back of the shop from the rear alley.

'There, that window goes into the back, then you can probably walk through to the main shop in the front,' he explained.

'When?' I said.

'Not now, it's still open. You won't be able to get out of the house in the evening so you'll have to do it on Sunday when it's closed.'

And that was that. He was really excited about the possibility of getting a new pair of size-nine waders on Sunday, and I was happy not to get beaten up for the rest of the week. The whole thing kind of excited me actually, and helped take my mind off my other worries. It was a different kind of kleptomania challenge and Nick was actually being nice to me. Hell, maybe we could even be friends – time would tell.

The weekend came and Aunty said yes when I asked if I could go for a walk. Nick had suggested that I stick tape all over the small window at the back of the shop before I broke it to stop the glass making a loud smashing sound. He'd given me a roll of parcel tape before I left the house and wished me luck.

I was vigilant about the job in hand: I made sure no one saw me sneak down the alleyway or climb over the small wall to gain access to the back of the shop, where I was now fairly secluded from public view. I also thought about fingerprints. If I used the tape, I'd leave my prints all over it unless I took the tape, complete with shards of glass, with me when I'd finished. But I had a better idea; I simply took my coat off, squashed it up hard against the small window and punched it. I heard the glass break and shards fell into the back of the shop, making a smashing sound on the hard floor inside. As I pulled my jacket away from the window, there were still some sharp angles of glass hanging down from the frame like lethal stalactites. I knocked them out using my coat, drew the dusty curtains to one side and then squeezed myself through the small aperture.

Once inside, I brushed myself down, put my coat back on and turned around. My jaw dropped and I stood there, gaping at the table in front of me. I'd never seen so much money in all my life! In hindsight, it probably wasn't that much, but to an 11-year-old kid all those pound notes, ones, fives and tens, and piles of silver and copper coins were an amazing sight. I stuffed all the notes in my trouser and jacket pockets, same for the coins. There must have been about £250 in total, and that went a long way for a child, especially in 1977. I wasn't really thinking about what I could spend it on, my only thought was that I had to have it. I wasn't entirely sure why, though it gave me a brief good feeling. For the most part, clothing, shelter and food were all taken care of by the children's home and Social Services – I just liked the idea of having that much money. I swiftly moved through the door and into the main shop area. Here, I had to be careful, as there were no shutters on the front section of the shop, just large windows that looked out onto the street. Although it was Sunday and this was a quiet side street, somebody could still pass by the shop and, if they saw a young kid helping himself to a pair of waders from the shelf, they would almost certainly call the police.

So I crept across the shop floor to the long metal hanger where the waders hung and went through them until I found a size nine. Relieved to find Nick's size, I unhooked them and went back to the rear of the shop, out of sight. I knew they would not fit in a carrier bag so I was just going to have to take them as they were. I pushed them through the small broken window and climbed out afterwards, relieved to see no one was waiting to arrest me outside. It crossed my mind to put them on and carry my shoes instead, but then I decided that this could look even more suspicious.

Back at Crag Bank I hid Nick's new waders under the hedgerows at the bottom of the garden. I went into the TV room, hoping to see him, but he wasn't there. So, I dashed up the stairs to his dormitory, where, upon my entering the room, he sat bolt upright.

'Did you get them?'

'Yes.'

'Brilliant,' he said, punching the air, 'where are they?'

'I hid them in the bushes at the bottom of the garden.'

'Show me,' he said, leaping to his feet.

When he saw them, he was ecstatic.

'Are they the right size?' he said.

'Yeah, nines … just like you asked for.'

'We've got to get them into the house, they can't stay out here,' he said.

Nick hatched a plan and got his younger brother, Billy, in on it. He told Billy to go to his dorm window and open it wide so that he could throw them up for him to catch, one at a time. I thought this was risky as it would mean standing just to the side of the large dining-room windows and, if Aunty or Uncle went in there, they would almost certainly see. Nick and I took one wader each and crept around the building to his dorm window.

'Are you ready?' asked Nick.

'Yeah,' said Billy, holding his arms out the window.

Nick launched the first unwieldy wader in the direction of Billy, who clasped his hands together, but missed. The wader hit the wall and fell to the ground. Nick and I looked around to make sure the coast was still clear.

'Catch it this time,' he said.

'OK,' said Billy.

Nick threw the wader up again. This time Billy caught it and pulled it through the window. Nick took the other one off me and repeated the process three more times until Billy caught it. Then we both ran back around the building and up to the dorm, where Nick tried on his new waders. He told his brother to keep watch in case Aunty or Uncle came up the stairs. I was pleased and relieved when they were a perfect fit. Nick loved them. He smiled at me and actually patted me on the shoulder and told me what a great job I'd done. I was so pleased; I could not resist telling him about the money. I figured I could buy my way further into his good books, so I emptied my pockets and started dropping notes and coins all over his bed. The look on his face was almost comical, it was a combination of shock and excitement.

'Where did you get all that?'

'It was on the table at the back of the shop.'

'Quick, we've got to hide it!' he said, gathering it up.

He grabbed his shoebox from the bottom of his wardrobe and stuffed all the cash and coins into it, putting his letters and postcards on top in case anybody looked inside. Then he hid it under some clothes in his wardrobe. I wasn't bothered that he had it; I didn't consider it my money anyway. As long as he was happy, more to the point, happy with *me*, that's all I cared about. But the happiness that Nick's happiness brought me didn't last.

Nick fast became spend happy. Every day after school he came home with new and fascinating items: sweets, pop, a new baseball cap, sunglasses, sweatbands and a new watch. It didn't take Aunty and Uncle long to realise that something was wrong, so they questioned him. He wasn't forthcoming to start with, but Uncle put paid to that with a few sharp clouts around the side of his head. So Nick told him everything – about the money, his waders and that it was me who broke into the shop and stole it all. Aunty didn't hesitate to call the police.

The shit was about to hit the fan.

Chapter 13

Perry, The Liverpool Supporter

Because I was already 'in care', the police handled my burglary with a little more tact. Instead of steaming in all-guns blazing, they liaised with Mrs Clements and the staff at Crag Bank. Because I'd told Aunty the truth about the burglary, the police didn't feel the need to question me, and therefore avoided triggering my anxiety and sending me into a deeper depression. Aunty told me off and punished me by taking away all my privileges. Uncle gave me a stern talking to and Mrs Clements came to see me to find out why I had done such a thing, then it was all over and forgotten. I thought that was the end of it as the police didn't come to see me again and the weeks rolled along.

Nick had spent most of the money, but had to hand over the remainder, along with all the goods he'd bought. Somehow, this ended up being my fault so, as far as Nick was concerned, all bets were off. He hadn't really become my friend; I'd been naive and stupid to think so. For a few brief weeks his plan had kept him off my back and he hadn't beat me up, but he soon returned to his old ways. If anything, he hated me more than ever now as I'd got him in trouble – at least that's how he saw it.

At first, it was just the odd punch as we passed in various hallways and corridors, while Aunty and Uncle were not in earshot or sight. But sometimes he would wait for me around the corner from Crag Bank and beat me up on my way home from school. As for school, well, there were a few new faces since I was last there, who soon learned that I was from the local home, so the bullying started up again. However, Philip, and those boys in my class who had witnessed my violent pencil stabbing attack close up, still gave me a wide berth and I continued carrying a visible pencil in my top pocket to remind and deter them.

There were two new boys who'd started, older and bigger than me, who, like Travis from London, had recently moved to the area. I later found out that they started on the same day and both came from Sunderland. Because of this, and the fact that they were the same age, they became good friends and stuck together. Soon the pair of them thought it would be a good idea to start a reign of terror against the kids from the home. Phoebe and Martin got it worse than me, first with name-calling, 'turban head', then punches and then full-on beatings in the playground. Pretty much every time I saw Martin in the playground he was crying. They didn't touch Billy because they knew Nick would come and find them and beat the crap out of them but they saw me as an easy target.

Back then I still looked a little malnourished. Due to my anxiety disorder and depression I was not eating as well as I should have been and so I looked about three years younger than I actually was. The two new boys, Trevor and Lenny, were despicable excuses for human beings – they cared for nothing, hadn't an ounce of compassion and showed no remorse for their despicable actions. They were always in the headmaster's office getting the cane, but it didn't seem to bother them. It was as if this cruel punishment was all part of the fun as far as they were concerned. When they hit, they hit really hard. It was almost as if they were trainee boxers.

The first time Lenny punched me he caught me square in my right eye. He was left-handed and I didn't see it coming. If he'd hit me any harder I'm sure my eye would have exploded. The pain was excruciating, it throbbed like anything; in agonising pain I squealed and fell to the ground. He didn't stop there either; he kicked me in the face. It was only due to my hands cupping my eye that his shoe didn't take half my face off. Instead, it felt like it broke some of the fingers of my left hand.

'Lenny Griffiths!' shouted Mr Baines, running across the playground. 'You just can't stop yourself, can you? If there's trouble, you're there.' The teacher then turned his attention to me, still squealing in pain on the cold concrete. 'Let's have a look at you,' he said, stooping down and moving my hands away from my face. 'Bloody hell!' he exclaimed, on examining my face. 'Come on, let's get you patched up,' he added, helping me to my feet. Then he turned to Lenny. 'You little bastard,' he said, clouting him hard around the side of the head, 'get upstairs and wait for me outside the headmaster's office. Move it!' he added, giving him another smack around the head to encourage him on his way.

'Come on, son, you'll be alright,' he told me.

Mrs Valentine – the school's appointed nurse – cleaned my face and hand in a room that was a makeshift nurse's station. My eye was swollen and black and blue. Again, my cheek had a nasty scrape from the toe of Lenny's shoe and the skin was all grazed, scraped, raw and bleeding from the full force of the kick, but, luckily, none of my fingers was broken.

'You poor, poor thing!' Mrs Valentine said.

She really did sympathise, not only because of the regular beatings, which she knew about due to the numerous times she'd patched me up before, but because she also knew that I stayed at Crag Bank – she could see that I didn't belong there and she felt sorry for me. Once, she gave me a hug, and with that, I cried buckets into her blouse. I found myself seeking love and compassion wherever I could, because I certainly wasn't getting it from my own mother. Although I still clung to the hope that she loved me, I wasn't thinking about her quite as much during this time. I was too busy watching my back, avoiding beatings, and generally in full-on survival mode as I fought and struggled my way through every painful day.

Whenever I'd taken a beating at school, Nick left me alone for a few days back at Crag Bank. I could almost have thanked the bastard for that, a glimmer of deranged compassion.

Two days later a new kid arrived at Crag Bank. His name was Perry and he was nearly 15 years old. Perry took an instant liking to me and took me under his wing, treating me like the kid brother he never had. A Liverpudlian, he was a huge football fan (he supported The Reds, of course). Perry and I talked a lot, about loads of things. He turned me onto football and taught me everything about the game; he told me who all the Liverpool players were. Soon we became best friends and did everything together. He loved that I was really into football now and showed an interest in his team. We'd go for walks after school and at the weekends. Best of all, he was a stocky lad and knew how to handle himself. Nick sensed that he had competition and that he might not be top dog anymore and his suspicions were right. One day after school, he waited just up the road from Crag Bank. He jumped out and ambushed me as I walked back from school.

'Just because you've got a new friend doesn't mean you're safe from me. I can get you any time I want, and I haven't forgot about the trouble you got me in,' he told me.

'But I didn't get you into trouble, you—'

His fist striking my mouth cut me short.

'Just remember that,' he said and left me there, holding my swollen and split lip, bleeding all down the front of my school shirt.

When I got back, Perry was the first person to clap eyes on me as I stumbled into the hall. He came rushing over.

'Nigel, what happened?'

'He hit me again.'

'Nick?' he said. He knew that Nick had beaten me up and bullied me in the past, but during the past week since Perry came to the home, he had kept a relatively low profile, until now.

'Right!' he said, storming off upstairs to Nick's dormitory.

'Did you fucking hit Nigel?' I heard him shout. Then I heard lots of tussling and banging.

'What in God's name's going on up there?' shouted Aunty, from her seat in the TV room. She came running out and paused when she saw me standing in the hall with a bleeding mouth. 'What happened to you?' she said. But the ruckus from upstairs sounded all too violent for Aunty to stop and question me more, so she hot-footed it up the stairs to see what all the noise was about. 'Stop this commotion right this instant!' she shouted.

Uncle came out of the office and ran up after her.

'OK, you two, break it up right now!' shouted Uncle.

Aunty came back down to tend to me. She examined my split lip and told me to go up to my room and wash my face while she grabbed the first aid box from the office. As I passed Nick's dormitory I saw him sitting on the bed with a seriously bloody face. His nose was bleeding, his mouth was bleeding and he was clearly in distress; Nick didn't look happy at all.

'Get to your room, Perry,' said Uncle.

Unfazed and totally unharmed, Perry winked and smiled at me as he walked past to his room.

Aunty came up and decided my split lip was more than a Band-Aid could fix, so Uncle took me to A&E, where they patched me up. When I got back to Crag Bank, Aunty had told Perry to stay in his room, while Nick was feeling rather sorry for himself in the TV room. I glanced at him, and he glanced back, an expression that was neutral with no hint of a threat.

'Aunty, can I go up and see Perry?' I asked.

'Of course you can, love,' she said, knowing that Perry and I had bonded.

I ran up the stairs to his room, which was a single room like mine.

'Hi,' I said.

'You alright?' he said, jumping off his bed. 'Let me look at your face,' he added, moving in for a closer look. 'You'll be alright, Nick won't touch you again.'

'But what if he does?'

'I'll kill him,' he said.

I didn't think for one second that Perry would literally kill Nick, but his tone suggested he would beat him to within an inch of his life, and he'd threatened him with as much if he ever touched me again. Perry beating Nick's face to a pulp and his threat worked a treat. Nick never touched me again after that; in fact he didn't even make eye contact with me anymore, nor did his brother, Billy.

The weeks rolled by and, for a moment, I was genuinely happy. Perry and I were like brothers now. We talked about everything: stuff I liked, stuff he liked. He told me all about his life, and I told him about mine. Our conversations were always balanced and two-way. Perry had this really cool denim Wrangler bomber jacket that had so many Liverpool FC patches and badges sewn onto it you could hardly see the blue denim of the actual jacket anymore. He also wore Doc Marten air-cushioned-sole boots just like mine; only Perry's were deep red, while mine were black.

We even polished our boots together; he'd sit there with his tin of oxblood polish, while I dabbed my brush into my black polish, sometimes in his room, and sometimes in mine. Usually we'd talk about football during our boot-cleaning ritual and, as Perry was a Scouser and Liverpool had won the League for the previous two years on the trot, Liverpool, Anfield and Kevin Keegan were the most discussed subjects.

It was great. I had the best friend in the world and – for a brief moment – I was untouchable.

Chapter 14

Kleptomania

It was Tuesday, 7 March 1978, the day before my 12th birthday, and I was excited because Mrs Clements had phoned and told me she had £5 for me. Did I want the cash or would I like her to buy me something with it? I was really keen to own a pocket calculator and, suspecting there might not be a shop in Grange that sold them, I asked if she could buy one for me. Pocket calculators didn't really catch on until the mid-seventies and, even then, you had to go to one of the larger towns or cities to find a shop that sold them. Back then there were no home video games, consoles, computers or the like, and only three channels on TV. For me, a pocket calculator represented the epitome of portable technology.

I was getting a little anxious because a few weeks had passed and I still hadn't heard from my mum – no phone call, no letter, nothing, and it was my birthday. Mrs Clements suggested it might just be late in the post and she was confident I'd get a letter and a card from her in the next morning's post.

The next morning, during breakfast before school, my eyes constantly scanned the driveway, looking out for the postman. Then there he was, strolling down the drive, holding a stack of letters all bound together with an elastic band. I was convinced there would be a birthday card from my mum in that stack. Aunty went to the door to take delivery and came back to the dining room, snapping the elastic band away. She too knew how anxious I was about getting a card from Mum so she quickly thumbed through the post, looking out for something with my name on it. The pile she'd thumbed through was getting thicker, while the one she still had to thumb through was increasingly thinner. It was so painful, watching her thumb through the last two or three until all the letters were now in her left hand. She looked up at me and her expression said it all.

'Never mind, mate, it still might come in the second post,' said Perry, putting an arm around my shoulder.

The muscles in my face relaxed and my expression dropped, along with my shoulders. As I retreated back into my cave the rest of my body deflated.

'Perry's right, Nigel. It might come in the second post. I'm sure it will be here when you get home from school later,' Aunty reassured me.

But it wasn't to be. That day at school was another long one and afterwards I ran all the way back to Crag Bank, where Aunty and Mrs Clements were waiting for me. There was no card but it didn't matter now because Mrs Clements had come to see me, bringing with her a brand-new pocket calculator. Aunty had also arranged a birthday cake with candles for us to have after dinner and, on top of that, she told me that she was going to take me down into town on the Saturday to buy me a present, courtesy of Crag Bank.

Mrs Clements stayed and talked to me for an hour or so. She was full of sympathy for me. So too was one of her colleagues, a lady called Mrs Costello, who often reported on my life, which would form part of my ever-growing file. When I decided to write this book, I applied to child care services for a copy of my file, which was a two-inch-thick A4 affair containing over 250,000 words of reports, letters, dictated meetings about me, every letter that my mother had ever written to Social Services and lord knows what else – basically, my entire childhood life from birth to sixteen was in there. When I got to read it all, Mrs Costello had written, 'Poor little Nigel. His mother just doesn't see how disturbed he is'. In the same part of the file a Sergeant Gemmell from Ulverston police said, 'The boy hardly knows if he is telling the truth or not as he lives in such a disturbed world. Mrs Cooper does not have a clue what the boy is going through or what to do about it.'

After dinner I blew the candles out on my cake and it was devoured, then Perry and I went up to his room, where I could check out my new calculator. Perry was so cool, he seemed to know everything. He told me if I keyed in certain numbers then held the calculator upside-down, it would spell out words. I thought that was a brilliant trick, so I started to see what words I could make with my limited numbers/letters. One of the first words I found was HELL – very fitting and ironic under the circumstances. But if I thought I was in a living hell now, it would soon escalate to a whole new level. Misery would fast become a burning inferno not even my rivers of tears would be able to extinguish.

The next morning my mother's card arrived with a crisp £1 note in it, but somehow the moment had passed. She told me she'd try to come to see me the following week. In the meantime things had been brewing and plans were made, not only for me, but for Perry too.

The next evening Perry's social worker came to visit him. He was in Aunty's office talking for about an hour. When they eventually came out and the social worker left, Perry told me to go up to his room with him.

'Nigel, I'm going to be leaving here soon,' he said.

'What do you mean?'

'I'm going home.'

'What? When?'

'In two weeks.'

Instead of being happy for Perry, panic gripped me like a Boa constrictor around my chest. I knew Nick would come at me with a newfound fury and a fresh taste for blood and vengeance. Even though he had not troubled me since Perry's arrival, I could sense he was itching for it.

'What will I do without you?' I said.

'Don't worry, you'll be alright,' he told me.

But I couldn't see how, and when Nick heard the news, he started making eye contact with me again and there was a threatening look about them. The next two weeks flew by.

Perry was going home on a Saturday morning. His social worker came to collect him and his things, we said an emotional goodbye, and then he left. Nick was out in the garden, playing football with his brother. I had to do something before he got to me, so I asked Aunty if I could go for a walk.

'Yes, love, but not into town, OK?' she said, probably concerned I'd break into a shop or something.

'OK,' I said.

I ran upstairs, grabbed my coat and pocket money and headed out, careful not to let Nick see me. Against Aunty's advice, I did go to town, but I walked through the town to the railway station and jumped on the first train to Ulverston. I didn't buy a ticket because I thought the man at the ticket office might think it suspicious that a 12-year-old boy was travelling alone, so I sneaked past the barrier without him seeing me. At Ulverston, by luck, there was nobody manning the barrier so I could walk on through, unnoticed. I walked across town until I reached Beech Drive, where my mum and two brothers lived. Nervously, I opened the gate and made my way to the back door and entered the house.

Mum was in the kitchen; she was shocked and surprised to see me walk through the door.

'Nigel, what are you doing here?' she said.

'I don't want to go back to Grange, please let me stay here,' I said.

Although I wasn't crying, she could see that I was anxious and upset about something.

'What's happened?'

'It's Nick, he's gonna start beating me up again.'

'What do you mean, I thought all the bullying had stopped?'

'It did, but Perry's left, he's gone back home.'

'When did this happen?'

'Just today.'

My mum was aware of Nick's (and the other boys, as well as boys at the external school) bullying me, but she didn't really know the full extent of it, or just how violent it was. She was under the impression it was just boys being boys while the staff kept most of the goings on under wraps and woe betide anybody who dared say anything – what went on in the children's home stayed in the children's home.

'What's he doing here?' said Anthony, entering the kitchen.

'It looks like there's been trouble at mill,' explained Mum.

'Oh, great!' said Anthony, going back to the living room.

Trouble at mill, I thought. *I'd say it was a bit more than that.*

She just didn't get it; she had absolutely no idea what misery I was going through. Naturally, she phoned Crag Bank to inform them of my whereabouts. It was agreed that I could stay at home with Mum (to Anthony's dismay) until the Monday morning, when Mrs Clements would come to take me back.

I spent the whole of Saturday evening and a large portion of Sunday telling my mum about all the bullying and beatings I was getting, both at Crag Bank and at the local school. She was listening to me, but she wasn't really hearing me.

'Anyway, did you get my card?' she said, as if everything I'd been telling her was inconsequential in comparison, either that or it all just went over her head. It was useless, my begging and pleading with her not to send me back was clearly falling on deaf ears.

It would appear that my relationship with Anthony had got even worse in my absence. There was a lot of tension and jealousy as we both fought for Mum's attention. I hated it when he was around and wished he would just go out with his stupid mates and leave me alone. Things between me and my younger half-brother, Jonathan, were not much better. I resented him for coming into our lives and partly blamed him for my being sent into care.

When I was home I suffered a different kind of anxiety disorder, and there was still no demonstrable love from my mum and only hatred from Anthony and a distinct lack of connection with Jonathan. Although there was no physical pain at home, the emotional pain and the overwhelming feeling of being unwanted hurt just as much. To me it seemed they had all ganged up on me, blamed me for everything and made me the scapegoat; it just wasn't fair.

On the Monday morning Mrs Clements arrived to take me back.

'Come on, Nigel, let's get you back,' she said.

Just seeing her kind face was all too much for me and I started to cry. She put her arm around my shoulder and tried to comfort me for a minute while my mum stood there and watched from a distance.

'Come on, son, you'll be OK. I'm sure it's not that bad,' said Mum.

Mrs Clements led me from the house to her car.

'Oh, is there any chance you can give the DHSS a prod? I still haven't had Nigel's money and it's been a good few months now,' said Mum to Mrs Clements.

I'd later learn, from my very thick file, that Mum was more concerned about getting her money for me off the DHSS for when I was home on those rare weekends than actually having me home for the weekend. For her, the money was at least some saving grace. Yet, she seemed to spend it just on Anthony and Jonathan and bought them pretty much everything they needed. When it came to me, she'd ask Mrs Clements or somebody else at Social Services for the money. If Nigel needed shoes, it was Mrs Clements' responsibility; if Nigel needed a new jacket or trousers, she'd tell Mrs Clements and expect her to pull the funds or some sort of clothing allowance from Social Services; if Nigel wanted pocket money, Mrs Clements would arrange a weekly allowance out of the Social Services budget. She took no responsibility for me whatsoever; she treated me like an unwanted foster child.

So, I sat in the front of Mrs Clements' car and turned to see my mum wave goodbye from the front door. I didn't know what to think or feel, it was like I was trapped between two worlds, and the only one that felt truly comfortable was when I was in Mrs Clements' car, being transported between one and the other. How I wished those car journeys would never end, but they always did, and their final destination was always the same: bleak, miserable and hopeless.

Back at Grange, Mrs Clements said goodbye and left me with Aunty.

'Why did you run away, pet?'

'I don't like it here. Nick always bullies me and hits me, and now Perry's gone, it's gonna be worse than ever,' I explained.

'Nigel, you know I'm here for you if you need to talk and, if Nick bullies you again, you come and tell me, OK?' she said.

I smiled, but said nothing; if I told on Nick, he'd only beat me worse. Meanwhile, the clock was ticking away and eventually the other children came in from school, but there was no sign of Nick. The mild happiness his absence brought didn't last; he eventually arrived, 40 minutes late.

'Where've you been?' said Aunty.

'I had to stay behind,' he told her.

'Well, hurry up and get changed. Dinner's nearly ready.'

He went upstairs, giving me the eye over his shoulder as he passed.

That evening, no beatings came, and that night nobody came into my room. But the next evening I would find out why I'd been spared when he came to my room. I was in the TV room, under the watchful gaze of Aunty, for my own protection, when Nick came in and sat next to me. At first he was just watching TV, but when Aunty left the room to answer the phone in her office, he spoke to me.

'Come up to my dorm in five minutes. There's something I want to talk to you about … Don't worry, I'm not gonna beat you up. I won't do that anymore, but you have to do something for me,' he said, then got up and left the room.

Aunty came off the phone and came back to join us. I waited a few more minutes so as not to cause suspicion, then got up and went upstairs.

'Is everything OK?' asked Aunty, as I left.

'Yes.'

'Good,' she said, getting back to the TV.

I was anxious and more than a little scared as I headed up the stairs. It could still be a trap; he could be waiting in his room with his brother, waiting to attack me. But when I entered his dorm, Nick was alone, lying on his bed waiting for me. He got up and handed me a picture – a page torn from a catalogue, actually – with three bicycles on it.

'I want you to get me a bike like that,' he said, pointing, 'with cow-horn handlebars, just like those ones.'

'How am I supposed to do that? I wouldn't know where to start looking for a bike like that,' I said.

Also, I was trying to keep out of trouble, but somehow, trouble just had a way of finding me.

'Don't worry, I know where you can find one.'

'Where?' I said, expecting him to say he'd seen one locked to some fence at school.

'In town, the bike shop.'

'How am I supposed to steal a bike from a shop? They're all locked up.'

'Only the ones outside, the ones inside aren't.'

'But the shopkeeper will see me.'

'Look, it'll be easy! The bike I want is right next to the door and I'm gonna get Billy to help you.'

'How?'

'He'll go in first to look around, then you go in a minute later. He'll ask the shopkeeper a question and get him to show him a bike out the back while you take the one near the front door.'

I knew the shop as I'd browsed in there before, fantasising about bikes I could not afford. The shop was in two parts, the front part with lots of bikes on display, then a small step that went to another small shop-floor area towards the rear. If Billy and the shopkeeper were preoccupied in the rear part, I could quite possibly wheel the bike out, unnoticed, and ride off on it. It sounded a little risky, though.

'What if I don't?'

'Your fat friend, Perry, he broke my nose and busted my lip …' Nick reached into his patch pocket and took out a flick knife, one he'd bought with my stolen money and not told the staff about. He triggered the spring-loaded blade via the button near the top of the handle. 'If you don't, I'll do a hell of a lot worse than bust your nose,' he said, folding the blade back in and putting the knife away. 'So, are you in?'

'Yeah.' I was reluctant, but caught between a rock and a hard place.

'Good, next Saturday, when it's busy,' he said.

'But what will you tell Aunty? She'll want to know where you got it.'

'Aunty won't know about it, I'm gonna keep it locked to the railings over the back fence. I'll use it to go to school on and at the weekends, she'll never see it.'

The weekend came and the Mason brothers and I headed off to town. Of course, I asked Aunty if I could go for a walk first. Nick and Billy waited half an hour before asking to leave and then we met up at the bottom of the hill. We made our way to the bike shop and Nick pointed to the bike he wanted, just inside the doorway.

'I'll wait for you back at the bottom of the hill,' he said, leaving Billy and me to do the dastardly deed.

Billy went in first, but I could clearly see from the pavement outside that the shop owner was already out in the back room with two customers. I stepped inside the entrance. Apart from Billy (who was loitering in the most obvious way imaginable), there was just one other man with a younger boy, whom I assumed was his son. They were over in the other corner, looking at smaller bikes and facing the other way. I checked out the bike that Nick wanted: it was not locked up, just supported on a small metal wheel stand. The shop owner was also facing away from the main door, talking to two guys. I grabbed the cow-horn handlebars and moved the bike forward a few inches until the back wheel came free from the stand. If the owner came out at that time, well, I was just looking at the bike and wanted to try it for size, but he didn't.

My moving it off the stand didn't create any noise and the dad and his son were preoccupied with a small bike. I was scared stiff. My heart was thumping away, my adrenaline in overdrive mode; it was like a strange kind of rush. Then I saw Billy walk out of the shop. He'd lost his nerve and was heading back to meet his brother at the foot of the hill. *Chicken*, I thought. I struggled to swing my leg over the bike's crossbar in the tiny space that I had. I managed and it soon became apparent the bike was too big for me. But, if the shop owner came out now, I was still just trying the bike for size. I spun the left pedal clockwise and stopped it at the eleven o'clock position in preparation for putting all my weight down onto my left foot to get a good acceleration out of the door. Heart pounding, I scanned the shop one more time: Dad and son were still looking at the smaller bike and the owner was still talking to the two guys out the back, his back to the door.

I turned the handlebars to face the door and, being left-footed, put all my body weight down hard onto the left pedal. The bike started to move out the door, but slowly. It must have been in a high gear as I struggled hard to get the pedals going and the bike was taking an age to get up to any sort of getaway speed. I was out the door, onto the road and pushing like crazy to get the thing moving faster. I had a mental vision of the owner running out of the shop and catching me as I was not building up speed fast enough and I wasn't confident with how the gears worked; also worried I'd jam the chain in the cogs if I tried. It was painfully slow and hard work getting the momentum going, but eventually, it came.

At last, I was up to speed, hauling myself and the bike along the road at an uncatchable speed. I looked over my shoulder but I didn't see the shop owner coming out of the shop – I figured he was still inside talking to his customers and hadn't noticed, but I was sure he would spot the missing bike before the day was out. I felt a pang of guilt for taking one of his bikes, but I was also on a high for my efforts and I knew that Nick would reward me with a big smile and a distinct lack of beatings.

When I rode around the corner towards the foot of the hill, Nick caught sight of me and put both his hands up to his mouth in excitement.

'He did it, he fucking did it!' he said, putting his younger brother into a friendly headlock and ruffling his short hair.

'Was it easy?' he asked, admiring his new bike.

'Nothing to it,' I said, puffing and panting.

Nick patted me on the shoulder and laughed. I laughed with him and got off the bike so he could take up the saddle.

Unfortunately, expensive though it was, the bike was not enough for Nick. He had his eye on plenty of other items, in and around town: light-blue drainpipe trousers and a matching blue drape coat and a pair of beetle crusher shoes (like the ones worn by Teddy Boys), a pair of Bermuda swimming trunks (the 'in thing' at the time), not to mention a pair of Foster Grant sunglasses from the local chemist's shop. This was just for starters, and if I didn't agree he'd threaten me with his knife, beatings and telling Aunty about my shoplifting. The fact that I'd been doing it all for him was neither here nor there as far as he was concerned.

I was in deep now: every single weekend, and even some days after school I'd be in town, ticking off retail items from Nick's ever-growing shopping list. I was stealing everything he wanted and more. I'd go into changing rooms in clothes shops, taking in several items at a time, including his trousers that were too big for me. I'd put them on and then put my trousers back on over the top. I'd come out and hang all the items back on the rails, except the ones I was wearing under my clothes. The drape coat proved a little harder because it was so big. I ended up folding it over a couple of times and tying it around my waist by its sleeves. By the time I zipped up my top, I didn't look that much different, perhaps a little bulky round the middle, but not so much that anyone would notice, unless they looked hard.

Time and again I got away with it. I didn't know if I was an incredibly skilful and meticulous thief or just plain lucky but I got everything on Nick's list, and he kept on thinking up new things to add to it. The more I stole for him, the more he asked me to steal, and the more he threatened me if I didn't. Over the course of the next two months I must have stolen over 100 items from pretty much every shop in Grange. I got so confident I even went back to the bike shop and stole a padlock and chain for his stolen bike!

Soon, Nick was taking orders for some of his dodgy friends at school. I'd steal the items for him, and he'd sell them on to his friends for a fraction of their worth. It was getting out of hand and I didn't think I could keep up the pace, but I did, and in a way I wanted to: thievery was acting as a drug and fuelling my kleptomania. It was just like before when I first started stealing when I was only four years old. I still loved the idea of owning various inanimate objects for a brief moment. Stealing all these items for Nick filled an emotional void, as well as being a very good defence mechanism from all the bullying and beatings. Some things he even let me keep for a few days until his buyer had the money; I was actually enjoying myself.

Meanwhile, Aunty was getting suspicious, not only of all the items that Nick was acquiring, but she also suspected I must have had something to do with it. Sometimes when Nick and Billy got back to Grange after being at home on weekend leave, he would pull certain items out of hiding and tell Aunty he'd brought them back with him. It worked for a while, but she wasn't stupid.

Eventually I was caught when I let my guard down and became a little reckless. Usually I'd hide anything I stole in the hedgerows that ran alongside the back garden, and then either Nick or I would go out 10 minutes later and sneak them into his dorm. On this particular occasion I decided I wouldn't bother; instead, I figured I'd just walk right in the front door, pockets bulging. Aunty had never paid that much attention to kids coming in from town in the past, but she was starting to be a little more vigilant where I was concerned. The one time I decided to change my safe and proven tactic, she leapt to her feet from her chair in the TV room.

'Can you come into the office for a minute,' she said.

Nick was in the TV room at the time and suddenly looked very concerned.

'Now, I'd like you to empty your pockets out onto the desk,' she told me.

Oh, shit, this I did not expect. But there was no escape. I could turn and run – but where to? And I could hardly tell her there was nothing in my pockets because they were bulging. So, I proceeded to empty them and place various items on Aunty's desk: Brut 33 aftershave, a Swiss Army knife and a small cigarette lighter in the shape of a handgun. I even had an Etch-A-Sketch stuffed down the front of my trousers, all items for Nick, or for him to sell on to his mates at school. Oh, and two sherbet fountains and a box of Matchmakers for me. Well, I needed a sugar fix to replenish all that lost energy from my shoplifting expedition.

Aunty went ballistic. Her famous kind streak dispersed quicker than a snowflake in hell, and was replaced by a burning rage I'd never have imagined possible from her. After the initial bout of shouting, she eventually calmed down and started to talk more rationally.

'I really can't believe you've done this, Nigel. Just when I thought you were starting to make a little progress,' she said. She was still a little red in the face from her angry outburst, but at least she wasn't yelling at me anymore. 'Now,' she said, sitting down at her desk, pen in hand, 'I need you to tell me exactly where you stole these items.'

'In town,' I said.

'Yes, I know that, but which shops?'

'Aunty, I'm sorry, I didn't want to do it.'

'What do you mean?'

Convinced Nick would get straight on the case with beating me up again if I told Aunty the truth, I decided not to say any more.

'I just … I didn't mean it…'

She looked at me briefly, then put pen to paper.

'Where did you steal that?' she said, tapping the Etch-A-Sketch.

And so I told her each and every shop I'd stolen from as she noted them all down.

'How long has this been going on, Nigel? I want you to tell me the truth because I'm going to find out, one way or another. Do the right thing, love, and tell me everything,' she said, calmer now.

I diluted the story considerably; telling her I'd only stolen one other time. I wasn't about to tell her about everything I'd stolen for Nick – he'd sold half of it anyway and I'd only be opening a massive can of worms. I didn't need the stress, punishments or loss of privileges from Aunty and Uncle, and I know I didn't need the physical punishments that would inevitably come from Nick.

The following day, two policemen showed up just after dinner. When I saw those two large men, looking all intimidating in their dark-blue uniforms, I nearly wet my pants right there. They were there to question Nick and me, in that order. Aunty told Nick to go to her office. She instructed me to wait in the living room, as I was next.

Nick was quite the hard case and he was 16 years old now, so I didn't think for one second that he would tell the police anything. How wrong I was. He told them everything, everything I'd ever stolen, including the bike. By the time I went into that office they had a complete inventory of everything I'd stolen over the past few months. When I saw it all written down like that I was shocked – I didn't realise I'd stolen so many things. As I was still a minor, things would be handled a little differently. I was still in deep trouble and there was no way that the police were going to just slap me on the wrist. They would discuss it all with my social worker and go through the options.

What came next was not good – not good at all.

Chapter 15

The Magistrates

My kleptomania had got way out of control, for more than one reason, and now that Aunty had got wind of it she would no longer let me leave the home or go to town on my own, which meant I could no longer steal for Nick, which in turn meant he soon got back to his old bullying ways and started beating me up all over again.

Just when I was planning to run away to escape from it all, Mrs Clements came to see me to give me some news. Aunty had advised me during breakfast that my social worker would be there when I got back from school that day.

'Nigel, we're going to move you somewhere else,' she said.

'Why?' I said.

'Well, it's because of all the shoplifting, but we also think it would be better if you weren't around Nick anymore.'

'OK,' I said, relieved that I would not have to tolerate Nick's bullying anymore, but also anxious about where I would be placed next. 'Where am I going to go?'

'It's a place called Mill House and it has its own school.'

'Where is it?'

'It's in Carlisle.'

'Is that far?'

'It's about 75 miles away.'

'Oh.'

'But don't worry, I'll still be able to come and see you and I'll try and arrange for you to go home for the weekend as soon as you've settled in.'

'When do I have to go there?'

'This coming Monday.'

I suspected Aunty, Mrs Clements and her colleagues, and possibly the police had all come to the conclusion that Nick and I were a bad mix and it would be best if we were split up. Nick and Billy could not be moved because they were brothers with a bit of an age gap; it was easier to move me. Also, Mill House was in the middle of nowhere, at least two miles to even the local shop. And Carlisle city centre was a good three- or four-mile walk so they probably figured I would not be able to sneak off to town, shoplifting. The built-in school also meant that I would not be able to get into any trouble either at the school, or walking home from it. On the whole, I suppose they thought I would be better protected there, from myself, and others.

How wrong they were.

Sunday evening, I packed up all my things in preparation for leaving Crag Bank the next morning. Mrs Clements arrived at 10 a.m. I said my goodbyes to Aunty, Uncle and the other children, not that they really cared. As I walked up the drive with Mrs Clements, suitcase in hand, relief washed over me. Knowing that I would never have to come back to Crag Bank was a huge weight off my shoulders.

The drive from Grange-over-Sands to Carlisle took about an hour and a half. As usual, Mrs Clements showed great interest in me and she tried to assure me that Mill House was OK. Even though the journey was pleasant enough and I enjoyed talking to her, there was an underpinning anxiety. I had butterflies in my stomach, but not the nice kind, more the black moth kind – the kind there to warn you when something bad is afoot. My overall fate regarding Mill House and my imminent court debut had not been delivered quite yet, but it was in the post and in a few days I'd have to sign for it.

The final few miles of the journey was a long country road with a somewhat bleak view of flat barren fields and countryside. Eventually the car turned off onto the winding driveway that led to Mill House Assessment Centre, a place set up for children awaiting care places. Mill House looked just as bleak and cold as its desolate surroundings. The car stopped and I observed the decrepit main building and the adjoining buildings: the red brickwork of the Georgian building had seen better days, unlike the unfortunate children it housed.

The head of Mill House introduced Mrs Clements and me to the housemaster. We were shown around the various rooms starting with the living-room area, which was like a regular living room, only much larger and with 20 or so comfy chairs randomly placed around the walls. This was the general area where children would hang around and entertain themselves. Next we were shown the TV room, which was similar in size to the living room, only all the chairs were lined up like a mini theatre, with the television at the front. The dining room was also quite large, with about seven Formica-topped tables, four chairs around each one. Then came the three dormitories and a few separate single bedrooms.

'Am I going to have my own bedroom?' I asked.

'Yes, you're going to be in this one,' said the housemaster, opening my bedroom door.

It was similar to my room at Crag Bank, only a little larger. Stepping inside, I immediately felt the vibe of misery and suffering. I noticed that the small wardrobe and chest of drawers had knife carvings of previous occupants' names or initials. They hadn't bothered to wash all the felt-tip pen graffiti off the furniture either. Mrs Clements looked at me and gave a little forced smile.

'OK, you can leave your suitcase here for now. Let's go and have a look at the schoolrooms,' said the housemaster, leading the way.

There were two large schoolrooms, one for the older boys and another for the younger ones. I started to get anxious about which one I would be in as I was 12 years old now and I definitely didn't like the look of the older boys' class. There was a horrible atmosphere and they were all playing up, being boisterous.

'Vincent O'Brian!' shouted the housemaster from the doorway to the grown-up class.

Everybody turned around to face him, but then they all clocked me. I just wanted to shrivel up and hide behind Mrs Clements, but that would not look good so I toughened out their stares as they all psyched out the new kid – it was awful.

'Yes, sir?' said Vincent.

'You know not to use language like that in class,' said the housemaster.

'But, sir, he *is* an ar—'

'Just shut your trap and try and exert some of those useless brain cells of yours into learning something useful!'

'Yes, sir.'

'Come and see me after class, I've got a job for you.'

'But, sir—'

'Just do it!'

'Yes, sir,' he said.

As we turned to leave, I heard them all mumbling and sniggering away to themselves and I just knew that I was the trigger. What a disgusting place, full of disgusting kids! Already I hated it and I just knew that Mill House was going to be worse than any of the other three places I'd been to.

'Which class am I going to be in?' I wanted to know.

'You're going to be grouped with the younger children to start with,' the housemaster explained.

What a relief as I was at the borderline age and could quite easily have found myself in the older boys' class. Years later I would learn from my files that I was about three years behind with my education – hardly surprising, all things considered.

Mrs Clements left me in the capable hands of the housemaster, who was quite tall and seemed very strict. He spoke loudly with a volcanic timbre that rumbled through my spine whenever he was in close proximity. As always, I was incredibly upset when Mrs Clements left.

Monday afternoon and evening passed quite fast, but I was cautious and tried to keep out of the other boys' way. There were about 20 children in total, aged from 12 to 16, and from what I could see the majority were about 15 or 16. Most were boys, but there were about four teenage girls too. The first evening and night passed without a hitch as I settled in as much as was possible.

The thing is, I'm a sensitive Piscean and I come from a regular (be it poor and lower-working-class) family, who go about their lives in a regular way and I felt anxious and vulnerable. But these kids, like the ones at Crag Bank and Newbarns House before that, were mostly from hard council estate backgrounds with violent, druggy parents who would beat each other as well as their own children. For the majority, fighting on the rough streets and on their rough estates was a way of life. Being placed in care and sent to somewhere like this was their normality, a home from home where violence was a way of life.

Now that these kids were here, in care at Mill House, they were aiming to continue their screwed-up way of life, which meant looking for fights to prove themselves, trying to be top-dog, establishing the pecking order, and so on and so forth. Me, I wasn't like them, not even close. In every place I'd previously been I felt like I did not belong; I never fitted in and I was always the loner, or 'freak', as some children would come to call me. I felt alone, surrounded by chaos and anarchy.

None of the other boys made a move on me, but I could sense some of them were up for it and I suspected most were just weighing me up, figuring out my weak spots, mentally and physically.

On the Tuesday during breakfast I was informed that Mrs Clements would be coming to pick me up to take me to court in Ulverston. She hadn't told me about the impending court appearance before because she didn't want to increase my anxiety any further. My psychiatrist, Dr Nolen (whom I was still going to see in Lancaster, while at Crag Bank), had advised her that telling me would not only raise my anxiety, it might make me do something stupid too. Dr Nolen had some serious concerns about me. Already she'd reported her fears that I might harm myself, or much worse. She also thought that I might actually be schizophrenic, a consideration she would later dismiss. Dr Nolen could clearly see that I lived in my own world, a dream world cum fantasyland, and that I needed a lot of sessions to nurse me out into the real world.

It was a long nerve-wracking journey from Carlisle to Ulverston. Eighty-five miles and nearly two hours later we arrived at Ulverston Juvenile Court. I desperately needed the toilet – I was in fear of losing control of my bladder through nerves. Mrs Clements booked me in first and then waited for me while I visited the bathroom. Relieved no longer to be about to wet myself, I headed into the large waiting area with her. To my utter horror, the Mason brothers were sitting right there, among several other rather unsavoury-looking teenagers.

My God, I really don't belong here, was my first thought.

Because of my age, the magistrates were understanding and sympathetic to my needs and, like Mrs Clements, didn't want to put me through any undue stress so I was told to sit in the waiting area while she went in to discuss with the magistrates and police the best course of action. Although she was only in there for about 20 minutes, it seemed much longer as I waited for her to return with the verdict.

She came out and quickly informed me that I'd been given a conditional discharge, which basically meant, stay out of trouble or else. I was so relieved.

Mrs Clements drove me all the way back to Mill House and we arrived just in time for me to join the others for dinner. While I sat eating, I caught the eye of a girl a few tables away. She looked about the same age as me and gave me a little smile while chewing her food. I treated the smile with caution, but that caution was unnecessary, as time would prove.

The next day, it started, just as I knew it would. Three or four of the older boys had taken a dislike to me. They didn't like the way I preferred to hang around the staff, nor the fact that I did not mix and preferred to keep myself to myself. The way I dressed was different to everybody else too (I was still emulating Hugh Cornwell and The Stranglers). The older boys started calling me names and giving me a hard time, 'freak' being their preferred label for me. Soon the name-calling turned into thumps, then harder punches, then kicks and then full-on group beatings, where three or four of them would launch a physical assault on the 'freak'. Relentless, with no escape, it was far worse than anything I'd experienced before. Those kids were vicious and mean; most of them were from Newcastle and hard as nails; even their strong Geordie accents were intimidating. There was more opportunity for these boys to carry out their unprovoked attacks on me, as we were often left alone in the TV room or lounge while the staff went off to the staff room or for a cigarette or to attend to some other chaos somewhere else in the building. Then there were the toilet rooms, dormitories and other unstaffed areas.

I only ever sat in the TV room once. I was sitting a few rows from the back, watching *Top Of The Pops*, when halfway through Boney M's 'Rivers Of Babylon' an older boy smashed his knuckles into the back of my head. The pain was excruciating. I couldn't help myself and started to cry. My tears were a combination of the pain and emotions: I just wanted to go home, I didn't want to be there, I didn't belong there either. For a whole variety of reasons I was the odd one out. This crying episode did not go down well at all and it instantly told all those hard cases that I was an easy target. It was hell, and it would show no sign of easing up.

Then a tiny miracle happened: Hugh and The Stranglers came to rescue me via 12 brand-new songs on their third, and latest studio album, *Black And White*. Just for me (and the first 75,000 people to buy the album) there were three more songs on the free 7-inch limited edition white vinyl single, containing the tracks: 'Walk On By', 'Mean To Me' and 'Tits'. As soon as I heard about the new album I just had to have it. I pestered the staff until they finally agreed to let me phone Mrs Clements, whom I begged to buy the album before the limited edition black and white vinyl versions with free white vinyl single sold out. She agreed and took the money out of my allowance. Two weeks later she brought it with her when she came to see me.

After Mrs Clements left I hurried to the living room, where an all-in-one-style record player sat in the corner. There was a stack of house records piled next to it, most out of their inner and outer sleeves, just lying around, getting scratched. Like everything else around there, no one had any respect for anything, not even themselves. There was no way my new Stranglers album was going to remain there with this scratched-up pile of unloved records! I picked a quiet time after dinner when everybody else had gone outside to play on the zip wire and swings. A first hearing of a new

Stranglers album was a very special moment indeed. Besides, these therapy sessions were between Hugh and me, and nobody else was welcome, especially that lot – they wouldn't understand Hugh or his music, anyway.

I lowered the cheap tone arm onto my pristine black and white swirly limited edition coloured vinyl record and listened intently. Hugh was back as his guitar riff kicked in, followed quickly by Jet Black's drums and JJ's bass line, laying down a nice bed of sound for Dave Greenfield's fast-fingered organ melodies. Then he spoke, singing/shouting out the lyrics to the first song on side A, 'Tank'. Two minutes and 57 seconds later, the first song was over. Before I'd really had a chance to get into it or understand it, Hugh was done. His warm-up out of the way, now it was time to get 'Nice 'N' Sleazy', the track released a month earlier as a single, alerting me to the upcoming new album. This single mesmerised me in the same way as 'Down In The Sewer' from the first album and when Dave's keyboard solo kicked in, oh, wow! It was the most amazing sound I'd ever heard as he played various notes while altering their sounds by sliding sliders and turning dials on his, then, high-tech keyboard.

But it was the last song on side B, 'Death And Night And Blood', that grabbed me and ended up being my favourite on the album, even though Hugh himself did not sing this particular track. This song was about the weirdest Stranglers number I'd heard to date, and I loved it. It oozed the strangest of atmospheres with its clipped verses collapsing into an evil-sounding chorus, while maintaining that typical Stranglers style I'd grown to love.

During this 40-minute therapy session, in 12 parts, all the evils of Mill House and its residents dispersed. I was in my own world again, and this time I was not coming out. After the stylus reached the end of side B, I carefully put my album back in its sleeve and it was while I was doing this that the girl who had smiled at me during dinner entered the room.

'Hi,' she said.

I turned around to look at her. 'Hi.'

'What are you listening to?'

'Oh, just a new album I got.'

'Can I see?'

'Yes,' I said, handing it to her.

'The Stranglers,' she said, flipping the cover over.

'Do you like them?' I asked.

'They're alright, yes,' she said, handing it back. 'You're Nigel, aren't you?'

'Yes. How do you know my name?'

'I've heard the staff calling you,' she said, smiling. 'I'm Susan.'

Susan and I talked a little more and learned the usual stuff about each other – where we were from and a little about our backgrounds and how we found ourselves at Mill House, the usual stuff. And there it was, I'd made an unlikely friend.

Susan went off to her bedroom while I took my album to mine and hid it away under my bed until the same time tomorrow. I went through the ritual of playing *Black And White* every single day after the others had gone outside to play, then a member of staff informed me that my social worker was coming to collect me again the next morning to go back to court in Ulverston. In the meantime, my mother seemed to have vanished off the map and hadn't been in touch with me for quite a while, not even a letter.

Exactly two weeks after my first court appearance I had to make a reappearance, though why I was not sure. I thought all that business was over and done with, but apparently not: there was the little case of a care order to be put in place.

So, the next morning Mrs Clements picked me up and drove me to Ulverston Juvenile Court for the second time. This time I had to go in as the magistrates wanted to see me, but I didn't have to say anything – well, not much anyway. They addressed me by my first name and sounded very friendly, something that was increasingly alien to me the more I was passed from pillar to post, from psychiatric unit to assessment and observation centre to children's home, back to psychiatric unit, then to children's home, then to another assessment centre – a different brand of brutal cruelty, abuse and torture at each one.

I didn't quite understand what the magistrates said or what exactly had happened, but Mrs Clements explained it all to me on the way back in the car. I'd been put onto a place of safety order, with immediate effect, with a care order to follow – a care order that would last until I was 18 years old. From now on, Mrs Clements and her team would make all the decisions about me.

At the time I didn't know if this was a good thing or not, but later I would learn that she was the person in all of this who prioritised me. But her hands were tied a lot of the time and she could not magic some foster parents out of thin air, there were simply none available. Well and truly in the 'system' now, I knew that I would not get out until at least my 16th birthday, when I'd be thrown out into the big wide world with my institutionalised upbringing and no proper education to boot.

My mother owed me a childhood, and it was my God-given right to have one, but I never got it.

Back at Mill House, the weeks passed and I kept myself to myself and avoided the other children (especially the older ones) like the plague. Although Susan had befriended me, we didn't see that much of each other because she hung around with the other girls for the most part. I really was a loner now, but then again, I always had been. I was not about to find a social circle that I fitted into here, and I was beginning to think I never would.

Chapter 16

Near-Death Experience & Runaway Puppy Love

One evening after dinner I was alone in the living room playing my record when the housemaster came in.

'Hello, Nigel, what are you up to?' he said.

'Just listening to my record,' I told him.

'Look, I don't think it's doing you any good, hiding away like this all the time. Why don't you try and mix with the others a little more?'

'They don't like me, nobody likes me.'

'Well, perhaps if you tried a little harder to mix in they wouldn't pick on you quite so much.'

'I don't want to try harder, they're not my sort of people. I prefer being alone.'

'Nigel, with that attitude you're just going to make life very difficult for yourself. Now come on, turn the record off and come outside with me.'

'But I don't want to, I'm happy here.'

'I'm not going to ask you again. Turn it off!'

So I did as he asked and took my record off and put it back in its sleeve.

'Can I put my record away in my room first?'

'Yes, but then I want you to come straight outside to mix with the others, OK?'

'Yes,' I said, but I didn't want to. I hated pretty much everyone in that place, most of the staff included, except Susan. After putting my record back under my bed, I ambled towards the side door, which led out onto the large, open garden area to the side of the building. It was quite a vast open space, about half an acre, and had a zip wire, swings, a large rope climbing frame and a long rope suspended between two large oak trees. Three girls (including Susan) were standing talking to a female member of staff, while most of the boys were being boys, generally scrapping and indulging in aggressive play. Some of the older ones were giving each other dares to pass away the time.

Ericson was the first to notice me when I came out. He was with another, older boy standing next to the rope suspended from the two trees. After nudging his mate he gestured towards me with his chin. Ericson was 15 years old, but looked older. Punk through and through, he was tall and had a spiky dyed-blond punk hairstyle. He was really into the Sex Pistols, The Damned, Generation X and The Jam, to name a few. I'd seen him around and, although one of the top dogs, he never singled me out or bullied me, though he did act hostile towards me in the company of his friends for their benefit. I couldn't quite figure him out entirely, so I treated him with the same caution that I did everybody else.

'What's the new Stranglers album like?' he said.

Ericson liked The Stranglers too, but not as much as the Sex Pistols.

'It's good, not quite as good as the first two albums, but close,' I said.

'You wanna do what we're doing?' he said.

'What are you doing?' I asked.

'Swinging on this – you just hang from the middle and we'll swing you.'

'No, thanks.'

'Go on, it'll be fun,' he said, smiling.

His smile seemed half genuine. I looked over at the housemaster, who gave me an encouraging nod.

'OK,' I said.

I moved over towards the middle section of rope. It was suspended between two large trees about 20 feet apart. The rope was tied about nine feet up the trunk of each tree and the lowest part of the suspended rope was about eight feet off the ground so I had to jump up with my arms high to grab it. I hung from the middle of the rope while Ericson and his friend stood on the wooden benches under each tree, reached up and grabbed the rope.

'Ready?' he asked.

'Yeah.'

They both started to swing the rope back and forth and at first I only swung gently, but then they began to swing it harder and harder, building momentum until I was swinging about 10 feet in each direction and going up pretty high too. I hung on with all my might. If I fell, it could be very bad: although the surface was grass, the ground was hard.

'Stop, stop!' I said, but they didn't, they just laughed and swung me harder and higher.

At the peak of the swing I was about 15 feet off the ground. I didn't know what to do and I was struggling to hold on; I was losing my grip. I had to let go, but I had to choose the right moment to do so, while close to the ground so I waited until the back swing. Instead of letting go while I was moving fast, I thought it would be safer if I let go while moving slowly, just before I reached a peak. Just past the backwards swing when I was about to approach the highest peak, with the slowest momentum, I let go. But I got my timing wrong and my body carried on backwards with momentum, flying up and through the air. Then I started my descent from a height of about 15 feet. I came down backwards and landed awkwardly on the hard ground. The impact smashed the air out of my lungs and winded me badly.

As I lay on the ground, unable to breathe, I struggled to suck in even a minuscule amount of air, but it would not come. My lungs and chest would not work, I could not breathe in or out – it was as if my respiratory system had crashed and frozen then refused to boot up again.

A female member of staff had witnessed what happened and she could tell that I was in distress. About 30 seconds passed by and still I couldn't breathe – I just lay there, grunting, as I struggled for breath. I was in trouble and if something didn't happen, and fast, I was going to die right there on the ground, miles away from home, surrounded by people who hated me.

I could feel my life slipping away. My head started to feel fuzzy. The female member of staff knelt down next to me, but there was nothing she could do. She just watched with a perplexed and concerned look on her face. Another 10 seconds or so passed and the world started to fade to black. I heard the woman shout to get the housemaster's attention. My eyes closed and I was convinced I was going to die. They say no one knows your body better than you do, and I knew my body and it felt like I had just seconds left to live. Then it happened in an instant: as if by magic, my respiratory system kicked back in. I gulped air deep into my lungs. Daylight started to come back and, several gulps of air later, my breathing had returned to normal.

'Are you OK?' asked the female member of staff.

'He's OK,' said the housemaster.

She stayed with me for a minute to make sure, while the housemaster got back to what he was doing before.

'Are you sure you're OK?' she persisted.

'I think so,' I said, standing up.

'Are you OK, Nigel?' said Susan.

I hadn't noticed her standing to the side.

'Yes, thanks.'

'It looked really bad from over there,' she said. 'I'm really glad you're OK,' she added, smiling.

I smiled back.

Exactly what had happened when I hit the ground I don't know, but the wind was knocked out of me and it took a good minute before I could breathe again. It really did feel as if I was on the brink of death.

Ericson came over and said, 'You were winding them up, weren't you?'

He truly believed I was joking around. But I didn't say anything; I just smiled.

After my accident, Susan and I spent a little more time together, though not publicly, and certainly not while any of her friends were around. But here and there we grabbed moments together and we talked.

I never saw Susan smile at any of the other boys and often I would catch her disapproving looks when one of the others, girls included (equally violent and repulsive in their own way), did something disgusting, violent or just plain idiotic. The other boys didn't think Susan was anything special to look at, just an average girl-next-door. But I could see what they could not: to me she was amazing. I could sense something in her that was lacking in every other kid in there. She had love and compassion in her heart and, although she joined in with the others and sat in the TV room with them, I knew she was just playing the system, pretending to fit in to avoid becoming a victim, unlike me. But I could also see that, like me, she really lived in her own private world. She was not like the rest and had not come from a typical dysfunctional or violent background.

Susan was depressed and miserable too and, even though she appeared to be part of the girl pack, she was at the bottom of their pecking order and still took some stick every now and then. Like me, she was also in care through no fault of her own, a victim of circumstances, and like me, there were no foster carers to take her in. Since Susan had been in my life I wasn't craving my mum's love quite so much. I suppose she was a kind of substitute for the love and affection I still desperately longed for. I had to take it where I could find it and Susan was there. She was the first person, excluding Mrs Clements, to show me any kind of attention or compassion for as far back as I could remember. But it went both ways for I listened to Susan and showed her compassion too.

Susan had a pair of small matching gold sleeper earrings and she suggested I pierce my left ear so I could wear one of them. She even offered to do the piercing for me using a long, thick sewing needle (which she sterilised first in boiling water) and a couple of ice-cubes held on the front and back of my ear lobe for five minutes to help numb it. I was quietly confident that, even without any numbing, I would be able to handle the pain. Surely it would be a walk in the park after everything I'd already endured in my life. She did a brilliant job and I didn't feel a thing. While sterilising the needle, she also dunked one of her sleepers in the bowl of boiling water to kill any germs before putting it in my freshly pierced ear.

And that was it: Susan and I were now connected via a tiny hoop of gold.

A few more days went by and the physical and mental abuse from the other kids became too much for me to handle so I decided to run away. Susan could see how upset I was and I ended up telling her that I planned to run away that very day. She asked if she could go with me. I said yes.

It wasn't the first time I'd run away from a place like this, and it wouldn't be the last. They weren't secure detention centres so getting out was pretty easy; it was all down to timing. Susan was happy for me to plan our escape and I loved the fact that she had total faith and confidence in me. This was a first in my life and made a refreshing change from the usual knocks I got from both staff and boys: 'Cooper, you're shit', or, 'No, you can't join the football team, you'll be crap' or, 'No, you can't join in, you'll only be rubbish' and even, 'Shut up, Cooper, what could you possibly know?' Well, the one thing they failed to realise was that you have 'one' mouth and 'two' ears for a reason: while they were busy shooting their mouths off about all manner of things, I was sitting quietly, learning. And, believe it or not, I was actually learning something from their stupidity: I learned that I was not like them, and never wanted to be like them, so it was important that I did not mix with them or try to emulate them in a way that lemming teenagers often do. So, I alienated myself even more, even though they turned on me for it. But Susan wasn't like the rest of them and, although young, the pit of my stomach told me that I was developing feelings for her in that young, puppy love sort of way. It certainly wasn't what I'd call a romantic involvement; we simply comforted each other in the cruel, loveless environment we found ourselves in.

I'd planned for Susan and me to run away on Saturday morning for several reasons, one of which was that there would only be a skeleton staff on duty as around 30 per cent of the children went home for the weekends and the structure was quite loose and not so disciplined. After breakfast on a Saturday it was a general free-for-all and the kids could be in the living room, TV room, bedrooms, dorms, or outside in the grounds, playing. The skeleton staff kept a general eye on things, but it would be quite easy to get a 90-minute head start before anybody noticed our absence and we could get quite far in that time.

We'd decided to travel fairly light, just the clothes and jackets we were wearing and all the money we had, which was a little pocket money, so getting from Carlisle to Newcastle would require a bit of skill and care. Although Susan was not from Newcastle, her parents now lived there and that was where she wanted to go. Naturally, I wanted to go home to my house in Ulverston, which left us with something of a geographical dilemma. However, even then I was incredibly chivalrous so I told Susan I would escort her all the way home to her house in Newcastle first. My plan involved us sneaking out of Mill House undetected, then doing the four-mile walk along the B6264, ducking into the hedgerows to hide whenever a car passed, sneaking through the ticket office at Carlisle railway station and getting a train to Newcastle, while evading any ticket inspectors during the journey. Once at Newcastle, Susan had told me her house was about 15 minutes' walk from the station. I'd see her to her door before heading back to the railway station to get a train back west across the country to Ulverston, which would mean a change or two. All in all, about 200 train miles and about 10 walking miles, all undetected.

Everything was going swimmingly. We got to Newcastle and managed to get out of the railway station undetected and all the way to Susan's house. During the walk from the station to her house we held hands and didn't speak a single word. Every now and then Susan or I would give a gentle knowing squeeze of the other's hand. I didn't want that walk to end, but all good things seemed to.

That walk was to be one of my typically euphoric heavenly moments between two ever-waiting nightmares. Arriving on her street, we stopped about 10 houses from where she lived. We decided that I should not go up to the door with her as her parents (assuming they were relatively responsible) would almost certainly take me in and call the police. Perhaps they would call the police when they saw their daughter standing at their front door too, but

Susan thought not. We stood and faced each other and, I'm not quite sure how it happened, but we were now holding both hands and standing very close.

'Will you be OK getting home?' she wanted to know.

'Yes, I'll be just fine.'

Then we looked at each other during an awkward pause before Susan leant forward and kissed me on the lips. She tasted every bit as good as she looked, all peaches and cream. Although the kiss was only brief and with closed mouths, my heart raced and that was it, I was in love.

She gazed into my eyes and ran a finger down my cheek: 'Thank you, I'll never forget you,' she told me.

'Good luck,' I said, then I turned and walked away.

It was the last time I ever saw Susan Finch.

Back at Newcastle train station, things started to go horribly wrong. Two police officers were waiting for me. Mill House had obviously discovered that Susan and I had gone AWOL and had informed the police, who in turn had put a constable or two at Newcastle railway station – and, quite possibly, Ulverston railway station too. Fact is they grabbed me just as I was entering the station.

'What's your name?' asked one of the tall, intimidating officers.

At first I didn't answer. I just stood there, his hand gripping my upper arm, hard.

'Don't lie, son, or you'll just make things worse for yourself,' he told me.

With that, I answered.

'Nigel.'

'Nigel Cooper?'

'Yes.'

'OK, come with us,' he said, escorting me to their police car, where they put me in the back and closed the door.

'You know, we're getting sick and tired of picking up little bastards like you. We're not a fucking taxi service, you know!' said the other officer.

I was stunned by his aggressive attitude towards me. He was so angry I thought he was going to lean into the back and hit me.

'We've got better things to do with our time, do you understand?' he added.

I just sat there on the back seat, trembling and trying not to wet myself through fear.

'Well, guess what? We're not fucking driving you all the way back to Carlisle, no fucking way! You're going to stay here for the night until somebody can come and collect you tomorrow,' he went on.

Oh, shit, I thought. That didn't sound good at all. Did he mean I was to spend the night in a police cell at Newcastle police station? I dared not ask, I just sat there and kept my mouth shut.

But I didn't spend the night in a police cell, although I wish I had. Instead, they took me to a local remand centre for children. It was a secure, lock-down place where there was no escape, like a detention centre for kids. The policemen dropped me off and left me in the capable hands of a rather angry-looking man who reminded me of a prison officer.

'Come with me,' he said, gripping my upper arm just as the policeman had.

He squeezed really hard and it hurt like hell, but I was too scared to say a word. The angry man marched me along a cold, stark corridor painted a bright sickly green – it made my head hurt, just looking at it. He took a large bunch of keys off his hip clip and opened a sturdy wooden door with a small letterbox-size observation window.

'In!' he ordered, shoving me in the back to encourage me on my way. 'This is what happens when you run away. You can stay in there until you're collected tomorrow morning. It's lunchtime, but guess what? You're not getting any! Somebody will bring you something to eat at dinnertime. Until then, I suggest you sit there and have a long, hard think about if you're going to run away again.'

He slammed the door and turned the key.

It appeared for every brief moment of happiness that I experienced, an onslaught of misery followed. If life had a design, mine was seriously messed up. Was I destined for complete and utter misery? Just when I got a whiff of joy, it was quickly snatched away from me, and then the onslaught of misery and abuse came back, worse than ever. My brief snippets of happiness were nothing but a transition, a two-second cross dissolving from one bleak scene to another.

The next morning another man came to let me out and took me to an office, where I had to wait with another member of staff while somebody came to collect me from Mill House. They'd obviously been given the heads-up on their time of arrival as I was only kept waiting for about 15 minutes before one of the staff from Mill House arrived to take me back. He was one of the regular house staff, only now he'd taken on a slightly different persona for the benefit of those waiting with me. As with the policemen, as soon as the car door was closed he yelled some abuse at me and vented his frustration at having to do the 120-mile round trip to come and get me, but he eventually stopped shouting after a short time to concentrate on the journey.

Back at Mill House, I was put under closer supervision. The staff were instructed to keep a close eye on me; they had to know where I was at all times. It seemed like every 10 minutes somebody was sticking his or her head around the living-room door or into my bedroom, which I was now locked into during the night.

A few days went by and I'd been thinking about Susan non-stop. I couldn't understand why she had not been brought back.

It was too much, I couldn't stand not knowing anymore, and so I plucked up the courage to ask one of the staff. I chose a female member of staff as I figured a woman would be more amenable and sympathetic to my needs.

'Susan, she's left. She's not coming back,' she said.

'I don't understand.'

'She was due to be transferred somewhere else next week, anyway.'

'Where is she now?'

'I'm not sure, I think she's staying at home with her parents until after the weekend, then she'll move to her new place.'

And that was it; I'd never see or hear from Susan again. The only ray of warmth and compassion I'd experienced from one of my peers at Mill House had been extinguished and taken away from me. Now all I had to look forward to was the bleak, cold winter ahead, not that I thought things could get any bleaker or colder around there. But they could, and they did.

Then came the news from Mrs Clements that my mother was moving down south to London. All at once I felt everything die inside of me.

Chapter 17

The Suicide Attempt

The reason my mum had decided to move down south to London so suddenly was down to her latest boyfriend, Keith, who lived just outside of London. Although he was married, Mum was infatuated with him and didn't mind being the 'other woman', though at the time she was convinced that he was going to leave his wife to marry her instead. Although Keith lived near London, he was often in Cumbria on business, which was when Mum had met him in a local pub.

Keith had everything – a white Lotus sports car, his own business, tons of money – and he was handsome too. Mum had only been seeing him for a few short months when she came up with the idea of moving to London. She figured they could see each other a lot more if she lived nearer to him. Keith had also told Mum that Anthony and Jonathan would have a better life in London. It seemed I was never part of her plans, but what was new? I'm not sure what she told him about me. I remember him being there when I went home one weekend and I really liked him. However, Mum and Keith spent most of that weekend smooching, and whenever I tried to grab a little of his or her attention, Mum just snapped at me.

It all happened remarkably fast: my mum put in for a council exchange and almost immediately found a suitable person to swap with her. Although the family from London came up to view my mum's house in Ulverston, Mum didn't fancy the long journey to London to look at her prospective house. Instead, she chose to go by the photos that the London family had sent her in the post.

Mrs Clements convinced my mum that I should be part of the move and that it would be damaging and detrimental to me if I were not involved. Already I was alienated from my family and feeling more and more distant from them with each passing year. She could see how devastated I was by the news of the imminent move and so, with my mum's approval, she arranged for me to go home for the weekend to see her.

Mrs Clements collected me from Mill House one Friday afternoon to take me home, but it wasn't long before my visit started to go horribly wrong. As usual, things with Anthony went badly and the all too familiar pattern of Mum ignoring me followed. All I could do over the weekend was wander the streets with no sense of purpose.

My life was worse than ever and I wanted to die.

That's it, I thought. At the time it appeared that death was the only way out of my nightmarish predicament, the only way I could escape having to go back to Mill House on the Monday morning, as well as escape the family who obviously didn't love me or want me around anymore. All at once everything became clear. Although I didn't know it at the time I was now in transition from sadness and despair to full-on clinical depression, with a serious case of anxiety disorder thrown in too. But the clock was ticking and I had just the weekend to plan my own suicide before they hauled me back to Mill House.

Back then, considering the mental state I was in, death did not scare me; in fact, I positively welcomed it with open arms. The way I saw it, I'd be reunited with my sister and father, the only two family members who ever really loved me. I'd spent all day Saturday trying to figure out the easiest and, more importantly, painless way to kill myself. There is one definitive built-in defence system that can stop a person from killing himself, and that's the pure 'will' to survive. As humans, we have all sorts of built-in defences that can deter and prevent death, where adrenaline kicks in and we stare death in the face and beat it. But for me, I didn't have any 'will' left: I had nothing and no one to live for, nobody loved me and the love I had for my mother was starting to fade. Depressed, unloved, hated and unwanted, my life was destined to be a slow-baked, lovelorn cake made up of the following ingredients: misery, torment, anguish, anxiety, uncertainty and depression, with a large topping of bleak, long-lasting darkness. I had nothing to live for, and even if I did come out the other side when I eventually left school, I would not have had a proper education or gained decent grades. With no qualifications any prospect of carving out a good life for myself would be next to zero. Essentially, come Monday morning, I'd be back in the so-called care system – FFL (Fucked For Life).

Although I'd lost the will to live, trying to mastermind a quick, clean and painless way of killing myself just a few months before my 13th birthday was not an easy thing to do. I'd thought of everything, but all the options seemed fraught with agonising pain, even if momentarily. I didn't want to suffer any more pain, no matter how brief. Saturday came to a close and I'd spent the whole day locked in my thoughts, unable to find a solution. That night I didn't sleep well, unable to switch off as I lay there thinking until eventually I fell asleep during the early hours of Sunday morning.

The bright light streaming in through my bedroom window penetrated my eyelids, forcing me out of my slumber and back into the painful reality of life. I sat at the kitchen table pondering to myself as I ate a bowl of cheap branded cornflakes drenched in watery Five Pints powdered milk, still with the lumps in it.

'You're quiet this morning, Nigel,' noted Mum, as she pottered around the house. 'Something troubling you?' she added, more out of something to say than genuine concern.

'Yes, actually, there is,' I said.

'Oh well, never mind. Why don't you go out for a walk?'

She didn't care that it was cold outside and she didn't want to know what was on my mind, she was too busy. I was pondering the fact that Sunday was the last chance I had to end my miserable life before D-Day on the Monday, when I would return to Mill House. So, go for a walk I would. I finished up my cornflakes, grabbed my jacket and headed out the door. But I didn't know where I was going to go. I just wandered aimlessly, with only morbid thoughts for company. First, I crossed the road and headed over towards the swimming pool, walking its perimeter before heading off into open farmland and no-man's land. I was walking and thinking, sitting for a rest and then thinking some more before walking and thinking again.

Although I tried to reason with myself and did my best to think positive thoughts and snap out of this negative state of gloom and depression, I just couldn't. Mill House was not the caring children's home for unfortunate kids that its façade suggested. For me, it was dystopia, a living nightmare with no let up. There was no escaping the misery, the abuse, the beatings, the bullying, the punishments from the staff, the belittling and cruel torments. It was relentless; no way on earth was I ever going back.

I'd been walking around for about two hours when I noticed an old building, a few fields away. As I got closer I saw a series of smaller outbuildings too. It was an old farm, but still in use. Parked out in front of the main building was a Workhorse Land Rover, so somebody must have been home.

I'm not sure why, but I decided to have a snoop around the smaller outbuildings. Perhaps it was curiosity, or maybe my kleptomania was taking over on autopilot again. The first outbuilding was more of a wooden shed than an outbuilding. Unlike a regular garden shed, this was larger and more substantial in construction, with a concrete floor and large double-doors at the front, big enough to park a tractor inside. There was a locking bolt system on the outside of the wooden doors, but the padlock was hanging by its open shackle with the key dangling from it; an invitation if ever I saw one. Inside were various metal cabinets and shelves, bits of agricultural machinery, boxes and some general junk. There was a musky dense smell about the place, with damp on the walls and visible mould on some of the old furniture.

At the back was an old wooden wardrobe. I was nervous, the adrenaline coursing through my veins. Someone could come out of the main house and catch me at any time, but I felt compelled to look inside the wardrobe. These were old buildings in the middle of nowhere: who knows what could be inside, and how long the contents might have been there?

I opened the wardrobe door and the first thing I saw, standing upright, leaning against the back left-hand corner of the wardrobe, was what looked like a 12-bore, double-barrelled shotgun. Without hesitation I picked it up and admired the beautifully carved wooden stock, so old and well used. It felt so smooth as I ran my right hand over it while holding the barrel in my left. I noticed a small box on the top shelf of the wardrobe; it was faded, red and blue and had an image of a shotgun cartridge on the side. Convinced the box would be empty, I reached up and grabbed it, just managing to wrap my fingers around its girth. I slid it forward to the very front of the shelf and pulled it off. The weight of it took me by surprise and it almost fell to the floor: it was heavy as a brick. I leaned the gun back in its place and opened the lid of the box. Inside were 20 or so red plastic cartridges with brass heads. I removed one and could not believe how heavy it was.

This was the first time I'd handled a shotgun or held a cartridge in the palm of my hand. Suddenly I was petrified, but somehow I held my nerve. And so I decided if I didn't think about it for long, opened the barrel and placed two cartridges inside, cocked the pins, put the barrel in my mouth and pulled the trigger, it would all be over. I was confident that I would not feel a thing; it would be over more quickly than the flash of a camera. To ease my state of mind and to comfort myself, I started to think about Lynda and my dad and how I'd be reunited with them.

I didn't know how to work a shotgun, but there were not that many moving parts so how difficult could it be? Besides, I'd seen the likes of John Wayne load cartridges into shotguns on many a Sunday Western on TV. I tried to bend the gun in half while pulling on the unlocking lever. It opened up to reveal two chambers. I pushed two of the red plastic cartridges into the chambers as far as they would go until all I could see were the dull brass heads then I snapped the gun closed with an audible locking click.

After a few more minutes of jiggery-pokery I was sure the gun was armed and ready to be fired – but not in there. I wanted to be found soon afterwards, not three weeks later in an old outbuilding, so I took the gun outside and sat on an abandoned piece of old agricultural machinery. I was within clear sight of the main farmhouse and, if there was anybody home, they would definitely hear the gun go off. If they were not home, they would see my body in their front yard when they returned. In hindsight, I suppose a rational-thinking person would have stopped to consider how upset the people who lived there would be to find my corpse lying in their yard, but, then again, I was not rational or in my right mind. So I sat there, cocked gun in hand, wrestling with my thoughts. Mentally, I was being pulled this way and that, my emotions in turmoil. My head felt like a pressure cooker about to explode. I wanted somebody to be here, somebody who loved me, to hold me; to wrap their loving arms around me and tell me everything was going to be OK, but it didn't take long for me to realise that was never going to happen, not in this lifetime. So I turned the shotgun around and put the barrel into my mouth – I wanted it to be quick, with no mistakes.

The barrel was long so attempting to place it against the side of my head was fraught with issues. Trying to hold the long gun out to the side with an outstretched arm while attempting to maintain aim with a shaking arm was too risky – I could get it all wrong and end up with brain damage or something. I figured with the barrel in my mouth, pointing towards the roof of it, the shot would go upwards and directly into my brain; I couldn't miss. So, I sat and wedged the gun's stock between my knees and positioned my right thumb over the trigger, ready to push down on it hard. At that point I started to sob, the taste of metal and gun oil in my mouth. The sooner I pushed down on that trigger, the sooner my misery would end, though. I checked one final time that the barrel was aimed towards the roof of my mouth, double-checked the angle of the barrel, then mentally said to myself, *please let there be a heaven*, and pushed down on the trigger until it clicked.

But there was no loud bang, no explosion, no life flashing before my eyes. For some unfathomable reason the gun misfired. There was a noticeable 'crack' as the brass cap of the cartridge detonated. With hindsight I suspect the cartridges had been in the outbuilding for so long they were damp inside and, because the gunpowder was slightly damp, it did not ignite. The cap detonating alone only had enough force to slightly move the wadding and shot, partially opening the crimp closure at the end of the cartridge, but not enough to send its contents up the barrel, through the roof of my mouth and into my brain.

As I sat there, shaking and petrified at what had just happened, a lady came out of the main house and started shouting at me. I was in my own world so I didn't hear what she was saying; it was just a muffled sound coming from somewhere. She ran towards me, frantically waving her arms about. Distraught, I dropped the gun and fled across the field, adrenaline flowing, heart thumping. My whole body trembled and I was crying my eyes out as I ran.

The rest of the weekend passed by swiftly enough. My self-absorbed mum had no idea how close I had come to dying and, on Monday morning, Mrs Clements arrived at the house to take me back to Carlisle.

Time flew by, and it wasn't long before the move to London was upon us. The removal van wasn't huge and had only three seats in the front: one for the driver and a bench seat where Anthony and my mum would sit, Jonathan squashed between them. This meant that I was stuck in the back of the van with just a large rubber plant for company. The journey was long, dark, cold and unpleasant – an abridged 300-mile replica of my life. Unlike my life, this particular journey, including several pit stops for toilet breaks and sandwiches that Mum had made that morning, would end in about eight hours.

The journey was excruciating. Every time we stopped for a break the driver would open the back metal shutter and I'd have to clamber over furniture to get out. Thirty minutes later, I'd climb back in for another 90 minutes or so until the next stop.

I could hear Mum and Anthony laughing and talking to each other and the driver through the thin metal between the cab and the back. Once more I felt lonely and excluded.

It seemed a painfully long journey, but eventually we arrived in Kentish Town in north London.

'Ay oop, Nigel, we're here!' shouted Mum, banging on the metal behind her head.

I heard both the driver and passenger doors open and general excited chit-chat.

Come on, come on, let me out, I thought. But their enthusiastic chat continued for a minute. Everybody got to enjoy that initial moment together, while I was still cooped up in the back. Finally, the driver unlocked the metal roller shutter and daylight flooded in.

Standing on the pavement, disoriented, I allowed my eyes to adjust to the harsh December light. I was standing in the middle of a rather long street with huge terraced three-storey (plus basement) Victorian houses. Our house (or rather my mum and brothers' house) was made up of the basement and ground floor; the first and second floors were occupied by a middle-aged couple whom my mum would soon alienate by 'putting her foot in it'.

My family didn't have much to unload: some rickety old furniture, bedding, clothes and general boxes full of crap that my mum had acquired from charity shops over the years.

'Right, where's the box with the kettle? I'm gagging for a cuppa and a fag!' said Mum.

We proceeded to unload the van and plonk all the boxes down in the relevant rooms. I would be sharing one of the basement bedrooms with Jonathan during my Christmas vacation at home. Excited and sad at the same time, I was quietly praying this could be a new start for all of us; that somehow I'd be reintroduced into my family and it would all go so well that after Christmas Mum would arrange with Mrs Clements for me to come home for good. But it was not to be. The first few days went fine, but the rivalry for my mum's love and attention was increasingly fierce between Anthony and me. Although I was hardly ever there (48 hours once every two or three months), he never cut me any slack and seemed to hate me being there. Christmas morning, everybody leapt out of bed, really excited. It was the one time of year when Mum would throw a little bit of all those DHSS and Social Services department handouts back into the community, i.e. me. She'd half-fill a pillowcase with several chocolate bars and packets of snacks, a tin of nuts, socks, a colouring pad and pencils, perhaps even a bargain three-pack of T-shirts. Usually Jonathan was treated similarly, although his presents had perhaps more thought going into them. Anthony, being five years older than me, got much cooler stuff.

But the whole 'opening presents' ritual seemed to be over in 10 minutes and it wasn't long before I started to get anxious about going back up north to Mill House. For me Christmas didn't have any real meaning; in our house it wasn't even a time for 'family' as there was usually some bickering or disagreement over something or other and Mum and me really did not see eye to eye on anything. Her way of thinking was the polar opposite of mine: she had some strange ideas about things, and made some odd choices, always the wrong ones. She just never got anything right, not even accidentally.

By Boxing Day, Mum and I were quarrelling like crazy. For two whole hours I'd begged and pleaded with her to let me stay. I'd told about all the horrible things I'd been through and would have to experience again if she made me go back to Mill House. My tales of misery were getting her down and making her depressed. She said I was ruining Christmas for everyone and, if I carried on like that, I would not be allowed home for any more holiday breaks.

'But, Mum …' I persisted.

'Oh, just stop it! I'm sick of all your moaning and complaining.'

'Why don't you just phone Mrs Clements to come and take him away?' suggested Anthony, sticking his head around the door.

'Shut up, you!' I snapped.

He just stuck his tongue out at me and pulled a face.

'Anthony, go away, you're only making things worse!' she said.

'Looney!' he said.

'Mum, tell him,' I said.

'Look, just leave him alone,' she told Anthony.

'Mum, *please*, let me stay!'

'One more word out of you and I'll phone Mrs Clements and tell her to come and get you early,' she warned.

It was useless; I would have to go back to Mill House. Over the next few days, matters escalated as I didn't let up for a moment. The year moved into 1979 without my even noticing. I tried and said everything I could to get my mum to let me stay at home, but it was futile. Mrs Clements drove all the way down to London to collect me on Wednesday, 3 January, my holiday cut short because Mum could not stand my complaining and upsetting everybody for a moment longer. She didn't understand what I was going through and, what's more, she didn't seem to care – she thought I was making it all up and refused to listen to me anymore. I was so upset, but when I saw Mrs Clements, I accepted the inevitable.

Mrs Clements only stayed for about 10 minutes for a quick cup of tea before loading my suitcase into the boot of her car, and then we were off. No hugs, no kisses, just the cold shoulder. Once again I was an outcast.

I sat in the front of the car in silence as she navigated her way through the streets of north London towards the M1. Once we hit the motorway and the busy streets of London were in the rear-view mirror, I started to settle down a little and Mrs Clements and I began talking. It was a long journey all the way back up to Carlisle, but at least I wasn't stuck in the back of some truck, I was sitting in the front of a warm car with a wonderfully warm and compassionate lady who cared deeply about me.

Almost seven hours later we arrived at Mill House and I mentally prepared myself to go back into 'survival mode'. I'd cued up my fantasy world, plumped up my comfy chair on the moon and prepared to withdraw deep inside, deeper than I'd ever ventured before. My private therapist, Hugh Cornwell, was ready and waiting in a carrier bag under my bed. The minute Mrs Clements left, I'd be gone.

Chapter 18

The Peregrine Falcon

I'd only been back at Mill House a few days and my fantasy world was not holding up too well as the evils of the place found new ways to get into my world, brutal ways. There was nothing else for it; I had to get out of there. I nagged the staff until they finally agreed to let me phone Mrs Clements. I told her that I had to see her right away, that I was desperate and there was something I needed to tell her, but I had to see her in person. She must have sensed my desperation because she came up to see me the following day.

During the visit I pleaded with her to help me. I didn't care about the beatings I'd have to take from the staff for telling my social worker about all the abuse I was being subjected to. I was being abused and beaten regardless so I had nothing to lose now and, quite frankly, I'd given up caring. There was no way I was going to stay there any longer. But Mrs Clements thought I was exaggerating when I told her the horror stories – the violence, the sex. After she left one of the staff clouted me around the head about 20 times for 'telling lies' and later that evening some of the other staff beat me too: kicks, punches and even several whips of a leather belt for good measure. All the staff had their own 'code of silence' and expected the children to go along with it whenever they had family or social worker visits. For the rest of the day I was locked in my bedroom, without any meals, crying and abandoned, until the next morning.

January 1979 ambled along at a snail's pace and the last dregs of snow had all but melted into the ground, but my internal winter was about to get a lot colder.

It seemed that all my letters to Mrs Clements, begging and pleading with her to get me out of Mill House, had eventually paid off. But there was something I hadn't taken into consideration. Instead of arranging for me to go home, she and her team had found another place that they thought would be more suitable for me. It was just down the coast from Whitehaven, about 50 miles from Carlisle. So, I wasn't going home and I wasn't even about to be transferred to somewhere nearer my mum's house: I'd be stuck 320 miles away from London. Pelham House was located in the middle of nowhere, about four miles inland from the bleak village of Seascale. The chances of my going home for the odd weekend were increasingly remote, especially now that Mum was seeing Keith more often.

We were about two weeks into the New Year when Mrs Clements came back to tell me about this new improved place that I would soon be moving to. My housemaster came to get me out of class and informed me that my social worker was there to see me.

'Hello, Nigel. How are you?' she said.

'I'm OK,' I said, with a feeling of ambivalence.

Back then, whenever I said that I was OK, what I meant was, I'm still alive. Usually my housemaster, or another male member of staff was present during the initial hellos and, although I was past caring what they would do to me if I told tales, I could not see the point in banging on about the violent beatings, bullying, belittling and sex between staff and children anymore. Already I'd mentioned the violent goings-on two or three times to no avail, and having learned a hard lesson about telling tales, this was not something I wanted to replay over and over. So, whenever Mrs Clements asked me how things were and if everything was OK, I would just answer, 'It's alright, I suppose.'

'You can use the living room, if you like – there's nobody in there,' offered the housemaster.

'Have you played your new record yet?' asked Mrs Clements, spotting the record player in the corner.

'Yes, it's great. Thank you for getting it for me.'

'You're quite welcome. OK, we've found another place for you and, because you're getting a little older now, I thought it would be a good idea if I took you to see it before you move there.'

'Oh, I thought I was gonna be allowed to go home?'

'Nigel, I'm really sorry, but you know that's not possible,' she told me.

Despondent, I just gazed into my lap.

'Look, this is a lovely place. It's in the country and there's lots of wildlife,' she added.

Wildlife, I thought. I knew she meant well, but I really couldn't have cared less about wildlife at that time.

'Where is it?'

'It's just near Seascale, on the coast.'

'Where's that?'

'It's about 30 miles from Ulverston so it'll be easier for me to come and see you.'

'What about going home for weekends?'

'Well, it's quite a long way from London, but I'm sure we'll be able to arrange it for you to go home to see your mum sometimes,' she explained.

Later in life, I'd read in my file that it was a toss-up between Pelham House and a school for the maladjusted. The idea of my being placed in an institution that closed down during the holidays was quickly rejected after Mrs Clements had a lengthy conversation with my mum. It seemed the holidays would be too long and my mother did not want me at home for long periods of time so it was decided that I would be sent to Pelham House instead.

'Here, I've brought you something,' Mrs Clements added, handing me a large brown paper bag. 'I know you still like birds.'

I opened the bag and inside was an A3 artist's sketchpad with a pack of assorted charcoal pencils.

'Thank you,' I said.

'Well, I thought you might like to get into drawing. I heard you were quite good at art in Lancaster.'

'Yes,' I said.

Although the classroom at the Children's Psychiatric Unit in Lancaster only produced a very patchy and improvised version of an education, I did enjoy drawing and other art-related pastimes there. At the very least, drawing might provide another form of escapism.

'Maybe you could draw a bird?'

'Yes.'

Well, I still had my bird books from Lancaster, so I figured I'd pick out a nice bird of prey and try to replicate it in black-and-white sketch form.

Mrs Clements continued to tell me more about Pelham House in Seascale – how it was in the country with lots of wildlife and how it had great sports facilities – but I wasn't impressed. She told me she would be back the following week to drive me there to see it. At the very least I had another visit from her to look forward to, a 100-mile round trip in her car, which would also include us going into a café somewhere.

Above all, it would be a day away from this hellhole.

After dinner that evening I dug out my bird books from the wardrobe and flicked through the pages to find a suitable picture to draw. I found the perfect image of a stunning blue-grey peregrine falcon perched on a rock, looking out across farmland as if it owned it. The peregrine presented lots of intricate detail: bluish-black on the back and long pointed wings, with white to rusty coloured underparts and horizontal speckled bars of dark brown on its breast. It would be a challenge, but I loved this bird and knew a lot about it. The fastest member of the animal kingdom, it can reach speeds of well over 200 miles an hour during one of its high-speed dives as it attacks prey mid-air.

Having prepared my artist's pad and pencils, over the next two evenings I spent several hours drawing this magnificent bird in great detail. I didn't do too much smudging, just a little in the relevant places, choosing to maintain all that detail and sharpness as much as possible. When I was finished, I stood back to admire my work. It was seriously good. My attention to detail was incredible, even down to the sparkle of light in its eye; I'd missed nothing. Although it was black and white, you could almost see the bluish-grey. Mrs Clements was going to be so proud of me.

Unable to contain my excitement, I gathered up my pad and headed off to find a member of staff to show it to. The living room was empty bar two of the older girls, so I headed for the TV room, where several boys and a male member of staff were sitting, watching television.

'Mr Fletcher, look what I've drawn,' I said, proudly holding up my picture.

He glanced at it for a fraction of a second, then said, 'So bloody what. What do you want, a bloody *Cracker Jack* Pencil? Go on, bugger off before I rip it up.'

Well, what did I expect? 'Well done, son, that's amazing' or even, 'Wow, what a stunning drawing, you're an amazing talent'. Of course, I should have known better. Creativity and originality were totally discouraged here. What was I thinking? Why did I think for one second that anybody there would be in the least bit interested?

The fact that tens of thousands of public workers went on strike at the beginning of what would become known as the 'Winter of Discontent' or that Peter D. Mitchell had just won the Nobel Prize in Chemistry didn't mean anything to these people. They were more concerned about whether or not Sid Vicious stabbed his girlfriend, Nancy, to death in a hotel room, and they all found it highly amusing that the YMCA had just filed a libel suit against the Village People for their song of the same name. My peregrine sketch fell somewhere between inconsequential and who gives a toss? Still, I knew Mrs Clements would be proud.

I would have to wait almost a week before I could show Mrs Clements my drawing – an eventful week at that, though not in a good way. Meanwhile, the staff were doing everything they could to get me to interact with the other children. They thought it would be good if I sat in the TV room with them for a minimum of one hour in the evening. I didn't want to, for obvious reasons, but my protests fell on deaf ears.

The first evening went exactly as I expected it to. I chose a chair two rows from the back, one of the few available seats left, to watch some television. Two minutes later it felt like the top of my head had just exploded; the pain was indescribable. The closest I can get is that it felt like a handful of white-hot lead shot had been fired into my skull from above. In an attempt to get the pain to subside I clutched the top of my head and curled forward into the foetal position.

'Markson, stop fucking about or I'll knock you into the middle of next bloody week,' said the housemaster.

'Yes, sir,' said Markson, sniggering.

The bastard had whacked me on the head with the studded side of a football boot.

'You alright, Cooper?' asked the housemaster.

But I didn't answer for the pain was excruciating; my head was on fire and throbbing so hard I could hear it pulsating in my head. The housemaster came over.

'Let me see,' he said, pulling my hands away. He rubbed, hard, across the top of my head. Already two large bumps had formed. I felt his fingers move over them, which made me flinch. 'You'll be alright,' he said.

He then leaned over the chairs and clouted Markson around the head with his hand.

'Any more trouble out of you this evening and I'll give you the biggest bloody hiding you've ever had! Now, give me that football boot.'

Markson handed the boot to him. I was hoping he was going to smash it across his head – an eye for an eye – but he didn't, he just said, 'Little fucking bastard,' and went back to his seat.

'I'm gonna fucking get you for that, Cooper!' Markson muttered under his breath.

I just looked forward at the television screen and waited for the programme to finish so I could go to my room again.

Monday morning came and the housemaster had another idea to try to get me more involved. How I wished that they would leave me to my own devices. Every time they tried to get me involved with the other kids it just ended in disaster. This time the housemaster thought it would be good for me to be on hen duty for the week. Now this was a job usually reserved for the older boys, not because it was a responsible one, but because they liked doing it. Being on hen duty meant they could bunk off doing the other regimented chores of the morning, smoke fags and have sex with a girl of their choosing (girls would sneak off to be with whatever older boy was on hen duty that week), while the staff turned a blind eye. Naturally I would now be in the firing line because I was depriving the older boys of their fun and games around the hen house and allotments.

Being on hen duty also meant mixing up the slops left over from breakfast with a separate large bucket of hen pellets mixed with water. I was to carry two heavy buckets down to the hen house at the other end of the extensive grounds and collect up all the eggs while I was there, clean hen shit out of the nesting areas and lay down fresh straw. The whole chore generally took about 20 minutes, but the bigger boys somehow managed to make it last an hour.

During lunch on that first day I'd been on hen duty the bigger boys were furious with me.

'Cooper, you'd better get off hens tomorrow or you're fuckin' dead!' said one.

'Yeah, Cooper, you don't get to do hens, that's our job you've nicked!' another told me.

'What can I do? I've been told I have to do it all week,' I explained.

'Well, you'd better think of something. If you think your life's been hard in here so far, just wait and see what happens if you don't get off hens by tomorrow. We'll make your life hell!' he said.

Great, the housemaster had personally greased the pole that would slide me into yet another bucket-load of shit.

The next morning I didn't get out of bed. I pretended to be sick, but of course it didn't work.

'Look, Nigel,' said the housemaster, 'I know you're just trying to get off doing the hens, and I know why. But sooner or later you're going to have to stand up to those boys.'

Of course, why didn't I think of that? It was staring me in the face all the time. What was he thinking? If he knew of some magical way that a skinny 12-year-old kid could overpower four hard-as-nails 15- and 16-year-olds, I wished he'd let me in on the secret. I tried to plead with him, but it all fell on deaf ears. So, I was forced to get up and go and have breakfast in the dining room, where I was subjected to more threats and glares from the older boys.

After breakfast was over I went to the kitchen, where the cook gave me the large bucket of slops, then I went outside and mixed up another bucket of hen food before heading off down to the allotments. Unbeknown to me, I was followed by two of the bigger boys. I'd collected the eggs and just finished putting down fresh straw in the nesting areas when I turned around and there they were: Markson and Walker, the two nastiest boys in the place.

'Fucking told you I was gonna get you, Cooper!' said Markson.

'But I didn't do anything, it's not my fault, I've got to—'

WHACK.

While pleading my case to Markson, Walker punched me in the side of my face. Then Markson stepped forward and kneed me in the balls. I fell to the floor and they both kicked me several times in the ribs. All I could do was curl up into a tight ball and hold onto that tiny nugget deep in the pit of my soul. I tried desperately to get to the moon, but the onslaught of kicks prevented me from even getting off the ground. The kicks eventually stopped.

'Put him in there,' said Markson.

They each grabbed one of my legs and dragged me into the large wooden hen house, closed the door and bolted it from the outside. I was left to nurse my bruised ribcage on the floor, among 20 clucking hens and all the accompanying shit. It was early February and still freezing cold. I hadn't taken the eggs back to the kitchen either.

As I lay on the cold floor, locked in the hen house and in severe pain, I wondered how long it would be before one of the staff realised I was missing.

Chapter 19

From Code Red
to Code Yellow

If I'm honest, I would have been quite happy to lie there and die with the hens, but as I suspected, the staff noticed that I hadn't come back. Meanwhile, I managed to sit upright, but my ribs were sore as anything and it hurt to breathe. I'd been in the hen house for about an hour before one of the staff came looking for me, and if I hadn't shouted out, I'm not sure he would even have bothered to unbolt the door to check inside.

'What the bloody hell happened?' he asked, as if it was my fault.

'Somebody locked me in,' I said, standing up and clutching my ribs.

'Who?'

'I don't know.'

'And why are you holding your ribs like that?'

But I didn't say anything. At that stage I didn't want to antagonise Markson and Walker any more as that would surely result in further beatings.

'I don't think this hen thing is really working out for you, is it?'

'No, sir,' I said, silently praying that I would be removed from hen duties.

'OK, let's get you to class.'

And that was it. He knew damn well that I'd taken yet another beating but, as usual, the perpetrators would go unpunished. I suspect the staff (who, for the most part, were just as bad as, if not worse than the older boys) figured that it would be pointless punishing these bigger boys, for whom fighting, abuse and taking beatings was now a way of life; in fact some of them thrived on it. It sickened me to the core and whenever something like that happened it was just another reminder of how I should not be in a place like that.

By now I'd been in five institutions (including this one) for almost five years and I refused to allow those places to influence my life in any way. No way would I ever become institutionalised, unlike everyone else. So, as usual, I kept myself to myself as much as I could, given my predicament, and curled up into a tiny ball in my fantasy world. Once there, I hung onto that little golden nugget in the core of my soul with every ounce of inner strength that I had, and refused to let go.

I'd come to the conclusion that I was pretty much on my own and so I had to look after myself; nobody else cared and Mrs Clements' visits were no longer regular. I was just a 12-year-old kid and looking after myself in such a harsh, hostile and often violent environment was no mean feat. The only saving grace at Mill House was that I was excluded from all the sexual goings-on, be it with the other kids or staff.

I was aware of another vulnerable kid, about my age, who was involved in some sort of sexual activity with one of the male staff, but judging from the way he spoke of events, I suspect he was simply getting some sort of love and affection wherever he could find it, no matter how sordid and wrongful it might appear to someone on the outside. This particular kid's parents had disowned him a long time ago and the only visitor he ever got was his social worker, about once every three months. He had no home to visit at holiday times and he was desperate for love and compassion. Although the majority of the kids in these places were real hard nuts, always there were the odd one or two like me, who simply didn't fit into the barbaric regime.

At breakfast the next morning I learned that I'd been taken off hens.

'Walker, you're on hens for the rest of the week,' said the housemaster.

Thank God, I thought. At least my beatings, bullying, abuse and torments would be brought down a grade in severity from a Code Red (severe risk of beatings and abuse) to a Code Orange (high risk of beatings and abuse) or, if I was lucky, a Code Yellow (significant risk of beatings and abuse). For the record, the only time I was on a Code Blue (general risk of beatings and abuse) was during the weekends when a lot of the older boys were at home on leave and I don't ever recall being lucky enough to get down to a Code Green (low risk of beatings and abuse), not even briefly. The colour code system, incidentally, was my own creation, a way of interpreting the beatings. By coincidence, airports would later use the same colour code system for security.

So, I spent the next 26 hours on a Code Yellow until Mrs Clements came to drive me over to see Pelham House in Seascale. Based on the places I'd been shipped off to in the past, I was scarcely optimistic. However, at least I'd enjoy the 100-mile round trip with my social worker, which would take about an hour and a half in each direction.

Mrs Clements arrived at Mill House at 10 o'clock the next morning. The housemaster came to fetch me from the school class. As he walked me round to his office, he gave me a few words of advice.

'Now, remember what I told you about telling tales?'

'Yes, sir.'

'Good, because if you tell tales you'll only make things worse for yourself, *much* worse, do I make myself clear?'

'Yes, sir.'

'I'm glad we understand each other. Besides, you'll be out of here in a few weeks, so let's try and get along until you leave, OK?'

'Yes, sir.'

So, it looked as though I was going to this new place, whether I liked it or not.

'Hello, Nigel,' said Mrs Clements, 'are you ready?'

'Yes.'

During the journey she could sense my anxiety about the new place and tried to reassure me that she'd been there and spoken to the headmaster. She was confident that Pelham House would be a better place for me. Unconvinced, I didn't hold out much hope. A distinct pattern was starting to emerge with the various institutions I found myself in. Essentially, they were all just a slightly different flavour of shit, regardless of what dog's arse part of the country they happened to be located in.

About an hour and a half later we arrived. It really was in the middle of nowhere, one of those off-a-main-road/B-road/ winding-little-narrow-road/winding-track sort of places. Although Pelham House was a large, stately looking building with several outbuildings, it was well and truly hidden from public view by the surrounding dense woodland, beyond which was mile upon mile of never-ending open fields. Unless you knew it was there, you'd never find it.

Although it was February and the snow had all but melted back in Carlisle, the extensive grounds were a thick blanket of white. Somehow the snow looked quite at home here. It was as if the place was built for long, cold miserable winters. Pelham House would never escape winter, and winter would never escape Pelham House; it was a marriage made in hell.

The main building was of the Georgian period and resembled an enormous 15-bedroom stately home. My first thought was, *My God, does Count Dracula live here?* It looked intimidating and the only thing that seemed to be missing from this particular prison was a huge 12-foot-high wall around the perimeter of the grounds.

Mrs Clements parked the car in one of the many vacant spaces and we got out. It seemed much colder here, as if the temperature had dropped considerably since we left Carlisle, 90 minutes earlier. The icy winds welcomed me by biting hard into my face; it seemed the elements were letting me know where I was, an early warning. I just wanted to get straight back in Mrs Clements' cosy warm car and drive away from there.

'Are you ready?' she said, the cutting wind preventing her from smiling. But I said nothing; I just gazed at the place. I must have had a look of sheer terror on my face because she walked over to me and put her arm around my shoulder. 'Come on, at least give it a chance, you haven't seen inside yet.'

'I don't want to, I don't want to go in there – I just want to go home.'

'Oh, Nigel!' she sighed, genuinely sympathetic and concerned about me.

Reading my file in my forties, I learned that Mrs Clements moved heaven and earth to try to find foster parents for me, so I could live a 'normal' happy life like every other child, but there were simply none available at that time. Her hands were tied: she knew I didn't belong in those places, but what else could she do?

'Come on, let's go inside, at least it'll be warm.'

Somehow, I doubted that.

We entered the main building where the headmaster, Mr Burkinshaw, greeted us.

'Hello, you must be Nigel,' he said, extending his hand. I shook it. 'How was your journey?' he said to Mrs Clements.

'It was OK, wasn't it?' she said, aiming the last part of her sentence at me.

'Yes,' I said.

'Good, well how about I give you the grand tour of the place first, then we'll go to my office and have a talk and something to drink?'

'That sounds good,' said Mrs Clements.

And off we went.

'This main building is where the main offices are, but the assembly hall is also in this part and upstairs are the dormitories …'

We walked down the long corridor and around the corner, where Mr Burkinshaw opened one side of a double-door. 'This is the assembly hall,' he said, inviting us in. *Oh my God, it's huge.* There was row upon row of chairs, enough to seat about 70 people. The place was much bigger than anywhere else I'd ever been.

'How many boys are there here?' I wanted to know.

'Currently we have 54,' he said.

Holy shit. Fifty-four unruly, delinquent, dysfunctional boys from who knows what sort of backgrounds, what a nightmare!

I knew they were all boys and no girls as Mrs Clements had explained to me that Pelham House was an all-boys' school. It was about as far removed from a cosy little two-point-four-children foster family as you could get.

Next, he showed us the dining hall, which was quite a size. It had six elongated Formica-topped tables in three separate groups for the residents of the three houses. Each table had 10 chairs.

'OK, let me show you the dormitories,' he said, leading us up the dark-brown tiled stairs.

At the top of the stairs was a long corridor that continued round the corner in an L-shape, off which were several dormitories, each housing anywhere between five and eight boys.

'We'll probably put you in this one,' he said, stepping into a medium-size dorm with five beds in it.

When he said those words, I nearly wet myself with fear as the brutal truth hit home. *So, this is it, I'm definitely going to be coming here, and soon.* It was so depressing, the beds looked like those horrible white metal-framed single hospital beds. It wouldn't have surprised me in the least if I had learned that the beds had been donated from a Victorian mental asylum abandoned long ago. They were disgusting, nothing homely about them at all. Those beds were not designed to have a good night's sleep in, they were instruments of torture and misery.

'Let me take you over to your house. Pelham House can accommodate up to 60 boys, divided into three separate houses. You're going to be in Mr Booth's house …'

We went downstairs from the other end of the corridor and came out of a side door, then walked across a cobbled courtyard to get to the house where I'd be staying. There was a boy, about 15 years old, sweeping the courtyard with a stiff yard broom. He was wearing blue denim work dungarees with a thick jumper underneath.

'Good morning, Paterson,' said Mr Burkinshaw.

'Good morning, sir,' said the boy.

I only glanced at him as we passed, but I felt his eyes on my back as we walked towards the elongated wooden pre-fab house. Inside, Mr Booth was sitting in the television room, looking through some paperwork.

'Ah, good morning,' he said, getting up.

'Good morning, Mr Booth. This is Nigel, he's going to be joining you next week,' said Mr Burkinshaw.

With those words, Mrs Clements glanced at me and put her hand on my shoulder. Up until then I'd still hung onto a glimmer of hope that my having to start at Pelham House was not a foregone conclusion, that there might still be another option, but there wasn't. I could sense that Mrs Clements was not best thrilled about this either and I suspect it was her superiors who had decided, during a meeting, that Pelham House was the only place available. In my files, it was revealed that Lowgate House in Levens, Kendal, had been suggested, as had the terrible Broughton Tower School for maladjusted children in Broughton-in-Furness, but for one reason or another, I ended up being placed at Pelham House. It was *fait accompli*, I was a victim of circumstance.

'Hello, Nigel,' said Mr Booth, extending his hand.

'Hello,' I said, shaking it.

'Perhaps you could show Nigel and Mrs Clements around and take them over to the schoolrooms, then bring them back over to my office afterwards,' said Mr Burkinshaw.

'Of course,' said Mr Booth.

'Well, this is the television room,' he said.

The room was similar to other television rooms in any number of boys' homes scattered around the country: a TV in the corner with about 15 chairs positioned around the room.

Mr Booth then led us along the corridor, his footsteps reverberating and the pre-fab wooden floor flexing under his weight as he walked. On the right was an office with a lockable door and along the left were padded, built-in benches to seat about eight people. At the end of the short corridor was a large open living area to the right. It contained about 15 chairs around the walls and in the middle there was a pool table and a table tennis table. At the far end was an open floor space. In one corner was a record player with two separate speakers: one on the window ledge, the other on a small, round coffee table.

'This is the main living area,' he said.

'Well, this is nice, isn't it?' said Mrs Clements.

I forced a smile.

'Let me take you over to see the schoolrooms,' he said.

Outside on the courtyard, Paterson was still sweating over sweeping up.

'This is another house,' said Mr Booth, pointing to a door that led into another house to the right, but still part of the same physical pre-fab building. 'There are three houses, with about 18 boys in each. We think it's better to keep the groups a little smaller. And over there is where the toilets and showers are located,' he added, pointing to the far left corner of the courtyard.

He glanced at his watch. 'You'd better get a move on so you get this finished before lunchtime,' he told Paterson.

'Yes, sir,' he said, putting his back into it with more urgency.

We walked across the courtyard, then along a wide concrete path between some large open grass areas. As we walked I could hear a parliament of rooks cawing in two large oak trees, probably planted long before this place was even built. The oaks looked as though they'd been standing for several hundred years, surviving the harsh elements a thousand times over – I sort of knew how they felt. The rooks' caws grew increasingly louder as we neared a large concrete building that resembled an aircraft hangar. I looked up into the enormous gnarled trees and could clearly see the rooks, their black feathers with purple sheen. Like sinister witches, they cawed and cackled.

Mr Booth opened the door on the corner of the building and we entered.

'This is the P.E. area,' he said.

Oh my God, it was huge, about the size of a five-a-side football pitch.

It was cold and bleak inside. I couldn't quite get my head around it, but it felt colder in there than it did outside. The floor was grey concrete and the brick walls were at least 25 feet tall, with a metal structure roof.

'They do all sorts of physical activities in here,' he explained. I really didn't like the sound of that, I could almost smell the blood and sweat.

We walked through the P.E. area and out through another door that led into a corridor, off which were three classrooms.

Suddenly it was very noisy. We went down the corridor and off to the right. I could just about make out lots of boys through the frosted opaque windows. Loud and boisterous, to me it sounded like hell. I didn't actually see any of the boys, at least not in focus, and frankly, I didn't want to.

Then Mr Booth said the very words I was dreading: 'Let me show you inside one of the classrooms.' He opened one of the old wooden doors and popped his head in. 'Mr Winters, there's someone I'd like you to meet,' he said. He turned to me, 'Come on in.' *Holy shit! I really don't want to do this.* The classroom fell silent in anticipation of the new kid entering. I tried my hardest to stop my legs from trembling as I stepped inside.

'This is Nigel, he's going to be starting here next week,' he said.

'Hello, Nigel, well, I'll look forward to having you in my class,' said Mr Winters.

I looked right into his eyes as he spoke as I didn't want to look to my left at the 14 or so pairs of eyes fixed on me. What I had seen in my peripheral vision was enough. I didn't need to look to know what lay ahead; already I knew the score.

'Come on, let's get back,' said Mr Booth.

As I turned to leave, I glanced around the room and saw a mass of rather unsavoury-looking, rough and ready boys, most of them aged about 15 or 16. They were all sitting at individual, old-fashioned wooden desks, the kind with inkwells in them. As Mr Booth closed the classroom door I heard the mumblings and sniggering behind me.

Back at Mr Burkinshaw's office Mrs Clements had a cup of coffee. I didn't feel like drinking anything, my stomach was full of nervous butterflies and I felt physically sick. I didn't want to talk about my future there, I just wanted to get out of the building and into Mrs Clements' car and then away from that place as fast as possible.

'Don't look so worried, we'll get you straightened out,' said Mr Burkinshaw.

An imposing thick-set man, he had a military feel about him, which I soon learned to be true as he often made references to serving during WW2. He scared me – his deep, booming authoritative voice, chest-out dominant stature and overall deportment. I wondered what exactly he meant by that. I'd soon learn that Pelham House was a highly disciplined and regimented approved school for the very worst kind of wayward boy. It was the sort of place where corporal punishment was as good as it got. I think it would be safe to say that it was like a borstal for boys between the ages of 10 and 16.

Mrs Clements and I finally left and headed back across the bleak grounds to her car. For me it wasn't soon enough. We got in the car and the relief physically washed over me.

'That wasn't too bad, was it?' she asked.

'I don't want to come here,' I said.

'Oh, I'm sure it will be OK once you've settled in.'

'Please, I don't want to come here, I just want to go home to live with my mum.'

I continued to protest as she started the car. As we made our way along the winding driveway to the perimeter of the grounds, Mrs Clements tried to reassure me that it would be alright and that I really needed to give it a chance. I sat there in silence, listening to her well-meaning words as we headed out onto the little winding country road towards the main road back to Mill House in Carlisle, where I would remain for another week until whatever fate awaited me at Pelham House.

Chapter 20

Welcome To Dracula's Castle

The following week Mrs Clements came to Mill House to transfer me down the West Coast to Pelham House. The end of February was in sight, and my upcoming 13th birthday was just around the corner on 8 March, but something told me I wasn't going to particularly enjoy that day.

As Mrs Clements' Cortina pulled into the grounds of Pelham House, it looked just as stark and cold as I remembered from the previous week. As I got out of the car the cutting wind slapped my face. Even the weather was uninviting. As I walked across the car park, dragging my suitcase on wheels behind with the ice-cold wind whipping up a frenzy around me, all I could think about was my mum and brothers in their cosy warm living room happily sitting around a Monopoly board with a tin of biscuits, my mother oblivious to what I was going through, or perhaps she'd just decided not to think about it. After all, out of sight, out of mind.

'Are you OK with that?' said Mrs Clements, holding her coat collar around her neck.

'Yes.'

We entered via the main large wooden door at the front of Dracula's mansion. Inside we stood in the large, open hallway, but there was no one in sight.

'OK, you wait here, I'll see if I can find someone,' she said.

In her absence I stood there admiring the internal architecture, but the ominous vibes of the place told me that I was not in a beautiful museum on a sunny Sunday afternoon and there were certainly no loving families with happy children filling the halls, chambers and large, high-ceilinged rooms. A shiver ran down my spine and I thought about turning round, opening the door and making a run for it. But then the moment passed as I heard the footsteps and the voices of Mrs Clements and Mr Burkinshaw as they came down the corridor.

'Hello again,' said Mr Burkinshaw.

'Hello.'

'OK, Nigel, I'm going to go now,' said Mrs Clements.

'Oh,' I said, looking at my feet.

Then a hand smacked me on the back, almost knocking me off-balance.

'Don't worry, son, you'll be just fine,' said Mr Burkinshaw in his deep bellowing voice, which sounded several decibels louder in the large brick and marble hallway.

'I'll check in on you soon,' said Mrs Clements, smiling. But the concern in her eyes was clear to see. She left and headed back to her car.

'Right then, young man! Let's get you over to your house so Mr Booth can get you settled in.'

As I was led through the long corridor, out onto the stone cobbled courtyard and across to my house, I couldn't help thinking about Mrs Clements driving off the grounds without me and I wondered what was going through her mind at that exact moment.

'Hello again, Nigel,' said Mr Booth.

'Hello.'

'I'll leave you to it,' said Mr Burkinshaw to Mr Booth, who nodded in acknowledgement.

'Right, let's take your things up to your dormitory then it will be almost lunchtime.'

He led me out and across the courtyard to a door over in the far corner. We went up the stairs and along the corridor to my dormitory. It was the dormitory that Mr Burkinshaw had told me I was going to be in the previous week. Of the five beds, mine was the one closest to the corridor. Apart from the door to the dorm there were two large windows so you could see in from the corridor. There was also a window on the outside wall with white security bars on the inside.

'You can put your clothes in this wardrobe,' said Mr Booth, pointing to the single wardrobe next to my small single bed.

He stood there and watched as I unpacked my clothes and put them away. I felt sick, like I was in prison. It took all my willpower to stop myself from vomiting. I'd never felt so vulnerable and terrified in all my life.

'OK, let's get down to the dining room.'

I can't begin to tell you how nervous I was as Mr Booth and I made our way down the stairs to the dining room. Long before we even reached the dining-room door, I could hear the noise of 54 boisterous boys and the occasional shouts of male members of staff. When we got to the door, Mr Booth opened it and the volume spilled out into the corridor. As we entered, the noise started to come down a few decibels as they all noticed the new kid. The general rowdiness turned into mumblings as pretty much every pair of eyes looked over in my direction.

'Come on, you're sitting at my table,' said Mr Booth, leading me across the dining room to one of the long tables. 'You can sit there,' he said, pointing.

I took my seat with the other boys. Each of the three houses had two long tables, one for the older boys and another for the younger ones. The housemaster from each house sat at the table with the younger boys. I was seated at the table for the younger boys and I suspected I was the youngest there, apart from one boy, whom I found out later was 12, like me. The remaining seven boys at my table looked as if they were aged 14 or 15. Over at the other table the nine boys all looked 15 or 16.

I glanced over at the four tables of the other two houses and the age groups seemed identical, perhaps with the odd one or two that might be closer to 12 or 13. Not only was I the second youngest kid in the entire place, I was the newest kid too. What exactly did that mean? I didn't want to think about it. Right then I felt way out of my depth. The dining room reeked of aggression, hatred and testosterone.

Over the coming days I'd learn that most of these boys already had a string of criminal convictions to their names: TDA (taking and driving away), burglary, arson, GBH (grievous bodily harm) and other acts of violence, muggings, street gang crime, drug abuse, alcohol abuse, under-age sex. Then there were a few unfortunate 'problem children', but for the most part, from what I could see, they were career criminals in the making with a pretty impressive rap sheet already under their belts. Every other week someone or other was being collected by their social worker to attend court for some offence they had committed while on home leave or after running away.

After lunch the other boys all made their way back to the schoolrooms, while Mr Booth took me across to the house. I'd start school the next morning, but for the remainder of the afternoon I would entertain myself by playing pool while he caught up with some paperwork in the TV room, though he did take a break to have a game of table tennis with me. I sensed Mr Booth was a good man, though I'd soon learn that he was perhaps caught up in the system; because of this his hands were tied and he regularly had to turn a blind eye to his colleagues' wicked behaviour.

The afternoon passed slowly until eventually the boys from Mr Booth's house came piling in. Feet stamped along the wooden corridor of the pre-fab house while voices shouted.

'OK, settle down,' ordered Mr Booth.

About 10 of the boys bustled into the main living area, where I was now sitting. (I didn't want to be standing there, playing pool when they came in, I figured sitting would be safer.) Most of them ignored me, but one boy, aged about 14, came over.

'Hi, what's your name?' he said.

'Nigel.'

'I'm Harry,' he said. 'You want a game of table tennis?'

'No, I'm not very good,' I admitted.

I was only average, but I suspected (based on the time they probably spent playing) most of these boys were pretty good.

'Go on, I'll go easy,' he said.

'OK.'

I grabbed a paddle from the table.

'Ready?' he said, preparing to serve.

'Yeah.'

Harry delivered a gentle serve, which I returned quite easily. We kept up a tame rally, which must have lasted about 10 seconds before my return missed the edge of the table on his side and fell to the ground. His point, though I don't think anybody was really keeping score. Harry served again and we began another rally. He tried a few smashes, the majority of which were successful. I decided to maintain respect for my opponent, of whom I was cautious, by not trying such an aggressive smash. Our game concluded painlessly. Harry went off to chat to some of his buddies while I took up my seat again. Then another boy came over to introduce himself.

'Hi, I'm Jerry, but most people just call me "Linnet", though.'

'I'm Nigel.'

'So what do you think of it so far?' he said, sitting in the chair next to me. Jerry was the youngest boy in the place, four months younger than me.

'I don't know yet,' I said.

'Don't worry, you'll get used to it,' he told me.

Jerry was cheerful enough and always seemed to have a smile on his face. Maybe that was just his way of dealing with it.

'Where are the toilets?' I said.

'Come on, I'll show you.'

As Jerry and I walked out of the living area into the corridor, there were five boys sitting on the padded benches that ran half the length of the corridor. They were all smoking roll-up cigarettes. The office opposite the benches was open and Mr Booth was in there, supervising handing out the various tins of Golden Virginia and Old Holborn so the boys could roll their own (you were allowed to smoke at Pelham House as long as you were over 14). The tins were identifiable via the various custom jobs the boys had done to them. Some had scraped all the paint off with a knife so they were bright silver then painted their names on with gloss black paint. Others had even taken their tins over to the art class and painted on various band logos such as: 'The Sex Pistols', 'Sham 69', 'AC/DC', 'Black Sabbath'.

Jerry took me outside and along the side of the courtyard and through a door in the corner. Inside was a fairly grim grey concrete toilet block, more like an old unkempt public toilet in a rough neighbourhood. There was graffiti everywhere and it stank of urine, even though there was natural air-conditioning, courtesy of the broken windows, with the icy-cold winds howling through.

After using the toilet Jerry and I headed back into the house. The boys had all finished their roll-ups and had congregated in the living area except one, who was still sitting on the padded bench area. I walked behind Jerry along the narrow corridor back towards the living area. Just as I passed this kid, he leaned forward and my knee caught him.

'Hey, man, watch where you're going!' he said, shooting me a look and rubbing his arm.

'It was an accident,' I said.

'What did you say?' he said, jumping to his feet.

'I said, it was an acci—'

WHACK! He punched me in the right eye. It was as if my eyeball had exploded as one of his knuckles caught the dead centre of it, the rest of his fist colliding hard with the bone around my eye socket. I'd never been punched so hard in the eye before. I fell to the floor, squealing, hands cupped over my face. The culprit, Paterson, was 15 and quite stocky. As I lay there writhing on the floor, crying out in pain, one of the older boys, Ericson, came running out into the corridor. Most of the boys used their surnames when addressing each other, or various nicknames.

'What happened?' asked Ericson.

'Paterson punched him in the eye,' said Jerry, just as Mr Booth arrived on the scene.

'What the hell's going on?' said Mr Booth.

'Paterson punched him,' said Ericson.

'Why?' said Mr Booth.

'He knocked my arm when he walked past,' said Paterson.

'You little bastard, he's only new here!' said Ericson, stooping down to check me out. 'Let me see,' he said, prising my hands apart. But I could not open my right eye; it was stinging like anything and throbbing away. Tears streamed down my face out of my right eye.

'Bloody hell, sir, look at this!' said Ericson.

Mr Booth took one look at my eye then grabbed Paterson by his hair and dragged him out into the courtyard.

'Go and change into your work clothes, get the yard broom and get to work!' shouted Mr Booth, before returning to the house.

'Are you alright?' asked Ericson.

'Yeah,' I said, but I was in severe pain. The staff didn't think it was serious enough for me to see a doctor, or even the matron over in the main building. Your injuries had to be a hell of a lot worse than that to even justify a visit to the matron's office.

A punk rocker with spiky blond hair, I instantly recognised Ericson from Mill House. He'd been transferred to Pelham House about a month before me, but from what I could gather, he'd settled in pretty fast and ran around like he owned the place. I'm not sure why Ericson showed me compassion, perhaps it was because we were at Mill House together and he knew I liked some of the punk bands that he liked. Anyhow, he didn't stop at showing me a little compassion, as Paterson would find out later that night.

The rest of the evening was relatively uneventful. I sat in the corner of the living area nursing my eye and feeling rather sorry for myself while the other boys were split between the living room and the television room along the corridor. The evening passed and bedtime arrived. Mr Booth escorted us all out of the house and across the courtyard and up to our dorms. As we made our way across the courtyard, he ordered Paterson to put the yard broom away and go upstairs to get ready with everybody else. He had made Paterson sweep the courtyard (about 15 x 20 yards in size) three times over until there was not a single speck of dirt between any of the cobbles.

In the dorms we had to strip to our underpants, grab our towel, soap, toothbrush and toothpaste before heading back down the stairs and across the cobbled courtyard in the freezing cold in just our underpants into the shower/washrooms.

To my dismay, I learned that Paterson was in my dorm in the bed opposite mine. He entered, wearing his denim work dungarees, nudging me hard as he walked past.

'I'm gonna fucking get you for that!' he muttered.

'Nobody's going to be getting anybody!' shouted Mr Booth, who'd heard from out in the corridor.

Walking across the courtyard on a cold late February evening in just my Y-fronts and barefooted was not my idea of fun. The three separate houses took it in turns using the washrooms, otherwise 54 unruly boys all fighting for wash space or a basin to brush their teeth would probably be too much. As I stood there, getting washed with the other boys, a feeling of dread came over me as I wondered if Paterson would make his move on me that same night.

After washing we made our way up to our respective dorms, tiptoeing across the courtyard, trying not to get our bare feet dirty. I was to share my dorm with Linnet, Paterson and one other kid, whose name I didn't yet know.

Mr Booth handed his duty over to the night staff, of which there were two: Mr Normington and Mr Banister. The man who was on watch for the corridor with my house was Mr Normington, a large overweight man aged about 40. He wore dungarees over his jumper and black boots. I couldn't help thinking that his medium-length scruffy hair needed a wash; it was almost dripping with grease.

'All right, you lot, settle down now!' he shouted as he marched along the corridor.

Before I knew it, the lights had all gone out, bar some dim night-lights out in the corridor. About 10 minutes had passed and the kid in the corner was masturbating away furiously when Ericson came into my dorm. He went straight for Paterson's bed and, without warning, punched him right in the face. Paterson held his face and squealed in pain.

'You fucking little cunt, you leave Cooper alone or I'll fucking kill ya!' said Ericson, before exiting fast and making off down the corridor back to his own dormitory, leaving Paterson holding his face.

The next morning in the cold light of day I could see blood all over Paterson's pillow. Ericson had given him a serious nosebleed. The morning routine was identical to the one the night before, only in reverse: the night staff marched us, in just our underwear with no socks or shoes, downstairs and across the courtyard to the washrooms to get washed and brush our teeth. Then we'd go back up to our dorms and get dressed before going to the dining room for breakfast. All the time we were getting dressed, Paterson didn't look at me once, not even a glance.

After breakfast all three houses made their way over to the various classrooms. Although the boys from each house were kept separate during the evenings and had separate dorms, during school hours everybody was mixed in together. There was an English class, Maths class, and Art and Woodwork classes. The 54 boys were divided up between the four classes. I was put in the English class first. Each class lasted about 90 minutes and we did two classes in the morning, then two more after lunch in the afternoon. The only exception to this routine was Wednesday, which was P.E. day, and Friday, when we all worked on the vegetable allotments and took care of the general gardening duties around the extensive grounds.

The English teacher looked quite old (late sixties, maybe) and had a serious hunchback. His hair was silver and thin. Like most of the boys in there, he too smoked roll-ups, evident by the half-smoked roll-up stuck behind his yellowing ear and his silver-turned-yellow moustache. Everybody called him 'Dog-end' because he always had a part-smoked cigarette wedged behind his ear. Dog-end was quite insistent that everybody learned longhand writing, and he was a really good teacher. He would write out the entire alphabet in both capitals and lower case, in chalk on the blackboard on his pre-chalked-outlines. The class would have to copy what he did into our lined writing pads. It was the first time I'd learned how to do joined-up writing.

The morning went quite fast and before I knew it we were breaking for lunch. We made the 200-yard walk through the choppy wind, past the large oak trees containing the ever-noisy rooks, between the fields to the dining room before eventually heading back to class an hour later. My first class after lunch was Woodwork, where the other boys were all making small wooden footstools that they'd started two lessons ago so they had a three-hour head start on me. However, after 90 minutes I'd not only caught up with them, I'd even managed to overtake some of the boys.

The teacher had given me the plans and wood and the tools that I needed and got me going. There were some things the boys were not allowed to do, like use the electric circular saw and other dangerous tools. I'd cut and prepared the four legs required for my stool and taken them to the woodwork teacher to carve into shape using a special electric saw. He observed how fast I'd prepared them. No sooner had he sent me away with my four newly carved and shaped legs than I returned with the prepared top section. He couldn't believe it and was very impressed.

The following day we would finish our footstools with sponge padding and a fake leather top that had to be stitched down and tacked into place with industrial staples underneath.

'Well done, son,' said the teacher, noticing that I was the third person to finish out of a class of about 12 people, all of whom had started two lessons previously.

And so it went on, the days rolled by with the same old regimented routine. I'd witnessed a couple of fights break out here and there, usually two boys whose disagreement had become heated before turning into a full-on scrap, which often ended with a bloody nose, black eye, split lip or broken tooth. Somehow I managed to avoid such confrontations and, as in previous places, I tried to keep myself to myself as much as possible, though Jerry had kind of attached himself to me. He must have recognised that I was not like the rest and was relieved to be no longer alone. Before I arrived he was the sole subject of incessant bullying, but soon I'd be sharing that burden with him. But first, I'd be subjected to something worse … much worse.

Chapter 21

Let the (Evil) Games Commence

The weekend came and went, and the week began as usual. On the Wednesday, P.E. took place in the large concrete building that resembled an aircraft hangar. I'd only done P.E. once and we did five-a-side football but today I was in for a very special surprise.

Most of the boys had got changed into their rugby kit and one of the teachers had taken them all out onto the pitch for a game. Some general gardening duties needed doing so another group had gone off with the gardener to do that. However, there were six of us left with three available male teachers with little else to do. So, that left me and five other boys, who were definitely the youngest at Pelham House. Linnet and I were both 12 and the other four boys were 13. So, we stayed behind in the large concrete gym with three members of male staff, who instructed us to go into the gym's changing/shower room and strip down to our underpants. When we came back into the gym there were three pots of paint and three brushes. Two of the men went off a second time and came back with three buckets, full to the brim with leather-clad cricket balls. Standing there, bare feet on the cold concrete floor, I started to shiver in the cold and tremble with fear. I knew something evil was about to take place because of the terrified look on Linnet's face and the tears that were starting to form in the other boys' eyes as they stood there, hands cupping their private parts.

'Linnet and Cooper, you're mine! Come over here,' said one of the men. 'Chop, chop!' he shouted. The other two men also had two boys each. Linnet and I came to the man, who promptly took up his paintbrush, stuck it in the tin and painted a large red 'X' across my chest. 'Turn around,' he ordered, then painted another on my back before repeating the process with Linnet. I could see the other two men painting yellow and blue crosses on the bare chests and backs of the other four boys. The different-coloured crosses distinguished the three teams of two.

'Right, go grab one of those brooms, you know the routine!' shouted the man in charge of Linnet and me. 'Right, Cooper, you'll soon get the idea! Go and grab a broom and stand next to Linnet,' he ordered me.

What the hell was about to happen? I wondered. By now, Linnet and the other four boys were crying audibly, but they were not pleading with the three men to stop whatever it was they were about to begin. Something told me they'd tried that before and it hadn't worked. While the six of us waited, wooden yard brooms in hand, over in the corner the three men chatted for a few minutes, each taking out money and putting it onto one of the wooden benches with a tobacco tin to stop the notes blowing away in any of the drafts that leaked into the place.

The three men each took one of the large buckets of cricket balls and stood about 10 feet apart from each other before taking out two of the balls, one in each hand.

'Right, is everybody ready?' shouted one of the men. His menacing voice echoed around the huge brick building. I looked at the others, perplexed.

The man doing all the ordering and shouting noticed. 'Linnet, show Cooper what to do,' he said.

Linnet looked at me, tears in his eyes, hardly able to speak a word, he was so choked up. The smell of fear was far stronger than the smell of paint on our bodies. Something told me that hell was about to be unleashed.

Gripped with fear, Linnet proceeded to explain and demonstrate what I was to do. 'You put the handle of the broom on the floor like this, then put your forehead onto the brush head and spin around.' He demonstrated this by running round in small circles with his face pointing towards the floor. 'Then when they shout "Run!", you've got to run down to that wall at the end of the gym and back,' he added, hardly able to talk as he struggled to hold back the tears.

'Right, when I shout "Go!" you spin as fast as you can until I shout "Stop!" then you run as fast as you can down to that far wall, then back to the middle as fast as you can,' ordered one of the men. 'Go!'

I put my forehead on the broom and shuffled round in a clockwise direction. 'Faster, Cooper!' shouted the man. After about 15 seconds he shouted, 'Stop!' I lifted my head up and felt the room spinning. 'Run!' he shouted. The others dropped their brooms and started to run, so I followed suit, only my body refused to go in a straight line, it involuntarily wanted to swerve over towards the left wall. Almost falling over, I could hardly stay on my feet. Then I became aware of cricket balls whizzing past me and bouncing off the brick wall to my left. I felt dizzy and sick, from the spinning and fear.

As I tried to obey the many orders being shouted at me I struggled to stay on my feet. 'Come on, Cooper, where do you think you're going?' the man shouted, as I slammed into the brick wall to my left. 'Move it, get back in the middle and run to that wall!' came another shout. I struggled to straighten up and maintain any kind of direction for the back wall. Then a cricket ball smashed into my right shoulder blade with what felt like the force and speed of a cannonball. More cricket balls flew past, so I put my hands up around my head to protect my skull. Another ball struck me on the hip.

'Faster, now run back to the middle!' came another order as I reached the back wall.

As I stopped to turn around another ball hit me in the chest. I started to run as fast as I could back towards the middle in the hope that the bombardment of cannonballs would cease once I got there. Another hit me on the upper arm and then another struck me in the midriff. It was pandemonium as cricket balls came flying at us from all directions. By the time I reached the middle the other five boys, having had more experience than me, were already there.

'Right, grab your brooms ... Well, come on, we still have half a bucket of balls left!'

'Please, sir, I don't want to,' said one of the other boys, crying.

'Don't you bloody well "please, sir" me, you little streak of piss, or I'll come over there and give you something to really cry about!' he threatened. 'Now, grab that fucking broom, you little shit!' As he did so, tears positively flowed. 'Now, spin!' And so we repeated the process, only this time it was worse as the dizziness had not worn off from the first time. It seemed like a much steeper mountain, much harder to run straight or fast. The other boys and I were hit about half a dozen more times as the men launched another full-on assault on us until eventually they finally ran out of balls.

'Right, let's tot up the hits and see who won,' said the main man as all three of them walked over to us. 'Stand up straight,' he said, examining my body, 'One, two, three, four ... turn around ... five, six, seven ...' he continued, counting. 'Eleven,' he said to one of the other men. Then he moved onto Linnet and went through the same process. 'Ten more hits here, which gives me 21 in total,' he said. Then he did the same with the remaining four boys. He was counting the bruises, scuffs, scrapes and other marks that the impact of the heavy cricket balls had left on our almost-naked bodies. 'You lucky bastard!' he told the man who'd got the most hits.

'Nothing lucky about it, skill, pure skill,' he smirked as he went over to the bench and pocketed the money.

'Right, you lot, go and get showered and dressed. I've got a little job for you.'

In the changing room I noticed the marks and bruises not only on my own body, but those of the other boys too. Of course, they would fade after a couple of weeks but the mental bruises would take longer … much longer. My shoulder blade was in agony from where a heavy cricket ball had smashed it. In the shower I struggled to get the paint off; it wasn't water-based.

'How often do they do this?' I asked Linnet, who was getting dressed next to me.

'It depends. This is the fifth time I've had to do it and I've been here seven months.'

Well, at least it isn't every week, I thought.

After we got dressed we all headed back out into the gym to find out what job awaited us.

Two of the men had left, the remaining one said, 'All right, you lot, follow me.' He led us back across to the main houses, then across the courtyard to the regular shower rooms.

Walking back to the house from the grim brick gym building I noticed how incongruous it was that the striking 18th-century architecture of Pelham House and its surrounding flora and well-kept grounds could seemingly conceal such a house of torment, horror and abuse.

Next to the shower rooms was a storage room with various buckets, scrubbing brushes and other cleaning products. We all had to take a bucket and scrubbing brush and some detergent, and then we were ordered to scrub all the floor and wall tiles in the shower rooms.

'Right, you've got an hour before dinner. Linnet, Cooper, you two do the floors, the rest of you do the walls. When I get back, I want this place to be gleaming,' he said, leaving us to it.

Being right-handed I struggled to scrub the floor on my hands and knees. Every time I made a circular scrubbing motion my right shoulder blade felt as if a nerve was trapped and crushing the surrounding muscle. I had to use my left hand, which soon started to ache. Also, the chemical detergent was beginning to burn my hand; there were no rubber gloves and it seemed they didn't go a whole bundle on Health & Safety here. All I could think about was seeing the matron to get something for the pain. It was only comfortable when I held my right forearm flat against my stomach; any other movement sent a sharp bolt of pain through my shoulder. The hour passed, painfully, and one of the men came to get us.

'Alright, put those buckets away, get washed and changed then make your way to the dining room!' he ordered.

I'd only been in the dining room for a few minutes when a fight broke out between two boys: Ericson, the boy from my house who defended me, and another boy from the house next door. They'd been eyeing each other across the dining room and had obviously interpreted each other's looks as hostile. The next thing I knew, both of them jumped to their feet, rushed across the floor and started throwing punches at each other. They ended up tussling round on the floor and smashing into one of the tables before two members of staff pulled them apart.

'You, plant your arse back on that seat and don't move!' said one man, dragging the other boy by the hair and pushing him down hard into his seat.

Mr Booth dragged Ericson back to our big boys' table and seated him. He straightened his shirt and hair, which was ruffled from the scrap. Mr Booth gave him a brief talking to before returning to my table. Ericson glanced over his shoulder towards the other boy and the other housemaster saw him eyeing his adversary again.

'Ericson, if you so much as glance in this direction again I'll rip your arm off and beat you over the head with it! Now turn around.'

Ericson duly obliged.

As I sat there eating I couldn't help but notice that pretty much every single boy in the place had DIY tattoos on their arms and hands that they, or their friends, had done with a sewing needle, a steady hand and a small bottle of Indian ink. Small swallows on the hand between thumb and index finger were common, so too were knuckles tattooed with dots and/or the letters A.C.A.B. (All Coppers Are Bastards) on their fingers between the knuckle and first joint. Names, initials, skull and crossbones, the odd crucifix with a snake wrapped around it, gothic roses and various football team initials and logos: LFC, MUFC, NUFC. This DIY skin desecration was one of many strange cultures that the other boys subscribed to that I didn't quite understand.

However, two older boys persuaded me to try it. I wasn't overly keen, but I thought if the other boys saw that I too had some DIY tattoos they might stop giving me such a hard time. How wrong I was. So, later that evening, with a sewing needle and a small bottle of Indian ink, one of the boys drew a small crucifix on my left arm, just below the elbow. He then proceeded to inflict hundreds of tiny jabbing pinpricks onto the pre-drawn image, each little stab taking some ink into my flesh. By now I was accustomed to pain so these pinpricks were a walk in the park. After about 10 minutes of continuous dipping and stabbing it was finished. Blood and ink was dripping down my arm but the other boy assured me that after a week, when the swelling went down and it healed over, I'd be left with a neat little crucifix. But he wanted to do another, so he went through the whole stinging process again, only this time tattooing my initials a few inches below the crucifix on the same arm.

As with the previous places I'd been in most of the boys at Pelham House were serious hard cases with attitude. Finding a like-minded person fell somewhere between rare and extinct. Apart from me, Linnet was about the only other person in there to have any humanity, civility or compassion. Don't get me wrong, not everyone in those places was an agro-seeking hard nut from a rough estate, there were a few sensitive, compassionate, loving types with intelligence, but they were few and far between.

Friday morning arrived and we were woken by the bellowing voice of Mr Normington. 'OK, you lazy bastards, out of your wanking chariots and down to the shower rooms!' followed by, 'Come on, come on, drop your cocks and reach for your socks!' That kind of talk from the night staff was about as intelligent as it got. Who knows what they did during the day when they weren't on duty? As I grabbed my things and made my way down to the washrooms with the others it dawned on me that I was the only person in here aware of the fact that it was my 13th birthday the day before. Nobody in here knew and they didn't want to know. It had come and gone as though it didn't exist.

After dinner, we were all allowed to go to the tuck shop to buy sweets with the pocket money provided by the school. It was the first time I'd done this and I was really looking forward to it. Each house took it in turns queuing up at the tuck shop, which was in one corner of the courtyard. Of course, we didn't have physical money; the housemaster simply had a notepad with each boy's allowance amount written in it. If you didn't spend your entire weekly allowance at once, it would roll over to the following week. It was rare that anybody did this, as there was usually only enough to buy a Lion Bar, a Mars Bar and a Twix, which is what I bought when I got to the front of the queue.

Just as I came out of the tuck shop onto the courtyard two bigger boys confronted me. One of them, Dean, was a real nasty bastard from Whitehaven. He pretty much ran things in our house and I always tried to avoid being in his vicinity, which was difficult because there were only two large rooms in the house. The other, who went by the nickname of 'Steel', was equally nasty.

'Hand 'em over,' said Dean, gesturing to my three bars of chocolate.

'Why?' I replied.

'Don't fucking "why" me, you little cunt, just give 'em here!' he said, shoving my shoulder back into the brick wall behind me, adding to the pain already there.

'Yeah, Cooper, give 'em here or you're dead!'

I'd already witnessed these boys throwing their weight around and I really didn't relish being on the receiving end of one of their combined beatings, so I handed over my chocolate bars.

'Now, fuck off, and if you say anything, I'll give you a fuckin' hidin'.'

I didn't say a word; I just made my way back to the house, empty-handed.

So, things just continued to worsen; I was to go through this trauma at least 50 more times.

An hour later, while Mr Booth and some of the other boys were in the television room, I was in the living room, chatting with Linnet. Dean walked in after the allocated cigarette time and he had with him what looked like a linen tablecloth. Immediately I got up to make my way to the television room to avoid him.

'Where do you think you're going? Get back in here and sit down!' he ordered me.

No one disobeyed Dean, or they would get the shit kicked out of them at his earliest convenience. I sat back down and watched as he systematically folded and rolled up his tablecloth to make a DIY whip.

'Paterson, go and get me a glass of water, now,' he said.

No sooner said than done. Paterson promptly returned with the water and handed it to Dean, who soaked the end of his tablecloth whip in it. He then proceeded to go round us younger boys one at a time, whipping us with the wet tablecloth. He had his whip/flick technique down to a T. He'd fling it forward, then snap his wrist back at the point of impact. The wet end of the tablecloth whipped across my arm and stung like a bitch, leaving a massive red swollen mark.

There were four of us that he'd whip: Linnet and me, for being the smallest and youngest, and Paterson and another kid of a similar age called Harry, simply because he didn't like them. He'd whip each of us about five times before moving onto the next. We had to sit there and take it; I'd hold my hands up to my face to protect my eyes while he aimed for my legs and arms. The bastard got off on this ridiculous game at least once a week, typically when Mr Booth was in the other room watching TV with some of the other boys.

The staff had their petty torments and abusive games too. As the weeks went by, the bullying intensified. Most of the boys had picked up on my speech impediment and gave me a lot of stick, imitating my slurry Ss whenever they passed me by. I couldn't get past more than a few days without one of the older boys hitting me or beating me up for some inconsequential reason. The least damage was done when I just let them beat on me, I soon discovered. I'd seen what had happened to Linnet when he tried to fight back once … once. Dean half-killed him, pummelling his face to a bloody pulp, before shouting, 'Don't you fuckin' dare fight back, you little cunt!' followed by more punches to the face. 'Do you fuckin' understand me?' Punch, punch. 'You take your fuckin' beating like everyone else!' Punch, kick, punch. Poor

Linnet was left crying and bleeding all over the cobbled yard for at least 10 minutes before the housemaster stumbled upon him. Of course, I couldn't say anything, even though I'd witnessed it.

'Cooper, get inside and don't say a fuckin' word or you're next,' he warned.

So, I took random beatings, and was bullied and abused with the constant taunts and name-calling.

The place was despicable and so too was everyone in it, except Linnet. I decided that 'Dracula's Castle' was too good a name. From now on, it would be given the far more fitting label of Colditz. The only difference between Colditz and this place was that here the abuse and punishment came from both the staff and boys.

A few more weeks passed and the abuse and brutality was unrelenting, to the point where I couldn't take it any longer. I felt trapped, isolated and cut off from the outside world. I had to get out before I was seriously injured, or even killed.

Run, run, run! screamed my mind and body, over and over. And so I did.

Chapter 22

London, Here I Come

The evening before my escape, I made my plans, which were improvised at best. As part of my defence mechanism, I'd become a relatively light sleeper. All manner of events could (and often did) take place during the night, through to the early hours. One of the bigger boys, called Brady, from the house next door to ours would frequently sneak down the corridor late at night to fight with Ericson. I'd hear the same ritual as often as three times a week.

'No, go away, I'm tired,' said Ericson.

'Come on, Ericson, get up,' said Brady.

'No, I'm trying to sleep.'

'Get up and fight!'

Most of the time Brady would give up after five minutes of provoking Ericson and head back to his own dorm. But sometimes he would persist to the point where Ericson would get so pissed off with all his prodding and poking and the verbal torments that he'd spring out of bed and there would be an almighty ruckus. The night staff, Mr Normington and Mr Banister, would come running and break it up. By then everybody was awake. The next morning at breakfast, one or the other, or both, would have a black eye or a bruised cheekbone. The one who didn't have a black eye or bruise would get praised and patted on the back by his pals on his table.

I decided I'd get out of bed and get dressed quietly, grab my jacket and sneak off before everybody else had woken up. If I woke up early, I could get a good head start before the staff noticed. I didn't have any money, just the clothes I stood up in and my jacket. This really was going to be an improvised affair; I'd just have to wing it and hope I reached London. The thought of how my mother would react when I turned up at her front door never occurred to me. I just knew I had to get out of this place before I got seriously hurt, and home was at the forefront of my mind.

The next morning I woke up nice and early. It was still dark, nothing and no one stirred. Slowly I got out of bed, praying the metal frame would not complain too loudly as I lifted my body off it. I got dressed, with one eye on the other boys in the dorm, and removed my jacket from the chair. After peeking round the corner to make sure the night staff were not in sight, I then stepped out into the corridor and made my way to the stairs in the opposite direction to where Mr Normington sat to keep an ear and eye on things. I tiptoed down the stairs in my trainers and gently pushed the door open, stepped through and nursed it closed.

Although there were windows all along the corridor to the dormitories, I doubted Mr Normington or Mr Banister would be standing there looking out onto the dark courtyard; they were probably catching a few winks in their comfy chairs. I walked across the courtyard with just the moonlight to guide me, then over towards the brick gym building and past the large oaks and the rookery. As I passed the old oaks, it was eerily silent. It wasn't even dawn so the rooks were mute. Apart from my sharp, built-in sixth sense, I also had a superb sense of direction. Like the birds, I instinctively knew which way south was. I remembered the way Mrs Clements had driven in when she brought me there and also seeing a sign to the local railway station. However, it was still a four-mile walk from Pelham House. I made it to the perimeter of the grounds to the small country road, where I turned right and headed off in the direction of the station, all the while listening and watching out for cars, prepared to dive into the hedgerows at a moment's notice.

It took me almost an hour to reach the railway station, during which time I disturbed two foxes, a Muntjac deer and several other forms of nocturnal wildlife. The station was unmanned so I walked through the barrier and onto the platform. I checked the timetable and noticed that the first train didn't come through for about another 40 minutes. As I didn't have a watch I had to assume the large clock on the platform was accurate. By the time the train arrived it would still be a good hour before the night staff woke everybody; by then I'd be well on the way and there would be no chance of my being picked up locally. The platform was open, windy and freezing cold. Being right next to the sea didn't help, nor did the harsh April weather. I stood there, hugging myself and pacing up and down to try to keep warm. What I would have given for a hot mug of cocoa!

The train eventually arrived for the first leg of my journey. This same part of the journey by car would have taken about an hour and a half, but the train was slow and stopped at every single tuppenny-ha'penny little town over the 70 miles of track, so it took about two and a half hours. Still, it was nice and warm in the carriage and it wasn't long before warmth started to come back into my windswept cheeks.

Back in the late seventies ticket inspectors on trains were few and far between, especially in the barren parts of Cumbria. However, a ticket inspector did hop onto the train two stops before I was due to get off. I craftily avoided him by hiding in the toilet, a trick that worked, this time, but I wasn't so confident I could get all the way to London like that. The second part of my journey was still 260 miles, which equated to about three and a half hours of train time, or more accurately, train time in which I'd have to avoid any ticket inspectors.

About an hour into the first part of my journey the sun started to rise as night dissolved into day. As it neared its end, I knew I would have to improvise again when I changed trains, but it proved fairly straightforward. However, there was one risky moment when I didn't know which platform to wait at and had to ask the man in the ticket office.

'Excuse me, could you tell me which platform I need for the train to London?'

'Platform three, on the other side,' he said, barely looking up as he sugared his coffee.

'Thank you,' I said, dashing off.

As I waited for the train that would take me to London's Euston station I suspected the staff back at Pelham House would now be aware that I was missing and would have contacted the local police and Mrs Clements. I prayed the train would arrive before a local bobby stuck his head in the station door and had a snoop round for a missing 13-year-old boy fitting my description. My eyes flitted from the main entrance to the station to the half-mile or so of empty track at the point where it vanished around the bend. Now it was simply a waiting game. What would get there first, the train or the local policeman? Then I saw the train, *my* train, appear on the bend of the track, half a mile away. It seemed to be moving in slow motion, or maybe it was just my mind playing tricks on me. When it pulled into the station a few passengers got off, but a lot more got on. The train had many more passengers than the previous one, but there were still seats available. I took an aisle seat close to the toilet, where I could watch out for uniformed ticket inspectors.

The initial jolt of the train as it pulled out of the station sent relief coursing through my veins. I relaxed and let out a quiet sigh as the immediate scenery out of the window picked up speed.

My long walk to the station, coupled with the adrenaline as I sneaked on and off trains and avoided ticket inspectors had made me hungry. I dismissed the thought from my mind and instead concentrated on happy thoughts about arriving home, where my mum would make me something to eat.

My luck was in. During the three-and-a-half-hour journey I didn't encounter a single ticket inspector. It was a long, dull journey and all I had were my thoughts for company. Most of the other passengers were only on the train for a few stops and those who stayed on there for longer had books or newspapers to read. Still, I didn't mind, I was excited to be going home and glad to be out of Colditz.

The train slowed for its final destination. I saw the sign, Euston, and my heart lifted. *I was here, in London, I'd made it*! Now it was just three short Tube stops (about five minutes) on the Northern line to Kentish Town and then I'd be home. I stood up before the train came to a halt and made my way to the door. Right there on the floor I saw a shiny silver 50 pence piece. What luck! I picked it up and thought about buying a bar of chocolate at one of the station kiosks. The train stopped and I lurched to the side, grabbing the wall to balance myself. I opened the door and stepped off the train onto the welcoming platform. It felt incredible and I wondered if Neil Armstrong felt this good as he stepped onto the moon; somehow I doubted it.

As I walked along the platform with the other passengers I noticed a ticket collector standing next to the narrow exit, collecting passengers' tickets as they walked through; it was all happening very quickly as the passengers bottlenecked at the platform exit. But people were walking through three-wide, the two furthest from the ticket inspector reaching across to hand their tickets to him.

OK, stay on the outside lane and duck through while hiding behind some of the other passengers, I thought.

My adrenaline kicked in again as the stampede of passengers grew closer and closer. Thirty yards, 20 yards, 10, nine, eight … *Please, God, let me get through*! My timing was perfect; I saw a gap between two of the passengers and the outer part of the exit. I bolted into it and walked through, unnoticed. He hadn't seen me; I was free and clear, I'd made it! Now, I was at the opposite end of the country to where I had been eight hours earlier. I saw the sign for the Underground, but first I'd reward myself with that much-deserved bar of chocolate. Well, it had been a very early start and it was now one o'clock in the afternoon so I needed a sugar fix. About 30 feet over to the left I saw a confectionery kiosk so I made my way to it. I scanned the numerous bars of chocolate and packets of sweets and decided on a packet of Maltesers. Just as I was reaching for it I felt a firm hand on my shoulder.

'Are you Nigel Cooper?' asked the man.

I turned around and noticed that the hand on my shoulder was attached to an arm, an arm in a dark-blue sleeve, a sleeve that belonged to a dark-blue uniform. Further still, a uniform bearing the British Transport Police logo. The officer's distinct pointed helmet confirmed that I was busted.

'Now, don't even think about lying, son. You fit the description perfectly and I'm only going to find out anyway.'

'Yes, sir,' I said, knowing I could not lie. He would have taken me away, checked me out and found out anyway.

Why the hell did I stop for those Maltesers?

'Come with me,' he said, leading me away by the arm.

We were walking in the opposite direction to the Underground sign. His grip wasn't that tight so I decided to try to make a run for it. After all, I hadn't come 330 miles for nothing. I yanked my arm away from him and made a bolt for it, but before I even got two yards the officer pounced and grabbed me again.

'Now look, son, don't make it any worse. You're in enough trouble as it is,' he said, tightening his grip on me.

He marched me across the concourse to the railway station's mini police station. It was more like a few offices and three small holding cells. I had no idea railway stations had such things, but I was about to be given the grand tour.

'OK, take a seat right there,' said the officer.

I sat down and reflected for a moment. All I could think about was if I'd not stopped to buy the Maltesers, if I'd simply headed straight for the Underground, he might not have spotted me. After all, I was at the kiosk behind another customer for a good 40 seconds before he approached me.

'Put him in number one with the other lad, they can keep each other company,' said another officer from behind his desk.

Officer number one escorted me to cell number one while officer two picked up the phone on his desk to make a call.

'In you go,' he said, gesturing me into the little cell. There was a boy in there already, a year or two older than me, 'and no fighting or I'll put you in separate cells, OK?'

'Yes,' I said.

'Do you understand?' he said to the other boy.

'Yes,' he said.

'Good,' said the policeman, locking the door.

There was a padded bench built into the wall, long enough for three people to sit on. As I sat down the kid said, 'Alright, mate, what's your name?'

'Nigel,' I said.

'I'm Duncan. What did you do?'

'I ran away.'

'From where?'

'A school up north,' I said, hoping he'd stop with the questions. I just wanted to be left alone with my thoughts. But he kept jabbering on and on, asking me loads of things and telling me about his crime – how he'd almost got away with stealing a lady's handbag in the station concourse, and he would have, had it not been for the two have-a-go heroes wrestling him to the ground. He had a crew cut and spoke with a cockney accent.

'Do you fight?' he said.

Christ, what is it with boys and fighting, don't they think about anything else? Maybe I was just a born pacifist, but beating the crap out of a fellow human didn't appeal to me any more than having it beaten out of me.

'Not really,' I said.

With that, he punched me in the upper arm, not really hard, just one of those macho bullshit punches to either test the water, or to assert himself as the top dog. Either way, I didn't care what his stupid motives were. I just ignored him like it didn't even happen and got back to thinking about my mum and my house, just three Tube stops from where I was.

'You're alright … don't worry, I won't hurt you,' he said.

What a little prick, he had absolutely no idea that after all I'd been through it would be impossible for him to hurt me. When you've been punched in the face hundreds of times, kicked in the head and ribs and abused every day for months on end the blows eventually numb. My real pain was on the inside.

After about an hour, officer two came to our cell.

'Right, young man,' he said, addressing me, 'your social worker's coming to get you. You'd better make yourself comfortable because you're in for a long wait.'

'Will I be allowed to go home to see my mum?' I wanted to know.

'No, you won't. You'll be taken directly back to your school,' he told me. 'Now, are either of you hungry?'

'I am,' said the other boy.

'What about you?' he asked me.

'Yes, please,' I said.

He left us to it again. The other boy, whose name I'd forgotten already, continued to chat. Frankly he was getting on my nerves and I wished they had put me in a cell alone. The officer returned about 20 minutes later with two pre-packed cheese and pickle sandwiches, two apples and two cans of Tango. I started to mentally rehearse my plea to Mrs Clements; if I begged and pleaded enough, I figured she'd take me to see my mum for an hour before driving me all the way back to Pelham House. After all, Mum's house was only a 10-minute drive away.

Three hours later somebody came to collect my cockney cell-mate and, three hours after that, Mrs Clements and her colleague, Mr MacGregor, arrived to take me back.

The cell door opened. 'Let's go, your social worker's here,' said the officer.

I got up and followed him out into the main office area – I'd been in the cell so long I'd almost forgotten what the front office area looked like. Mrs Clements and Mr MacGregor were standing there, waiting.

'Oh dear, why did you run away?' said Mrs Clements, putting her hand on my shoulder. 'Come on, let's get you back.'

Mr MacGregor and the two officers exchanged a knowing glance. As we made our way across the station concourse, outside and across the street to the car park, I pleaded with Mrs Clements to let me see my mum for an hour before the long drive back up north, to no avail. In hindsight I suppose she might have viewed my request as unethical, or thought that it would have been hard for her to tear me away afterwards; she would have been right.

The journey back was long and tiring and who knew what awaited me when I got back. I'd seen how the staff had punished other boys who'd run away, and it was not pleasant. It was one o'clock in the morning when we eventually pulled into Pelham House car park. I'd slept the last half of the journey on the back seat. We were greeted by the night duty man, Mr Normington. He was pleasant enough, at least in front of Mrs Clements and Mr MacGregor, who now had another hour's drive back to Ulverston.

I was exhausted, what a long day! I'd left at 5 a.m. and it was now 1 a.m. the next day, 20 hours later. And I never even got to see my mum. Talk about close, but no cigar!

'Right, get undressed and get into bed quietly. You'll be dealt with appropriately tomorrow,' said Mr Normington.

I got into bed and cried myself to sleep.

Chapter 23

Psycho Boy

The next morning when we got up I noticed a new addition to my dormitory. A previous boy who was in the bed over in the far corner was no longer there, but had been replaced by an older one. As we got our toiletries together in preparation for the washrooms, he glanced over at me a few times. I couldn't quite put my finger on it, but there was definitely something not right about him, something in those deep black eyes that made me shiver. His facial features didn't sit right either; he had a protruding Neanderthal forehead and a wide nose. He was quite tall, about six foot, and I guessed he was close to 16 years old. Although of a slim build, he looked strong.

After breakfast everybody else went over to the schoolrooms, but I was told to wait behind in the dining room. Eventually I was escorted up to the headmaster's office and told to take a seat in the hallway outside. After a few minutes the office door opened and Mr Burkinshaw stuck his head out.

'OK, in you come,' he said, closing the door behind me.

He walked over to the corner of his office and removed a long piece of cane from the umbrella stand.

'Right, you know that absconding is a punishable offence, don't you?'

'Yes, sir.'

'Do you know why we punish boys who run away?'

'I think so.'

'Well, let me explain it to you. It causes a lot of trouble for everyone. Every time a boy runs away, it takes up people's valuable time and resources, not only us, but the police and Social Services. Do you understand?'

'Yes, sir.'

'Good, because we're here to help boys like you, get you back in line, on the straight and narrow. Now, I want you to have a long, hard think about what you've done and all the trouble you've caused, young man.'

'Yes, sir.'

'In the meantime, pull your trousers down and bend over the desk.'

I just looked at him with pleading eyes.

'Come on, come on, I don't have all day! Let's get this over with,' he told me.

I walked over to the desk and pulled my trousers down to my knees. Just as I was leaning forward he said, 'Underpants too.' I looked over my shoulder at him, then to the long cane in his hand. 'That's right, pull 'em down – yours won't be the first bare backside I've seen and it certainly won't be the last!'

Shit, this is really going to hurt, I thought, pulling my underpants down.

Although corporal punishment and the cane was legal back then, it was supposed to be over the trousers, but here, they took corporal punishment to a whole new level. I leaned forward over the desk, clenched my fists and gritted my teeth.

WHACK!!! The whipping sound of the cane cutting through the air, the crack on my backside and the pain were instantaneous. *WHACK … WHACK … WHACK … WHACK.* Each strike was more painful than the last. He was putting everything he had into it. Tears ran down my face and started to form pools of salty water on his leather-bound desk. He must have struck me at least 20 times, far more than the recommended guidelines.

'Right, pull your pants back up and get on over to the schoolrooms! Don't expect any pocket money for at least a month either.'

Backside on fire, I pulled up my underpants and trousers then ambled out of his office. Each step, as I staggered down the corridor, exaggerated the pain. Burning hot, stinging and throbbing all at the same time, walking down the stairs made the pain unbearable. I stopped off in the washrooms to check out the damage in one of the mirrors. After dropping my trousers and underpants, I looked over my shoulder. My backside had so many swollen red horizontal lines on it that they were merging in places. I eased my pants back up and ambled over to the schoolrooms.

'Need a cushion, son?' asked the art teacher, noticing my discomfort as I constantly shifted my weight from one buttock to the other, to no avail.

'Yes, please, sir.'

'Well, you can't bloody well have one! It's called punishment. You might want to think about that next time you get any bright ideas about running away.'

The other boys sniggered.

Bastards, they're all horrible bastards, I thought to myself.

After school that day I couldn't see the scary new kid who'd slept in my dorm the night before. But later that evening I learned that the boy who was there previously had been moved to another school and, by coincidence, a new boy had been admitted to Pelham House the same day, the day I was locked in a police cell in London. However, this new kid was not in our house, he was in the house next to ours, but there were no spare beds in his house's dorm area, hence they stuck him in my dorm until other arrangements could be made.

Although his name was Travis Cunningham, it took only a week for the other boys to pin a suitable nickname to him. This latest resident of Pelham House would become known as 'Psycho Boy', and for good reason. He was definitely weird in an evil and creepy sort of way. His eyes seemed to be almost completely black and it was hard to separate the pupil from the dark surrounding iris. Like dolls' eyes, they were lifeless, with no hint of human emotion. There wasn't even anything human about the way he walked – kind of like a mannequin with one leg an inch longer than the other, ridged and lopsided.

Cunningham kept to himself, and he preferred it that way. Kind of like me, only I didn't have the violent psychopathic tendencies that he had, as we would soon learn. Sure, he went to class like everybody else and he took part in the various sporting activities, and did his share of toil, both indoors and out in the grounds, but he simply wasn't there. He bothered people, not by actually doing anything, just by being physically there. Because he was a loner, like me, I was quietly praying he might take some of the heat off me, but for some strange reason most people, including the bigger boys, gave him a wide berth. They too could sense that something was not quite right.

Every few months the local barber would come to Pelham House for three consecutive days to cut everybody's hair, one house per day. During this particular visit everyone would learn just how psycho Cunningham really was. It got round to his turn – his housemaster had sent him out to the empty office, which they had allocated for the barber. His hair was not quite shoulder-length, but heading in that direction. The barber had done one side when Cunningham caught a glimpse of his reflection in the mirror. Seeing his hair, longer on one side and shorter on the other, triggered something inside him and he flipped, big time.

He grabbed the barber's arm, prised the scissors from his fingers, stood up and proceeded to repeatedly stab him in the neck and chest with them.

We, and everybody in the house next door, heard the screams coming from the makeshift barber's shop. The staff, and some of the boys, rushed out into the courtyard to see what all the commotion was about. I ambled out behind the rush just in time to see the barber writhing about on the cobbled ground, desperately trying to protect his face and chest from Cunningham's relentless stabbing. Mr Booth and next-door's housemaster ran over and dragged Cunningham off him, but he wasn't finished yet; he tried to break loose from their grip, scissors still in hand. Next-door's housemaster drove his knee hard and high into Cunningham's balls. He doubled over and dropped the scissors, which the housemaster kicked away before kneeing him hard in the ribs, sending the boy to the ground. Strangest thing, Cunningham didn't react to the pain. Sure, his physical body reacted to the knee to the balls and the knee in the ribs, but that was all; his eyes told a different story.

'Jesus fucking Christ!' said next-door's housemaster, observing the bleeding barber on the ground.

'Ericson, go to Mr Burkinshaw's office and tell him to get out here right now,' said Mr Booth, turning to unlock the small office door next to the barber's room to phone for an ambulance. Meanwhile, next-door's housemaster had Cunningham face down on the cobbles, his knee dug into his back and his arm twisted, like some sort of wrestling hold. Every now and then Cunningham would writhe and try to get free and, although the housemaster was a big man, he almost succeeded. But then the housemaster would exert more pressure with his knee and twist his arm harder; all the while Cunningham's eyes gave nothing away.

From what I could see, the barber was lucky to be alive. Although he'd been stabbed two or three times in the side of the neck, Psycho Boy had missed the major artery. As for the stabs to his chest, they were all in non-vital areas around his collarbone and left shoulder. He was still bleeding all over the cobbles, though, and in an obvious state of shock and distress. Mr Booth tried to stem the bleeding with various cloths until the ambulance arrived. But it was the police who arrived first, and just in the nick of time as the housemaster struggled to hold the powerful boy down. The police restrained him, while the housemasters instructed the small crowd who had gathered to get back inside the houses. After that I don't know if the police cuffed him, arrested him, or what happened. All I know is that midway through the following morning Cunningham was back. Meanwhile, the barber had been patched up in hospital and was back at home, recovering. Needless to say he refused to ever return to Pelham House to cut anybody else's hair again.

During lunch Cunningham sat there eating his food as if nothing had happened and no one seemed to think that it was strange that, the day after what could be construed as attempted murder, he was back, had re-joined his house and was in class with everybody else. I guess, in hindsight, that's just how things were back then. It became clearer than ever that there was something seriously amiss with this system.

A few days later, Cunningham decided that there was only room for one loner at Pelham House. The fact that I didn't mix with the others and kept myself to myself whenever possible bothered him and, even though we weren't in the same house, it didn't make any difference as far as he was concerned.

'I don't like you, Cooper,' he told me one lunchtime when I was just hanging out in the corridor outside the dining room, trying to avoid people. 'Yes, you'd better watch your step. Yes, yes, *yes*,' he muttered in the most sinister dark tones I'd ever heard. 'Watch your step, yes, yes, *yes*.'

There were so many different shades of 'wrong' about him. The way he looked at you, or rather, didn't. He'd look across to another wall while addressing you, but just knowing that I was in his peripheral vision was enough to give me the creeps. Every now and then he'd glance into your eyes and hold his sinister glare for an uncomfortably long time before looking back across to the wall or past one of your shoulders into the near distance.

He looked at me with those malevolent black eyes; holding his stare, with an evil wry smirk. I knew he meant what he said, the only trouble was I really didn't know what he was saying. Truth was, he scared the shit out of me. I'd witnessed his barber-stabbing antics and I suspected he was capable of so much more.

'I don't understand,' I said, hoping for a clearer explanation of why he was so upset with me.

'You know exactly what I'm talking about, yes, yes, *yes*. Oh yes, yes, yes, *yes*,' he muttered. Then he went to lean closer to me. I flinched back just as his housemaster came out of the dining room.

'What are you up to, boy?' he said.

Cunningham said nothing, just glared at him.

'*Well?*' he persisted.

'Nothing,' said Cunningham.

'Well, go and bloody well do nothing somewhere else! Go on, git.'

Cunningham sloped off down the corridor with that strange walk of his.

'I know you, Cooper. You're a loner,' said the housemaster, 'but being a loner in here will make you vulnerable, especially to psychos like that,' he added, nodding down the corridor. 'That's why people form alliances in places like this, there's strength in numbers. You should have a little think about that before you alienate yourself any more than you already have,' he said, before heading back into the dining room.

The thing is, I could not relate to a single person in there, except for Linnet perhaps. So far in life I hadn't really found a social circle in which I felt comfortable, and there certainly wasn't anything social about this place. It was more like some sort of demented and deranged animal farm. I didn't belong there, I didn't fit in, the other boys didn't want me there, but there I was, stuck, like a tiny insect struggling in an enormous web of evil.

Friday arrived and it was tuck-shop evening, only I didn't have any money to buy anything for the next four Fridays as part of my punishment for running away, something that would have a knock-on effect.

Dean and Steel came into the living room looking for me.

'Why aren't you over at the tuck shop?' said Dean.

'I don't have any allowance, Mr Burkinshaw stopped it for a month as punishment for running away,' I explained.

'Come with me,' he said.

What now? I thought.

I followed Dean into the shower-changing rooms, with Steel close behind me.

'Well, if you can't give us sweets, you're gonna have to be punished instead,' said Dean.

'That's not fair, it's not my fault.'

'I don't fuckin' care,' he said.

I turned to leave, but Steel stopped me.

'Hold 'im down,' said Dean.

I struggled to get away, but Steel was big and strong and forced me to the floor. Dean knelt on my back and smashed one of the football boots he'd grabbed from a pigeon hole into the back of my head. What was it with my head and the studded sole of football boots? It hurt far more than the last time I was whacked in the head with a boot at Mill House. I put my hands over the back of my head to protect myself.

'Move your fuckin' hands,' said Dean, raised boot in hand.

Did he really expect me to move my hands to expose the top and back of my head for him? There was no way that was going to happen.

Dean smashed the boot down three more times onto the backs of my hands and knuckles.

'Now, you'd better have something for me next Friday, or else,' he said, lifting his weight off me.

Steel gave me a parting kick-in-the-ribs gift and they both left me there on the cold floor to nurse my throbbing head and swollen hands. Now that was just great; I was going to have to go through this torture three more times until my allowance was reinstated so they could take my chocolate bars off me again. The injustice of it all, from the older boys, the staff, the whole system, sickened me to the core and frustrated me beyond belief.

I was the ultimate example of a victim of circumstance, but things were about to get a hell of a lot worse.

Chapter 24

Psycho Boy, Part II

It was about seven o'clock in the evening, no different to any other mid-week evening, really. I'd headed out of the house across the courtyard to the toilets, just as I'd done hundreds of times before, only this time three other boys came in shortly after me. They weren't coming for me particularly, just three boys coming to use the toilet; only one of them was Psycho Boy (Cunningham). I came out of my cubicle and saw Paterson and Harry, with Cunningham standing about five feet away from them.

Now, Paterson and Harry had a strange kind of relationship, as in they were always fighting each other, typically two or three times a week. Both about 15 years old, they were hard cases and enjoyed fighting. They were constantly challenging each other, sometimes Paterson won and sometimes Harry won. Over the months they proved to be equally matched and one or the other often had a bloody nose or a black eye to prove it.

As I came out of my cubicle there was some sort of debate going on between Harry and Psycho Boy. In the meantime, Paterson, who was standing closest to the door, showed me the palm of his hand, gesturing for me to stay where I was, out of the way.

'Harry's a little girl, he's gonna run off and cry to the housemaster,' said Cunningham. 'Yes, yes, *yes*, little girl, yes, yes, *yes*.'

'I'm not a little girl,' said Harry.

'Little girl, yes, yes, *yes*. Go on, little girl, run away to the housemaster.'

'I'm not running anywhere,' insisted Harry, standing his ground with an angry look in his eye.

'Hmmm, yes, yes, *yes* … yes, yes, *yes*,' said Cunningham in his sinister low tone.

He glanced at me with those black eyes. That was all it took. The instant Cunningham took his eye off Harry, Harry lunged for him with everything he had. I could not believe that anyone would have the guts to start a fight with this maniac, but Harry did. But poor Harry only managed to get a few punches in before Cunningham overpowered him and punched him, hard, several times in the head and face. They ended up on the ground, where Harry was starting to look quite weak. Cunningham wrestled him into the position that he wanted him in. With Harry on his knees, arms flopped by his sides, dazed and confused by the powerful blows he'd taken, Cunningham got behind him and wedged his bleeding head between his legs, then he grabbed Harry's hair and pulled his head back. There was nothing Harry could do, he didn't really know where he was, but Cunningham wasn't finished yet and started to rain down hard punches with his clenched fist into Harry's upturned face.

Harry was one of the first kids to talk to me and he had offered to play table tennis with me on my first day. He had never been a part of the torrent of abuse and bullying that I had endured, yet there was nothing I could do to help him. His eyes were now closed and starting to swell up, his nose bleeding badly and his lip and both eyebrows were split and bleeding like crazy. I'd never seen so much blood in all my life; it was running down his cheeks, neck and staining his T-shirt. Paterson ran out to get help. I went to follow, but then Cunningham dropped poor Harry to the ground, lunged forward and grabbed me.

'Yes, yes, *yes*, Cooper. I told you to watch your step, yes, yes, *yes*,' he muttered.

His tones came straight from the pit of hell, those black eyes, that bony forehead, his wide nose, all making up that pale sinister face. He scared the hell out of me and I almost wet myself in fear right there. His long fingers gripped my arm; they were locked and could not be prised open, like an eagle's talons gripping a helpless rabbit. He swiped his leg across my calf muscles, sweeping my legs from under me, sending me crashing to the ground. Then he grabbed my hair and pushed my head back, slamming it into the concrete floor, almost knocking me out. Now he was on top of me, pinning me down, his knees either side of my shoulders. He lifted his fist up into the air and glared down at me, but I could not free myself, he was so powerful. But then the door was busted open and Cunningham spun around to see who was there: it was his housemaster.

'What the bloody hell's going on here?' he shouted, taking in the bleeding Harry on the floor and the rest of the horrific scene. He grabbed Cunningham by the hair and yanked him off me. 'Come here, you fuckin' mental psychopath!' he said, throwing Cunningham hard against the wall. The housemaster grabbed him by the collar and kneed him hard in the balls. Cunningham doubled over in pain then the housemaster drove his knee up hard into his face. His head and upper body flew up and back, then he dropped to the floor, his nose and several teeth busted, more blood, everywhere.

As with everything else in this place the staff would speak to the boys in a language they understood: violence. Around 95 per cent of the boys in this place (and all the other places I'd found myself in) actually enjoyed violence and fighting; out of every 20 boys there were, on average, usually only two or three who, like me, detested violence and kept out of the way. But for the most part, the other boys were all tough, horrible bastards so the beatings from the staff, or when they lost a fight to another boy were water off a duck's back.

At Pelham House the 'system' was designed not only to whip you into shape, but to crush you too, by whatever means. The brutality was unremitting and simply bred more violence, the whole system was crushing and I was tarred with the same brush as all the other boys. As far as the staff were concerned they didn't have any expectations of us; no one in there was ever going to amount to anything. We were all no-hopers so nobody ever bothered to try to teach us a different way of life, a better way; it was all about verbal and physical abuse. For me the worst part of it all was the fact that I was typically the youngest and the smallest in most of the places I found myself in. When I was eight, most of the other boys were 11 or 12; then, when I was 12, most of them were 15 or 16. I never stood a chance – I'd never be able to win a fight with a hard bastard three years older than me and much bigger. In a constant state of trepidation and anxiety I frequently locked myself into confined spaces, such as disused storage rooms, seeking some sort of sanctuary.

Mr Booth arrived in the toilets to assist the other housemaster. Several other boys and another member of staff also arrived on the scene. Luckily, I was fine, apart from a sore head and a bruised coccyx from where my backside hit the concrete floor hard when Cunningham took my legs from under me.

Cunningham was dragged away and they called an ambulance for Harry, who had come round, his face a bloody, battered mess. It looked as if someone had mistaken it for a piece of steak and got to work with a tenderising mallet. Poor Harry stayed in hospital overnight, but was back the next afternoon. He'd had stitches in his lip and both eyebrows, which were black and blue and incredibly swollen. His eyes were every shade of bruise and almost closed with the swelling, with just two tiny slits to view the miserable world through. Meanwhile, Psycho Boy was in the house next door, going about his life as 'normal'. The bastard didn't even get the cane and, from what I could gather, he wasn't punished in any way whatsoever for what he'd done. This was seriously fucked up. I ran away in an attempt to reach my mum in search of a small taste of love and compassion and I was punished, while Psycho Boy half-killed somebody and got off scot-free – twice. Perhaps they just didn't know quite how to handle him or figured punishment would have no effect.

Cunningham was still in my dorm, even though it was supposed to be only temporary. He didn't wait for things to calm down before he threatened me again. I'd gone out to the toilet, about the only place boys from other houses could bump into each other in the evening, and I hadn't seen Cunningham, who was loitering outside his own house. I was just about to unzip my fly when I heard his unmistakable tones.

'Ah, Cooper, yes, yes, yes. I told you to watch your step …'

I spun around and saw him blocking the door.

'Yes, yes, *yes* … watch your step, yes, yes, *yes*, watch your step, Cooper. There isn't room for both of us here,' he muttered, walking towards me.

I knew what he meant, two loners, or freaks. I looked around for a weapon as I knew I would not be able to beat him with my bare hands. Anything would do – an old, long screwdriver that I could drive into his eye, anything, but there was nothing lying around. I was fucked.

This was it: I was going to die, painfully. I was about to be on the receiving end of something similar to what poor Harry had undergone, only this time there were no other boys there to run and get help for me.

Then he spoke. 'You had a lucky escape last time, but I'm gonna let you off for now. This isn't the right place,' he said, glancing at the door, 'somebody might come in. But tonight, while you're sleeping, yes, yes, *yes*, I'm going to kill you, Cooper … yes, yes, *yes*. I haven't decided how yet … perhaps I'll put a pillow over your face and suffocate you, or maybe a knife, yes, yes, *yes* … a knife.'

Then he turned and walked out of there, leaving me trembling. I knew he meant every word he'd said.

I told Mr Booth about the threat, but he didn't take me seriously, no matter how much I pleaded with him to help me; it was futile. The thing is, Cunningham should not have even been in a place like Pelham House, he should have been somewhere more specialised, with a team of doctors and psychiatrists trained to deal with psychos like him. Most of the staff at Pelham House came from a uniform background: military, police, prison guard. It was more like a borstal than a children's care home. The staff just didn't have the qualifications or knowledge to recognise, let alone deal with, the serious mental issues of people like Cunningham.

I had to do something; the evening was passing and bedtime drew nearer. As I tried my hardest to figure out a way to escape certain death I was going out of my mind. I couldn't run away again as the staff were now keeping a close eye on me because they knew I was a potential runner. I could not leave the house without asking permission, even to go to the toilet – if I was not back within two or three minutes they would come looking for me.

It was getting later and later and I found myself pacing up and down between the living room and the television room. Then I saw it: Mr Booth had left his bunch of keys on the padded bench, a bunch of keys with his Swiss Army knife attached to them. I glanced up and down the corridor and found I was alone, but probably only for a few seconds more, so I grabbed the keys, stuffed them in my pocket and went back to the living room and sat down. The next hour passed and Mr Booth still hadn't noticed his keys were missing, but it was only a matter of time.

I asked if I could go to the toilet again, so I could remove the knife from the bunch of keys, but Mr Booth refused me because we'd all be going to the washrooms soon enough as it was almost time for bed. I was tempted to put them back for fear of him noticing and searching us all, a distinct possibility as the staff often searched the boys for one thing or another: money, cigarettes, makeshift weapons and other contraband. But I knew if I got rid of them I would have no defence against Cunningham. So I held my nerve and prayed he would not notice his keys were missing.

The time came, we were all hauled up to our dormitories to get undressed and ready to go back down to the washrooms. Cunningham was watching me as I got undressed, smirking and nodding, knowingly. He hadn't forgotten, psychos like him *never* forget. I still had to get the knife off the key ring, open up the longest, sharpest blade and hide it under my pillow. Once I was back in bed I'd hold the knife under my blanket and stay awake, I figured. If he approached my bed I'd stab him in the eye, but I knew I'd have to strike quicker than a coiled viper to take him by surprise. I even thought about the consequences of blinding a person in one eye, but what was that compared to my fate if I did nothing? It wasn't as if I hadn't tried to tell somebody, not that that would do me any good later in court, as I doubted Mr Booth would admit that I'd approached him about it.

Eventually, Cunningham left the dorm in his underpants, a towel rolled under his arm, glancing at me as he passed. I'd been taking my time getting undressed on purpose as I wanted a few seconds alone in the dorm. I kneeled down next to my bed and, with my hands near the floor, my bed obscuring the glances of anyone who might pass by along the corridor, I removed the knife from the bunch of keys. After thumbling around with a few blades, I eventually found a nice long pointy one, then, leaving the blade out, I hid the knife under my pillow and stashed the bunch of keys in the bottom of my wardrobe under some other things. I figured I'd put the keys back on the bench in the house the next day after school.

As I went down to the washrooms to get ready it was then that I had another idea. I don't know why I didn't think of it before. Just along from the washrooms was a metal door, which led into the boiler room; it was never locked. I'd been in there loads of times before, while trying to find a little sanctuary for myself. No one ever went in there, only for boiler maintenance – at least the boiler room was warm and safe. After I got washed I went back up to the dormitory with everybody else, got into my pyjamas and into bed, along with the others. I knew Cunningham would not make his move until after lights out – that would be too risky as the day staff had to hand over to the night staff, who in turn did a quick round of the dorms to check on everybody and do a head count.

Mr Normington stuck his head into my dorm and scanned the beds to make sure everybody was there before heading off down the corridor to repeat his head count in the other dorms. The instant the lights went out, I hopped out of bed, knife in hand in case Cunningham tried to jump me there and then, and sneaked out into the corridor.

'Cooper, where are you going?' asked Paterson, more out of curiosity than anything else.

It wasn't unusual for boys to sneak off to other dorms for one reason or another during the night, but it was uncharacteristic of me, hence his question, which I chose to ignore. I looked left and right down the corridor: the coast was clear and Mr Normington was nowhere to be seen. Tiptoeing as fast as I could to the end, I looked back and, to my relief, neither Paterson nor Cunningham had come out of the dorm. I headed down the stairs, out the door, across the courtyard and into the boiler room. The boiler room was relatively large, with lots of large boilers, thick pipes, concrete pillars and various freestanding units to hide behind. It was quite dark, just the moonlight coming in through the two small windows, but my eyes soon adjusted so I was able to see the whole room. I knew the layout well from going in there during daylight hours.

At first I just sat down on the concrete floor, which was quite warm, in the corner furthest from the door, but still with a clear view of the door and the rest of the room. About half an hour passed and no one entered. I figured Paterson couldn't care less and Psycho Boy wasn't about to come looking for me, he could kill me some other night. Generally, the night staff only came to check on us if there was a ruckus, they weren't that committed to the job.

I always woke up before the staff came to wake us, so I planned to head back up five minutes before this happened and loiter just outside my dorm. By chance, there was an old (working) carriage clock on one of the shelves so keeping time would be easy. If the staff asked me what I was doing when they came to wake us, I'd just say I'd been to the toilet. By then it would not matter and they probably wouldn't suspect a thing.

'OK, Cooper,' said Mr Normington, spotting me outside my dorm. 'Grab your things and get off down to the washrooms.'

'Yes, sir,' I said, re-entering my dorm. I grabbed my towel and toiletries.

'Cooper, where were you last night?' asked Paterson.

'I just went for a walk,' I said.

It was stupid, I know, but it was the first thing that I could think of.

'In this fuckin' freezing weather, you must be mad, man!' he said, thinking nothing more of it.

Phew!

Cunningham looked at me with a slightly perplexed expression on his face.

The boiler room was hardly comfortable, the only thing it had going for it was that it was toasty warm. Apart from that, the concrete floor was hard, which led to a restless night's sleep and there were rats too. I suspected that rats were either nocturnal, or just didn't like daylight as I'd never seen or heard any in the boiler room before, but within a few hours of my being in there two or three of the bloody things came out to introduce themselves.

My plan worked fine for the first two nights, but on the third night Mr Normington noticed I was not in bed and, torch in hand, decided to come looking for me. Who knows how long he'd been looking when he'd decided to check the boiler room, but there he found me, hiding in the far corner.

'What the bloody hell do you think you're doing in here, Cooper?'

'Nothing,' I said.

'It's two o'clock in the bloody morning so don't say nothing to me! What are you doing in here?' he persisted.

I went on to explain about Cunningham's threats to kill me while I slept; I also told him how I had sneaked down there after lights out and crept back upstairs five minutes before his wake-up call. He could see how scared I was of sleeping in the same dorm as Psycho Boy and he certainly knew his reputation. So I pleaded with him and, just when I thought he was going to drag me back up to the dorm, he came up with a solution.

'You know I can't let you sleep in here, don't you?'

'Yes, sir, but—'

'No buts, just listen to me. I'll consider letting you sleep here on one condition.'

'Yes, sir, anything.'

'Hell, I'll even bring some spare blankets from the storage room for you, that floor doesn't look very comfortable. Would you like that?'

'Yes, please, thank you, thank you, sir,' I said.

Great, I'd be spared death by Psycho Boy.

I could not believe he was going to let me sleep in there, and bring me some blankets to create a makeshift bed, wow!

'But there is a condition,' he added.

I just looked at him and waited for him to tell me what the condition was.

'Get up and come over here,' he said.

I obeyed.

'Now, stand behind me …'

Again, I obeyed.

'Closer,' he said, reaching behind, grabbing my forearms and pulling me up against his back. He undid the two strap buttons on his dungarees and dropped them before pulling down his underpants. Then he grabbed my right hand and pulled it around the front. 'You know what this is, and you know what to do with it,' he said, placing my hand on his erect penis.

'Sir, I don't want to,' I protested.

'Well, if you don't want to that's fine, I'll take you back up to the dorm to sleep with Psycho Boy … Do you want that?'

'No, sir.'

'Well, start tugging.'

Reluctantly, I obliged. I'd seen a lot worse in some of the previous places I'd been in and so I figured I was getting off lightly, all things considered. The vulgar deed didn't take long, thank God. He re-fastened his dungarees and left.

'Have a good night,' he said, closing the door behind him.

For a moment I stood there, then I started to tremble involuntarily, not really knowing how I was supposed to feel about what had just happened. I waited a few more minutes then went next door to the toilets to wash my hands. Back in the boiler room I tried to sleep, but I could not shake off the thought of what had just taken place.

I was in the middle of a nightmare, yet I was still wide-awake.

Chapter 25

The Evil Boiler Room

About two weeks passed and my boiler room arrangement continued. I'd sneak off about 30 seconds after lights out and an hour after that the big, fat, disgusting, middle-aged and greasy-haired Mr Normington would come down for his recompense. Yes, I minded, but, like sleeping with the rats, it was preferable to the alternative – either being smothered to death with my own pillow or having my throat cut with a Stanley knife while I slept. So, for now at least, I was willing to oblige and would fall asleep on the hard floor to the occasional sound of scuffling rats' feet.

Cunningham never questioned my nocturnal vanishing act and, oddly enough, he never attempted to follow me out of the dorm, probably because there would be too many witnesses, but I could tell it was frustrating him in that special way of his. Paterson couldn't care less where I disappeared off to, or what I was up to. But then things took a turn for the worse.

It was a Sunday night and I'd sneaked off down to the boiler room, as usual, but an hour later it wasn't Mr Normington who arrived, it was the other night watchman, Mr Banister. He too was middle-aged, but he wasn't fat like Normington, he was taller, thickset and strong looking. Although his torch blinded me, I could tell by his silhouette that this was not Normington, and when he spoke I knew straight away that it was Banister.

'Come on, boy, get to your feet,' he said, still shining his torch in my face.

'What is it?' I said.

'What is it? What do you *think* it is?'

'I don't know, sir.'

'Oh, I think you do! There's only one reason we let you sleep in here, so why don't you come over here and show me what the reason is? Well, come on, lad, I'm waiting!'

So I got up and ambled over to him.

'What do you want me to do?' I said, hoping he would tell me to go and mop a floor somewhere or clean the boot room, but of course he didn't.

'Oh, I think you know what I want you to do,' he said, undoing his belt and the top button of his trousers. 'Well, come on, you can do the rest,' he added.

'I don't understand,' I said, trying to delay the inevitable.

'Look, don't give me any fucking trouble or you know what's going to happen! Now don't be shy, just do what you usually do to Mr Normington.'

So I stood behind him in the same way as I'd done several times with Mr Normington. I prayed he wouldn't make me do it from the front because I didn't want to have to look at him, or anything else out front.

I'd learned how to block it all out, become robotic, and to see it as a means to an end. Whenever anything bad was happening to me, I simply went somewhere else in my head, usually the moon, where I'd lounge in my comfortable chair. Visiting the moon distanced me from the earth and the horrific reality of what was going on in my immediate vicinity. But even when I was on the moon, my thoughts, perspectives and attitude were changing and becoming increasingly unhealthy. From my comfy reclining armchair I'd look down at the bright-blue earth and imagine some evil, unearthly force from a horrific, non-existent version of the Old Testament. I'd imagine this force sending a bolt of fire to earth, ripping white-hot flames across the miserable planet's surface, killing everything on this godforsaken planet. All those evil, sadistic bastards who'd tortured, tormented and abused me would be getting it worst of all. They would scream as their hair caught fire and their skin started to melt off, and then, after a period of agonising pain, they would all die horrific agonising deaths. Nothing would survive.

Fuck the world! My world was an evil, sordid, despicable place full of torment, torture, beatings, abuse (both sexual and physical), and all kinds of other sadistic, sick goings-on. If you spend enough time in an institutionalised environment as I had done, eventually being abused becomes a part of you, or you become a part of it. The lines blur and after a while it all seems normal. You start to believe that this is just how the world is, even outside the walls of whatever place you find yourself incarcerated in. So, yes, why not let the whole miserable fucking planet go up in flames? But, hidden away in the depths of my soul lay a dormant belief that there was love in the world – and one day I would find it.

When Mr Normington nudged me awake with his foot, I was still half asleep. I had no idea what the time was; it was not yet light and I couldn't make out what he was saying. I had got the idea into my head that Normington and Banister would take turns, alternating nights. Now I was so tired and I could hardly keep my eyes open. Everything seemed surreal, which wasn't a bad thing, given the circumstances. I almost fell asleep while relaxing on my chair on the moon, but I was snapped out of it a few minutes later when Mr Normington pushed me away and buttoned up his dungarees.

I stumbled out into the cold, across the courtyard to the washrooms to wash my hands. When I got back to the boiler room the cold air and wash had woken me, so I lay there, unable to get back to sleep, and waited for daybreak.

Now my nights were just as bad as my days, but for a whole different set of reasons. There seemed to be no escape and at night all I could manage was a few hours' broken sleep, with two random interruptions that came at different hours every night. Just when I thought things could not get any worse, they did. After a few weeks, Banister was no longer content with hand relief from behind, on this particular night he insisted that I get down on my knees in front and take him in my mouth. For me this was a step too far and so I refused outright.

'Don't you dare refuse me, boy! Now kneel down,' he ordered me.

'No, I won't do that.'

'*Won't*? Yes you fuckin' well will! Now, I won't tell you again, boy, get on your fuckin' knees right now!'

'No.'

He stepped forward and clouted me round the side of my head.

'Do it,' he insisted.

'No.'

At this he grabbed me by my hair and pushed me to the floor.

'You know what's going to happen if you don't do this? I'll drag you back up to that fuckin' dorm and let the psycho have you. Is that what you want? Do you want Psycho Boy to kill you while you sleep? Do you, *do* you?'

'No, I don't, but I'm not gonna do this anymore.'

'You fuckin' little bastard,' he said, zipping himself up and buttoning his trousers. 'You make me come down here and waste my fuckin' time! Well, I'll show you what happens to people who waste my time, boy,' he said, removing the leather belt from his trousers.

He folded it in half and began whipping me with it. I curled up into a ball on the floor and put my arms and hands over my head to protect myself.

'Get those fuckin' arms out of the way!' he shouted.

'No.'

'No? I'll give you fuckin' *no!*'

He leaned down, grabbed my hair and pulled my head up, then punched me in the side of the face three times in quick succession.

'No, you dare say *no* to me, boy!' he said, standing up again and getting back to whipping me with his belt.

I lay on the floor, crying out loud, my face in agony from his hard adult punches, but he didn't care. He took a break from whipping me to kick me in the ribs and stomach several times before whipping me again until he was exhausted and could not continue. As a parting gift he kicked me in the face, sending a shooting, stinging pain right up my nose. I could feel and taste warm blood running from my nose into my mouth, but I was in too much pain and too exhausted to go to the washrooms to pack my nostrils with toilet paper.

In my half-unconscious state I didn't move from my spot on the floor; I didn't even have the energy to crawl back to my makeshift bed in the corner. I don't know if I passed out or fell asleep, but the next morning Mr Normington came down to get me when he noticed that I hadn't made my own way back up to the dorm. He saw all the dried blood and the large bruise down the left side of my face and told me to get to the washrooms to clean myself up.

As I stood in front of the washroom mirror, gazing at the elongated purple bruise and swelling on my face, I began to question if sleeping in the boiler room, with all that went with it, really was the lesser of the two evils.

Fuck it, tonight I'll take my chances with Psycho Boy, I thought.

During the day in the schoolrooms Cunningham was nowhere to be seen, which was unusual as I saw him every single day in school. He wasn't in the dining room for lunch and he didn't show up for dinner either.

Where could he be?

In the evening I went out to the toilets a couple of times and, while walking back to my house, I glanced in the open door of the house next door, but I didn't see him in the corridor. He could have been in any of the other rooms, but it was strange that I hadn't seen him all day or evening. Bedtime arrived, and in the usual regimented way, we all went up to our dorms to get stripped down to our underpants and gather up our toiletries. Not only was Cunningham not there, his bed was stripped to the bare mattress. From what I could see, his things had gone – at least his shoes, which were usually kept within sight at the foot of his bed – along with the few things he kept on the windowsill, but I couldn't see if his wardrobe was empty.

'Where's Cunningham?' I asked Linnet, who was getting undressed next to me.

'He's been transferred … probably to a nuthouse,' he said, laughing.

Linnet's relief was obvious.

'And about fuckin' time … psychopath would have ended up killing someone,' added Paterson, grabbing his towel and heading out the dorm.

'Great!' I said.

'Yeah, we can relax a little now,' said Linnet.

Well, I doubted for one moment that I'd be able to 'relax' but at least I'd still be alive. I headed off down to the washrooms, smiling inside. After getting washed I returned to the dorm and got into bed, only this time after the lights went out I stayed right where I was.

The Evil Boiler Room

No more Psycho Boy, no more rats, hand jobs or beatings in the boiler room.

As I settled down in the hope of getting my first decent night's sleep in about three weeks, suddenly the ancient metal-framed hospital-type bed seemed very welcoming.

The lights went out, apart from the dim night-lights in the corridor, and I closed my eyes. However, I was still nervous as I didn't know quite how Mr Normington or Mr Banister would react when they realised I was in bed in my dorm and not in the boiler room. After about half an hour I was still awake, but with my eyes closed. I heard a creak by my dormitory door; I didn't have to open my eyes to know there was a presence there. As I opened my eyes just a fraction, leaving a slit to see through, I saw Mr Normington standing just inside the doorway, motionless, just gazing at me. I knew it was too dark in the dorm for him to see if I had my eyes open slightly, and they were only open ever so slightly. He stood there for a short time and then, finally, he walked back down the corridor to take up his seat around the corner.

The next morning I heard Mr Normington yell his usual chants of, 'OK, you lazy bastards, get out of your wanking chariots and down to the ablutions … Drop your cocks and reach for your socks … Come on, come on!' Then he arrived outside our dorm, stuck his head inside the door and looked at me.

'Enjoy your night's sleep, Cooper?'

'Yes, sir,' I said.

'Good,' he said, in a tone that suggested he'd acknowledged the fact that now Psycho Boy had been transferred, I didn't need the boiler room and all that went with it anymore.

My instincts about Travis Cunningham would be proved right for it transpired my choosing to go through all that hell in the boiler room for three weeks was far and away the best choice. Fifteen years later I read in one of the national newspapers about a certain psychopath from a certain approved school in a certain part of the country who'd bludgeoned to death his former social worker by repeatedly battering him in the head with a hammer. He then killed the first policeman on the scene by stabbing him several times in the stomach, before rushing off to his girlfriend's house to kill her too – lucky for her, she was not at home at the time.

The police caught up with him the same day and now he will spend the rest of his life in a special prison for the criminally insane.

Chapter 26

Et Tu, Hugh!

Mrs Clements arrived to collect me in her car on Friday morning. After I'd spent two months writing letters in which I repeatedly begged her, she'd arranged for me to go home to London for a long weekend. She would be driving me down south on the Friday and I would get the train back up myself on the Tuesday as it was a bank holiday and the school didn't mind if I missed one day. I'd been warned that I would not be allowed home again if I didn't return, and I knew what the punishments would involve too. With this in mind, they had trusted me to return to Pelham House after my home leave.

After breakfast I was led to Mr Burkinshaw's office, where Mrs Clements was waiting.

'Hello, Nigel,' she said with a huge smile on her face.

'Hello,' I said.

'Are you looking forward to your weekend in London?' asked Mr Burkinshaw.

'Yes, sir,' I said.

'Well, you'd better get going then, you have a long journey ahead,' he told me.

'Yes, sir.'

'Come on then,' said Mrs Clements, putting her hand on my shoulder.

It was brilliant, it felt like nothing else on earth as we pulled out of the grounds and away from Pelham House. I sat in the front with Mrs Clements and, as usual, we had some great conversations on the way. However, I omitted to mention any of the evil goings-on at Pelham House for two reasons: one, I was embarrassed and, two, I knew there would be serious and almost certainly violent consequences if Mrs Clements expressed her concerns to Mr Burkinshaw or my housemaster. But I felt as free as a bird as we drove down the motorway, stopping twice at service stations on the way.

The 310-mile journey took nearly seven hours, including stops, but we eventually arrived at my home in Kentish Town. Mrs Clements knocked on the door and it was answered by Jonathan, who was now eight years old; she and I went inside and into the living room, where Mum was busy trying to tune in the new rental television that had been delivered an hour earlier from Rumbelows. Anthony (now 18) was up on the flat roof, making adjustments to the aerial to try to get a better picture. Even though Mrs Clements and I had been travelling for hours and were in dire need of a cup of tea, my mother was too preoccupied with shouting out of the open front window up to Anthony on the roof. 'No, it's still a little bit snowy,' she yelled, while looking across at the TV from her position at the living-room window. 'That's it … no, you've lost it, go back a bit!'

But Mrs Clements just looked at me and smiled while waiting patiently for my mother to stop faffing about and come and give her son a hug.

'Oh, bloody hell, we had it then!' she muttered, and then, 'Anthony, go back a bit, you had it!' she yelled in the direction of the roof. And so went the fiasco for about another 10 minutes until Anthony finally got the aerial into a position that rendered a half-decent picture.

'Bloody hell, what a palava!' said Mum, finally turning round and seeing Mrs Clements and me standing in the doorway to the lounge. 'Oh, dear, bloody televisions! Nothing's ever easy, is it?'

Mrs Clements didn't seem to have an answer for her.

'Hello, Nigel,' said my mother, finally giving me a much-needed hug, 'now, would you both like a nice cup of tea and a slice of cake?'

'That would be lovely,' said Mrs Clements.

But I didn't really know what to say, or feel; I felt like a stranger and the hug didn't radiate. It felt like I was in somebody else's house. Anthony arrived in the kitchen.

'Hi,' he said, directed at Mrs Clements.

He glanced at me with a fake half-smile and went to the sink to wash his hands. This wasn't quite what I expected – I'd painted a nicer picture than this and somehow I didn't feel like I was at home. Maybe my love for my mother was starting to fade a little, or perhaps I was coming to the stark realisation that I was all alone in this world, even Mrs Clements' involvement in my life was less than it used to be. From now on I would just have to look after myself.

Over the course of the weekend and the Bank Holiday Monday I was left to my own devices, except on the Sunday when Mum, Jonathan and I went for a walk in Regent's Park. It wasn't the weekend I'd hoped for; my mum was preoccupied with her own things and even spent all of Saturday evening until late with her friend Trish, who lived next door at the top floor. I was only home for three days so you'd have thought my mum would at least give up her weekend for me, but it wasn't to be. At least Anthony was not around to pick on me or call me names – he'd recently moved out into a bedsit with his girlfriend.

So, Tuesday arrived and it had been arranged that I'd make my own way back to Pelham House on the train. I took the Tube from Kentish Town to Euston, then an overground train, eventually arriving at Oxenholme station near Kendal, before finally getting a bus to Pelham House. Having to voluntarily walk back up the driveway to Pelham House was one of the hardest things I've ever had to do.

One month rolled into another and it was business as usual; nothing had changed, nothing ever would change or so it seemed. But then something happened, a small ray of light shone on me. It was September 1979 and The Stranglers' fourth studio album, *The Raven*, was released. I wrote a letter to my mum begging her to buy it for me and send it in the post. Although the older boys would not let me use the record player, I knew Ericson would like to play this new album because, for him, The Stranglers kind of fell into the Punk scheme of things, and he was still really into his punk rock music.

My letter was written on the Monday and posted on Tuesday. I figured Mum would get the letter by Friday, then pop out to buy the album from the local independent record shop at the bottom of her street on Kentish Town Road on the Saturday. Perhaps she would delay sending it until Monday, or Tuesday when she had time, and then I'd get it by the middle to the end of that week. I had it all worked out and waited in anticipation; I could hardly wait to see what Hugh and The Stranglers had written for me. The week passed, so did the weekend, as did the following week, but still no sign of any record.

I asked my housemaster, Mr Booth, if I could phone my mum. There was a telephone next door to the house in a small office alongside the cobbled yard for the purpose of the boys speaking to their parents or social workers. Sometimes the parents and social workers called the boys, and sometimes, rarely, the boys themselves were allowed to call their parents or social workers. I generally got to call my mother once a month, and occasionally she would call me. Mr Booth agreed and at seven o'clock that evening he escorted me to the small office and dialled my mum's number, which was written down with the other boys' parents' numbers on the wall.

'Hello,' said Mum.

'Hi, Mum, it's Nigel.'

'Oh, hello, how you doing?'

'OK, did you get my letter?'

'Oh, yes. You know, I just haven't had the time and money's been a bit tight, can it wait a bit longer?' she said.

My heart sank; she hadn't bought the record or sent it. There I was, waiting keenly, rushing back to the house after school to ask Mr Booth if there was any post for me. 'Nothing today,' he'd say. How could she do this to me? Didn't she realise there was so little to keep me going in this place and that album would serve as a lifeline, for a short while at least?

'But Mum, please, I really want it.'

'Look, I'll see how much money's left when I get my widow's allowance next week, OK? But I can't promise anything.'

I just stood there in the cold office, deflated, looking out onto the cobbled yard with nothing to look forward to but misery.

'Are you there?' she said.

'Yeah.'

'Look, I'll write to Mrs Clements and see if she can help.'

'OK,' I said.

'Anyway, I've got to go. Jonathan and I are going out to buy some fish and chips from the takeaway, but I'll talk to you soon, OK?'

'OK.'

'Alright, Nigel, tatty bye.'

And that was it. I still had nothing to look forward to and I'd been left with the mental image of Mum and my bastard half-brother walking hand-in-hand down to the fish and chip shop. After coming off the phone to her I was usually left feeling more depressed than before. Knowing she was spending money left, right and centre on the cinema, fish and chips and whatever else took her fancy at the local Thursday market in Queen's Crescent made me so angry. Why, oh why, couldn't she throw me a little charity once in a while?

So, I gave up all hope of getting some therapy from Hugh; I got my head down and got back to the miserable grindstone. But then, two weeks later, a package arrived for me: a 12-inch flat cardboard package. Could this be it? I went into the living room, gently opened it and removed the black album cover with an image of a raven in the middle and that famous handwritten Stranglers logo in the top right-hand corner: 'The Stranglers' in bright red and *The Raven* written in a white, medieval-style font. I couldn't help thinking that Mrs Clements had a hand in this.

Just as I turned it over to look on the back, Ericson came over. 'What did you get?' he wanted to know.

I looked up and could see that he was quite excited at the arrival of my new album. Strangely enough, nothing ever happened to my Stranglers albums because Ericson liked them and he could beat up most of the boys in there so no one else dared touch them.

'Come on then, let's play it,' he said, walking over to the record player.

After taking the inner sleeve out, I removed the shiny 12-inch piece of vinyl. For a second I held it in my hands, observing the grooves and the label in the middle and checking that the spindle hole was perfect, with no scraggy bits of vinyl from a dodgy hole-punch on the production line. It all looked perfect on both sides, so I handed it to Ericson, who took it by the edges and placed it on the record player before gently lowering the arm onto the record. I was pleased that he had as much respect for vinyl as I did and knew how to handle records. He turned the volume up and we sat down next to each other and listened to it. The other boys who were in the living room with us could take it or leave it and continued to play pool, table tennis or just chatter.

Oh my God, what's happened? What's with all the weird experimental tracks?

It was barely recognisable compared to the first three Stranglers albums, which had served me well, both musically and therapeutically – but this? It sounded like Hugh and The Stranglers had moved away from their edgy, no-holds-barred, hard-hitting music. Hugh had moved over into experimental musical waters, and they were waters that I didn't particularly want to swim in. He really didn't have much to say to me anymore and was spouting on about social and political issues with his newfound musical styles.

'Dead Loss Angeles' and 'Nuclear Device' were the closest thing to 'typical' Stranglers tracks on the album. 'Shah Shah A Go Go' was just too repetitive for me, while 'Men In Black' and 'Genetix' were just too damn strange and avant-garde. As for 'Duchess' … well, it sounded like The Stranglers had attempted to write the most commercial-sounding pop song ever, and they'd succeeded. In all my life I never heard such a mainstream song; no hard-core sensibilities whatsoever. I could almost say the same for 'Don't Bring Harry'. As Ericson lifted the vinyl off the record player and handed it back to me, I couldn't decide if *The Raven* was utterly intelligent, or a collection of experimental studio out-takes that should, for the most part, have been banished to B-sides.

Over the coming weeks Ericson played my record a couple more times, but in my current state of mind, there was only one way to see it: Hugh had abandoned me. It would probably be at least a year before another Stranglers album arrived. I doubted that Hugh and the band would return to the style of music to which I'd become accustomed.

boy

Apart from the odd rare visit from Mrs Clements, I was now on my own.

P.E. day arrived and the staff at Pelham House had had a brilliant new idea. They'd spent some of the budget on some new sports equipment – well, two pairs of boxing gloves, actually, thinking they'd introduce boxing into the sports curriculum.

'Alright, everybody, go and get changed, only no shirt tops, just shorts and trainers,' said one of the staff.

There were 16 boys in our particular P.E. class, which meant there would be eight fights.

'Right, Ericson and Jones, you two can go together,' said the P.E. teacher, looking for the next two boys to match up. 'Harry, you can go with Paterson.'

That made sense as Harry and Paterson were always fighting anyway. I was standing as close to Linnet (and vice versa) as possible, in the hope that we would be paired up. There was no way he would pair us up with anybody else as they were all two or three years older than Linnet and me, and way bigger.

'Linnet, you go with Parker.'

Oh, shit!

'And Cooper, you can go with Clifford.'

Great, Andrew Clifford was probably the tallest kid in the place, and, although he didn't usually go around picking fights, he sure as hell finished them. I'd only ever seen him in action twice, so I knew I was on a hiding to nothing; I doubted I'd even have the reach to get up to his face. I looked over at the P.E. teacher, with a questioning look in my eye.

'What's wrong, Cooper? Get over there, boy, and stand next to Clifford,' said the sadistic bastard. Matching Linnet and me up with much older, bigger and stronger boys was all part of his sick game.

Ericson and Jones went first. They gloved up and stood in the ring that had been chalked out on the floor in advance. The teacher didn't have a whistle to act as a bell, nor did he have a stopwatch to time the rounds; already he'd decided the boys would fight until one of them won.

'OK, off you go,' he said.

And so Ericson and Jones started moving around. Ericson got the first punch in, nothing serious, just a jab, then Jones retaliated with a jab of his own.

'Come on, Ericson!' shouted a few of his mates.

Nobody shouted for Jones, probably for fear of Ericson beating the crap out of them later. I just stood there and said nothing. Ericson got in a few more punches to Jones's face, chest and ribs, but then Jones threw a punch that landed right in the middle of Ericson's nose, but it didn't bother Ericson, who continued. It was a relatively even fight and it soon became clear that both boys were getting tired on their feet as they started to amble and throw slow punches with no aim. Ericson had blood running down his mouth from a nosebleed too.

So, there they were again, the so-called 'care' staff, breeding ever more violence.

'OK, that's enough,' the P.E. teacher finally said. 'Jones, go with Ericson and help him get cleaned up in the showers.'

Increasingly anxious, I just wanted my fight to be over and done with. A few fights on, and it was my turn.

'Cooper, Clifford, you're up!'

I was handed a pair of gloves from one of the previous fighters.

'Good luck, Cooper,' he said, pissing himself laughing.

I looked across at Clifford, whose face carried a blank expression. Perhaps if I just danced around a little and threw a few light jabs in the direction of his chest he'd go easy on me, but then I'd come across as a total pussy for not even trying. Getting beaten up by a bigger boy in day-to-day life was perfectly acceptable, but this was something else; I had to try or there'd be hell to pay. So, I decided the instant the teacher said 'Go!', I'd fly in as fast as I could. Arms, legs, fists, head, I'd go for it with everything I had. What the hell? I was probably going to get killed anyway so I might as well try.

'OK, you ready?' said the teacher.

I leaned in slightly and prepared to spring forward like a sprinter off the starting blocks. My only chance would be to take him by surprise. I'd gone through it in my head, now all I had to do was try to put my plan into practice.

'Go!'

At the precise moment the teacher said 'Go!' Clifford looked down at his feet as he stepped forward. Great, he'd taken his eyes off me. Before the echo of that single-syllable word had trailed off the teacher's lips, I'd pounced forward, pulled my right arm back and thrown my gloved fist in the direction of Clifford's face as hard as I could. He looked up just as my glove made contact with his jaw. Strangest thing, he was actually rattled and momentarily dazed, so I didn't give it a second thought. I hit him again, this time catching him just under his left eye. I was manic with my speed and frenzied punches; perhaps it was pent-up anger from all the beatings I'd taken. My unexpected success whipped up a storm among the small crowd.

'Go, Cooper!' shouted one.

'Look at him, he's fuckin' crazy!' shouted another.

'Cooper, Cooper, Cooper, Cooper!' came the chants. I could hear the crowd chanting in hysterics and disbelief at what they were seeing, a skinny 13-year-old kid landing punch after punch on Clifford, a 16-year-old six-footer probably double my weight.

I threw another punch, then another. But then Clifford lifted his gloves to block my punches before throwing one of his own. I wasn't guarding the left side of my face and he caught me hard, rattling my jaw. Instinctively, I stood back and put my glove up to my face. Going into defence mode was a big mistake. Clifford launched a full-on assault and the next thing I knew he was raining punches all over my head and face. Then, he grabbed me and got me in a headlock and started punching me in the face again, only this time I could not duck or move. Although I could not break free, the teacher allowed the bout to continue as more and more blood poured from my nose. I tried to protect my face with my gloves, but only managed to block about half of his punches, the other half finding their way through to my head and face. And then it was over; Clifford released my neck from his arm lock and like a sack of spuds I dropped to the floor. I suppose he went ballistic due to my embarrassing him and managing to rattle him and get in so many punches, and having geed up the crowd like that.

'OK, Cooper, get to the showers and get cleaned up, then get over to your house,' ordered the teacher.

In the shower I checked my face in the mirror: my lip was slightly split, my nose would not stop bleeding and there was a cut just below my right eyebrow. As I stood in the shower, I watched the blood run off my face and chest and around my feet and down the water hole. Afterwards I had to stick two small wads of toilet roll up each nostril to stem the bleeding.

I was sitting on the padded bench in my house when, by chance, the matron came over to see one of the other boys. She took one look at me and said, 'Oh, bloody hell! Come with me, son, we need to get your face looked at,' taking my arm. A chubby, middle-aged lady with a kind heart, unfortunately she didn't come to the houses that often and so the only time anyone got to see her was if they were injured, badly, then a member of staff would take them over to her nursing station in the main building.

Mr Booth was in the television room as we passed.

'I'm taking this one over to my office to get his face cleaned up,' she explained.

Mr Booth nodded in acknowledgement. We got halfway across the courtyard when Matron saw the P.E. teacher talking to one of his colleagues.

'What the bloody hell have you monsters been doing to these kids this time?' she said.

'Oh, put a sock in it, woman! It's all part of their growing-up process,' he responded sharply, dismissing her.

'You cruel buggers!'

'Just preparing them for the real world, it won't do 'em any 'arm.'

'Oh yeah, what bloody world would that be then? Bloody barbarians, the lot of you!'

But they just sniggered to themselves.

'Who's rattled 'er cage?' said one, taking another drag of his cigarette.

'Come with me, son, let's get you looked at,' Matron said, turning to me.

Up in her nurse's station she patched me up but, while she was tending to my battered face, I cried and fell forwards into her arms. She stopped what she was doing and hugged me back; I was so grateful for that.

'It's OK, son,' she said, squeezing me and rubbing my back.

I was overwhelmed.

'I want to go home,' I said, sobbing into her white nurse's jacket.

'I know you do, son, I *know*. You know, if I could take you home myself, I would. This is no place for a boy like you, you don't belong here – any damn fool can see that. Listen to me, son, don't let these bastards break you. Just hold on and you'll be out of here before you know it.'

I could have stayed in her arms forever.

Chapter 27

The Selfish Giant

The boxing matches didn't stop. In fact, the staff started betting money on the outcome, as they did with their sick cricket ball assault game. When the betting happened, Linnet and I found we were less involved in boxing and were put into some other activity group, possibly because the outcome would be too predictable against the bigger boys. Linnet, like me, got a lot of stick from the older boys – in fact, I think he probably got it worse than I did. But one day he'd had enough and he snapped, and I knew exactly how he felt. If you are constantly bullied, picked on and tormented day in, day out, eventually you'll reach your limit.

Paterson had been picking on Linnet all evening; he'd punched him several times and made him cry, he'd called him every disgusting name imaginable and just didn't let up as he continued to poke, prod and generally annoy him. Usually the pool cues were kept locked away in the office and only came out when some of the boys wanted to play. Mr Booth or another member of staff would usually be in the recreation room at the same time to supervise. However, they didn't lock away the billiard balls, which were always left on the pool table and in the six net pockets.

Poor Linnet had come to the end of his tether, and it was clear to me that he just couldn't take it any more. But what he did next was both surprising and shocking. He'd asked Mr Booth if he could go to the toilet, but then he'd run off up to his dorm, removed his pillowcase, stuffed it down the front of his trousers and returned to the living room, where he would sit and bide his time. At eight o'clock, most of the boys went off to the television room to watch a programme; Linnet remained in the living room with me and one other boy.

At five minutes to nine, just before the programme ended, Linnet removed his pillowcase, walked over to the pool table and placed four billiard balls in it. He spun it around so the balls ended up packed tightly at one end then wrapped the other end around his right hand twice to get a good grip. Afterwards he waited just inside the doorway, out of sight. He glanced over to me and smiled through his inner torment. The other boy and I just looked at each other. I had an idea what Linnet was about to do, but I did nothing to stop him; I was quietly praying his plan would work and that he would not be outsmarted by Paterson.

Two or three boys came rushing into the living room, past Linnet, not noticing him, before Paterson ambled in. Linnet walked up behind him, drew his billiard ball-filled pillowcase over his right shoulder and swung his right arm forward and down as fast and as hard as he could. The billiard balls smashed against Paterson's skull with a horrifically loud crack, so loud it made me wince. Paterson fell to the ground, clutching his head, but Linnet didn't stop there; he smashed the balls down onto his head again and again.

CRACK, CRACK, CRACK!

'Linnet, what the fuck are you doing?' shouted Steel, running over and dragging him away from Paterson.

Mr Booth came running in just in time to catch the aftermath.

'Bloody hell, sir! He hit Paterson over the head with this,' said Steel, tipping the balls out onto the pool table and holding up the pillowcase.

Mr Booth took one look at Paterson and instructed Ericson to go and fetch the Matron fast. Meanwhile, Paterson's head was bleeding all over the place. His hair was sticky claret, so too was the carpet where he lay. Although he wasn't unconscious, he wasn't moving either. The matron arrived and took control of the situation, and by now Paterson was a little more alert. After assessing the damage to his head, she pressed a towel up against the gashes to slow the bleeding and asked Mr Booth to phone for an ambulance.

When the Matron got Paterson to his feet, he almost passed out and collapsed again, so she sat him down in a chair and waited with him for the ambulance.

'Nigel, go and get a bucket of hot soapy water and a scrubbing brush,' said Mr Booth, who, being one of the half-decent members of staff, often called us by our first names.

A minute later, I returned with it.

'I've got it,' I said.

'Good, now clean that up before it soaks in and stains permanently!'

Oh, I wasn't expecting to have to get down on my hands and knees and scrub all Paterson's blood out of the carpet, but I did so, reluctantly. I scrubbed and rinsed, and scrubbed and rinsed, trying to lift as much of the sticky red stuff out of the carpet as I could. It took ages. Meanwhile, Mr Booth gave Linnet a stiff talking to. I was pleased to note that he didn't hit him or punish him. Mr Booth knew how much Linnet and I had to suffer so I suspect he thought it was a little bit of justice that he would let slide, this time. Although Linnet didn't get punished, I myself was about to – but for something else, something I'd entirely forgotten about.

By the time I'd finished scrubbing half a pint of Paterson's blood out of the carpet it was time for bed. As I arrived at my dorm, Mr Normington, the night watchman, was standing next to my wardrobe. He lifted his hand and jingled a bunch of keys at me.

'Care to explain how these got into your wardrobe?' he said.

Oh shit, Mr Booth's keys!

I'd totally forgotten that I'd hidden them in the bottom of my wardrobe. I meant to put them back on the bench, but with one thing or another I'd forgotten. Not knowing what to say, I said nothing.

'Come on, let's go down and see Mr Booth.'

Oh shit, I'm in trouble!

We went into the shower rooms, where Mr Booth was supervising.

'Mr Booth, I've found your keys,' said Mr Normington.

'Oh great, where were they?'

'I think you should ask this young man,' said Mr Normington, looking at me.

'Well?' said Mr Booth.

The other boys in the shower rooms stopped and waited, along with Mr Booth, for my answer.

'I don't know, sir,' I said.

'Well, they were hidden in the bottom of your wardrobe,' said Mr Normington.

'Did you take my keys?' said Mr Booth.

But I didn't answer; I just nodded yes.

'Where's the Swiss Army knife?' he said, taking the bunch off Mr Normington.

'It's under my pillow, sir.'

'Can you supervise here for a few minutes?' said Mr Booth to Mr Normington.

'Sure.'

Mr Booth marched me up to my dorm and lifted my pillow; there it was, folded away. I'd kept hold of the knife just in case Cunningham came back – after all, his transfer might have been temporary and I wasn't about to take chances.

'Why did you take them?' he said.

'I just wanted the knife, sir.'

'For what?'

'Protection.'

'Protection from whom?'

'Psy— Cunningham, sir.'

'Well, Cunningham isn't here anymore so you won't be needing this, will you?'

'No, sir.'

'Right, I'll think about your punishment tomorrow, it's too late for me to get into this right now.'

'Sir?' I said.

'Yes?'

'Is Cunningham gonna be coming back here?'

'No, he's been moved somewhere else.'

It was good to have that confirmed, at least.

The next day, Mr Booth had some chores lined up for me. On alternate days for a week I'd have to spend every evening after dinner brushing the courtyard and scrubbing the tiles in the shower rooms. I'd get the stiff yard broom and start at the top left corner of the cobbled courtyard and begin by sweeping down the slight incline with a repetitive forward brushing motion to get all the dirt out from between the cobbles. Then I'd go back to the top and repeat the whole procedure, brushing a section roughly 14 inches wide at a time until I'd completed the entire courtyard, which took over an hour. It was one hell of a workout.

The next evening I'd have to scrub the tiles in the shower rooms with a scrubbing brush and disinfected water, with no gloves. This took considerably longer, about two hours, and was serious toil. When it came to punishments, I was tarred with the same brush as everybody else – there simply was no individuality around there. But it wasn't the first time I'd had to brush the courtyard or scrub the tiles. Once, while on gardening duty, the gardener/maintenance man who taught us about all things horticultural had made me scrub the washroom floor with a toothbrush because he caught me chomping on a stick of rhubarb that I'd pulled out of the ground. I was on my hands and knees for three hours that evening. Making jobs extra-difficult like this was commonplace, even for the smallest of offences. Some of the staff just liked to make our lives as difficult as possible, it seemed.

The night watchman, Mr Banister, even made me come down at six in the morning to brush the yard, not for any particular reason other than frustration on his part for I was no longer sleeping in the boiler room. I'd brush the courtyard at dusk to the ghastly soundtrack of the rooks cawing vociferously in their rookery as they prepared for the day. Listening to those harrowing sounds in the early mornings as I walked across the cobbled yard in my underpants, my clothes tucked under one arm in the freezing-cold weather, will probably stay with me for the rest of my life. Today, whenever I hear a parliament of rooks cawing away in a rookery, I'm transported back to my time at Pelham House.

Spring was broken up by a visit from my mum and Jonathan. Mrs Clements had arranged everything for Mum – the train tickets, a bed and breakfast a few miles away from Pelham House, everything. As my mother usually pleaded poverty, she had even pulled funds from somewhere to pay for the whole trip.

Mum and Jonathan arrived at the B&B mid-evening, spent the night there, then the next morning I went in the school minibus to collect them and bring them back to Pelham House. We didn't do an awful lot, just walked around the grounds, and I showed Mum my house and dorm. But we talked, mostly about her stuff and what had been going on in her life.

Later in life, I read in my file that Mrs Clements spent ages persuading my mother to come and visit me, but she just kept complaining that it was too far. If Social Services hadn't paid for the train fares and B&B she wouldn't have bothered at all. I did explain to Mum, briefly, why I was so unhappy at Pelham House, but I wasn't going to ruin her break by making a big deal out of it. It was futile anyway. I think she saw the trip as more of a little holiday to a nice B&B by the seaside for two nights, courtesy of Social Services, as opposed to visiting her estranged son. She told me how lovely the B&B was and that she and Jonathan had had a lovely meal and they could see the sea from their bedroom window.

How nice for the two of you, I thought.

That was the only time during my 11-month stay at Pelham House that my mother visited me.

Early that evening one of the staff drove Mum and Jonathan back to the B&B. Within half an hour of them leaving, Dean got out his makeshift whip and busied himself whipping me, Linnet and Paterson to entertain himself. So I tried to leave.

'Cooper, get back in here,' he said.

'But I want to go and watch TV.'

'I don't fuckin' care, get back here, *now*!'

I ambled back towards my seat and huffed.

'What did you say?'

'Nothing,' I said.

'Good, 'cos if you did, I'll fuckin' kill ya!' he said, pushing me and knocking me down into my chair. He stood back and proceeded to whip me with his 'tablecloth' whip. As usual, I held my hands up to protect my face.

'Move your fuckin' hands!'

I didn't, so he stepped forward and punched me on top of my head.

'I said, move your fuckin' hands out of the way, *now*!' he said.

Fuck this, I thought.

I jumped to my feet and ran out of there.

'Cooper, get back in here,' he said, trying to mute his voice so Mr Booth didn't hear from the TV room at the other end of the corridor.

But I didn't – I just ran into the television room and sat under the watchful gaze of Mr Booth. There would be hell to pay, but I'd had a relatively enjoyable afternoon with my mum, or at least I'd had a break, so I wasn't about to let him extinguish my brief moment of happiness quite so fast. The thing that frustrated and annoyed me most was knowing my mum was in a B&B less than five miles away, enjoying an evening meal with Jonathan, oblivious to the torment that I was going through at that exact same moment.

And so it continued, the abuse, the beatings, the bullying, the endless name-calling and belittling, the cruel and unusual punishments from the brutal military staff. It just didn't let up, not even for a morning or an afternoon.

Summer came and went. The next thing I knew we were into autumn and the clocks were being put back. Dark evenings had returned, though my miserable existence was dark all the year round.

The weather was miserable and cold, but it felt like that every month of the year. I'd been a resident at Pelham House for 11 months and saw five seasons come and go yet I don't recall a single summer or even a hot sunny day. It was like something out of the Oscar Wilde story 'The Selfish Giant' – always it seemed to be winter, regardless of the time of year. It was either snowing, hailing, sleeting, raining, frosty, or just torrential wind storms whipping up piles of leaves into mini tornadoes. Inside the various buildings the staff were just as cruel as the giant in the story, only they never had a change of heart, nor did they take a great axe to knock down the wall. The key difference in this particular story was that there were several giants at Pelham House, dictators of their own private little empire, and the children were on the inside and most of them just as evil and sadistic as the giants.

Then something happened that would change everything.

It was the first week of December and Mrs Clements and her colleague, Mr MacGregor, came to visit me out of the blue. Not for any particular reason, though, with hindsight, I suspect Mrs Clements just felt sorry for me, stuck out there all alone, and she knew my mother wouldn't bother coming to see me again. She brought me some sweets, chocolate, a bird book and, to my amazement, a seven-inch record. The single was called 'Making Plans for Nigel' by XTC, which had been released a few weeks earlier. I knew the song as it had been played on the radio several times and all the other boys used to tease and torment me about it. There was no way I'd ever be playing it, not here. Still, it was a nice gesture.

Mrs Clements and Mr MacGregor spent a few hours with me in one of the visiting rooms. She could clearly see how depressed I was and I tried to tell her how unhappy Pelham House was making me, without explaining about all the evil goings-on for fear of being beaten and punished by the staff, should she confront Mr Burkinshaw with my complaints. Caught between a rock and a hard place, I was confident, if I told her about everything that went on there, she would get me moved but I couldn't do so because of the immediate consequences. But she could see it in my eyes, I could tell by her sympathetic and concerned expression. The time came for them to leave, and I had no idea how long it would be before she would return. I could, potentially, be stuck there until I was 16 years old – another 30 months, which I knew I would never survive. As I went back over to my house, Mrs Clements and Mr MacGregor visited the head, Mr Burkinshaw, before making their way back to Ulverston.

Back in the house, almost immediately Dean and another boy started bullying me. Mrs Clements would soon be leaving in her car and I'd be stuck there with this continuous stream of abuse, potentially for another two and a half years. I'd rather be dead, I decided. Once I managed to escape Dean and his friend, I made it to the television room, where I sat, in Mr Booth's company, contemplating.

'Sir, can I go to the toilet?'

'Yes, but don't be too long.'

So I headed off, but not to the toilet. Instead, I sneaked around the courtyard and headed over to the car park. There I saw Mrs Clements' red Ford Cortina. I went over to it and laid myself down underneath the bumper, directly behind the rear wheels. Her car was parked in such a position that she would have to reverse out, but she and Mr MacGregor would approach the car from the front because that was where the small pathway was that led to the main building.

I wanted to die and what better way to go than at the hands of the one person in the world who genuinely cared about me? So I lay there and waited for them to return to the car, get in, start the engine and reverse over me. I considered all things and had positioned my neck up against the offside rear tyre. Although a car weighing over a ton driving over my neck might not decapitate me, it would certainly bring my miserable life to an end. Deeply depressed, I was not thinking straight. I hadn't given much consideration to the actual outcome – it was an impromptu suicide attempt, thought up during a dark moment.

After about five minutes, I heard Mrs Clements and Mr MacGregor talking, their voices and footsteps progressively louder. Then, eventually, the car doors opened and they both got in and slammed the doors. Thank God they hadn't noticed me! My heart started thumping and I wanted to get up, but then I thought about what I'd be getting up for – more abuse and cruelty – so I held my nerve and stayed put behind the wheels of the car.

The engine started and sounded quite loud from underneath the vehicle as the noise reverberated through the exhaust, back box and out of the tail pipe. I could smell the exhaust fumes, which I was confident I'd only have to smell for a few seconds longer. Then I heard Mrs Clements put the car into reverse, its body jolted slightly on the spot as the gear engaged, but then the car relaxed as she took it out of gear. I heard the sprockets of the handbrake grind then the engine stopped and both doors flew open. Before reversing, Mrs Clements had checked her rear-view mirrors and seen my feet poking out from the back of the car.

'Nigel, what on earth are you doing down there? I could have run over you!'

'My God, son, what was going through your head?' said Mr MacGregor. 'Come on, get up, son,' he added.

'Nigel, are you OK?' said Mrs Clements.

I didn't know what to say, but I realised then I'd made a terrible mistake. Not because I didn't want to die, I did. I'd made a mistake because I hadn't stopped to think about the effect it would have on poor Mrs Clements. If I'd thought about it longer and harder, I wouldn't have put her through such an ordeal. I could see that she was shocked by my actions to the point where she was almost hyperventilating. She was clearly in some distress and obviously upset, probably for more than one reason and torn between her own racing heart and emotions and her genuine concern for me. The fact that I was in a dark place and not thinking straight was my only saving grace.

'Why, Nigel, *why*?' said Mrs Clements, her hands cupping my face.

'I don't want to live anymore.'

'Oh, dear Lord! Why, what's happened?'

'I don't like it here, it's horrible.'

'But I thought you were getting on OK?'

'No, I'm not,' I muttered. At this I burst into tears and grabbed hold of her.

They walked me back across the car park to Mr Burkinshaw's office and told him what had just happened. I was convinced I was going to be in a whole heap of trouble, but strangely, his usual sergeant-major voice dropped a few decibels as he spoke with Mrs Clements and me about what had taken place.

So, I didn't die that day, just like I didn't die when I fell off that abandoned warehouse roof and through a greenhouse onto a concrete floor, or when I stuck a shotgun in my mouth and pulled the trigger, or when I was thrown 15 feet in the air off a rope swing and landed awkwardly on my back. But something else happened, something quite miraculous.

About a week later I got a phone call from Mrs Clements, telling me there was another school that they were thinking of transferring me to. It was in Hertford, about 20 miles outside London, which would make home visits a little easier, she explained. I nearly hit the roof with excitement.

Years later I read in one of Mrs Clements' reports that the headmaster at Pelham House, Mr Burkinshaw, was connected to the headmaster at Danesbury School in Hertford and, after speaking with Mrs Clements first, he contacted the head at Danesbury to discuss the possibility of my transferral there as soon as possible. I also read in my file that Mr Burkinshaw had said that the head at Danesbury School thought along similar lines to him.

Mrs Clements asked me if I wanted to go and visit this potential school, but I declined simply because, if it was a real possibility, I didn't want to delay matters by a few weeks while arrangements were made for me to visit. I'd rather take my chances for it couldn't possibly be any worse than this place.

Phone calls were made, meetings held, Christmas came and went, and four weeks later, on 7 January 1980, I moved from Pelham House in the north of England to Danesbury School in the south.

My 11-month sentence of relentless abuse and cruelty at Pelham House was finally over.

Chapter 28

Welcome to Hell

My last weekend at Pelham House couldn't have passed any slower if God himself had physically grabbed the earth with both hands and stopped its rotation. I knew on the previous Thursday that Mrs Clements would be coming to pick me up first thing on the Monday morning to drive me down south to my new school in Hertfordshire. It was 7 January and outside it was freezing cold. The ground was a blanket of sparkling hard frost and the ice-cold winds bit hard into my face as we walked across the car park for the last time to Mrs Clements' Cortina.

I got comfortable in the front and put my seatbelt on.

'How are you feeling?' she asked, fastening her seatbelt.

'Great,' I said, smiling from ear to ear.

She smiled back, knowingly, and started the car. We headed down the windy driveway and out onto the country road, away from Pelham House. I can't find the words to express how I felt as the car drove off the grounds of Pelham House and out onto that small country lane. It felt incredible knowing that I was never going to have to return to Pelham House, and that, after the 300-mile journey, I would be just 30 miles from my mum's house in north London, which would make going home on the odd weekend that much easier.

We were soon on an A-road, which, in turn, would eventually join the motorway. The further we got from Pelham House, the warmer I started to feel, and it had nothing to do with the heating in Mrs Clements' car. It was as if I'd been dead during my stay at Pelham House and now I was slowly being brought back to life. That tiny nugget of hope in the pit of my soul to which I'd clung so desperately was now spreading outward through my entire body.

'It's lovely to see you smiling again,' Mrs Clements said, glancing across at me.

I knew I was heading out into the great unknown with this new school, which I still hadn't seen, but at least I would be closer to home and I figured nowhere could be as bad as Pelham House. I had everything to smile about, for now at least, so I just sat back and enjoyed the six-hour drive in the company of a lady who truly cared about me.

I was so happy, the journey passed in no time at all, even with the toilet breaks. We entered the county of Hertfordshire, then the town of Hertford, before finally arriving at Danesbury School, which sat at the top of a hill. The town looked quite pleasant, even classy, in that quintessential English sort of way. Not the kind of location where you'd expect to find an approved school.

There was an aged gardener working just inside the grounds, which were vast and incredibly well kept. He saw our car and came over to open the enormous gates to let us in. We drove through, with Mrs Clements saying thank you through her open window as we passed, and headed along the winding driveway. There was a large football pitch complete with field markings and goal posts to the left and a substantial, two-storey Victorian building to the right and three separate, but identical, much newer buildings straight ahead. We pulled into the car park to the right alongside the older building, where we were met by the headmaster.

'Good afternoon, how was your journey?' he asked.

'Very good, thank you,' said Mrs Clements.

'You must be Nigel. Welcome to Danesbury,' he said, extending his hand to me.

I shook it. As he squeezed my hand firmly he reminded me of Mr Burkinshaw from Pelham House; indeed they could almost have been brothers, or maybe even served together during WW2. This new head was also in his sixties but, despite his age and short stature, he was equally intimidating with a deep, loud and authoritative voice. He could have been ex-military.

'Let me take you over to meet your housemaster,' he added.

The three newer buildings were the houses where the boys lived and slept, each with its own name: Greys, Reynolds and Harris House. I was going to be in Greys House, which was closest to the playground and the main Victorian school building. The three houses were exact replicas with a television room, recreation/lounge room, dining room, kitchen, office, toilets and a storeroom on the ground floor. Upstairs was a bathroom, shower room, three large dormitories, three single bedrooms and a staff bedroom with a lockable door where the night duty staff would sleep. Also on the ground floor was a two-bedroom flat, where the housemaster lived permanently with his wife in his live-in job.

Across the playground the central Victorian building housed the main offices at the front of the building, all the school classrooms towards the rear of the building, and upstairs was the girls' living quarters. Greys, Reynolds and Harris buildings each housed around 14 to 16 boys, while the upstairs quarters of the main building housed around 15 girls. In total there were around 63 children, the majority of them boys. Most were a motley crew of majority whites, with some blacks, Irish, and one or two whose nationalities eluded me. But, regardless of nationality or skin colour, they all had one thing in common: they were either dysfunctional, delinquent, unwanted, unloved, violent or generally messed-up boys and girls who were the offspring of already messed-up dysfunctional, druggy or violent families.

Danesbury School was an approved school that was designed to attempt to fix those children who were clearly beyond all parental control, by whatever means the school and its staff saw fit. It didn't take long for me to realise that Danesbury was similar to Pelham House in more ways than I would have liked. It was regimented and strict and the staff dished out corporal punishment, brutality and hardship for no good reason. As for the boys, well, they were pretty much the same as the ones from Pelham House, only with southern accents, mostly London.

I was introduced to Mr Mears, the housemaster in Greys House. In his mid- to late thirties, he seemed nice enough. Immediately I felt at ease in his presence, in a way I had years previously with Mr Richardson at Lancaster. Mrs Clements didn't stick around long, understandably, as she had a long journey back up north.

'OK, Nigel, I'll be in touch to see how you're getting on,' she said.

I knew that she would not be able to come down south to see me very often, if at all. Suspecting this might well be the last time I saw her, I grabbed hold of her and gave her a big hug, which was reciprocated. But I knew I could not hold onto her forever as Mr Mears was standing by.

'You take care of yourself, OK?' she said.

I could have sworn I saw a tear well up in her eye.

She quickly turned to Mr Mears: 'Right, I'd better be on my way, I've got a long journey ahead.'

'OK, we'll keep you up to date with Nigel's progress,' said Mr Mears.

Saddened, I watched as she left and disappeared around the corner. I felt like it was the end of an era for Mrs Clements and me. Now torn, I was no longer sure I'd made the right choice: did I want to be closer to my mum, or Mrs Clements? All I knew was that I wanted to cry. Already I missed her and knowing she was going to be 300 miles away felt like something had been yanked out of me. Suddenly there was a void in my chest and I wasn't confident that my own mother could fill it, or even wanted to.

Mr Mears showed me around the house and the dorm where I'd be sleeping and told me a little about the place, then he gave me a tour of the gym and main building with the schoolrooms, where most of the boys and girls were in the various classes. The classrooms resembled regular classrooms that you'd find at a regular school. They had classrooms for Woodwork and Metalwork, Art, Technical Drawing, Maths, English, History, Home Economics and Typing, the latter two reserved solely for girls, though in time I'd manage to muscle my way into the Home Economics class. The large indoor gym had a tough parquet floor where the boys did circuit training, played indoor football and various other P.E. activities.

After I'd been given the grand tour, Mr Mears took me back over to Greys House. He sat with me in the television room and did some paperwork while I sat deep in thought. It wasn't long before the Greys House residents came rushing in from the schoolrooms – I heard them before I saw them. Mr Mears got up and stuck his head out into the wide corridor.

'Can we have a bit of bloody decorum, please! There's no need for all that racket, just go upstairs and get changed ready for dinner … quietly,' he said, loud enough for those already halfway up the stairs to hear him.

He gathered up his papers and returned them to his office, leaving me alone in the television room, feeling rather vulnerable and anxious. I really didn't want to be sitting there alone when all those boisterous boys came bumbling in. But I was, and they did.

The first kid who rushed in saw me sitting there.

'Oh,' he said, surprised to see me.

He rushed right back out again almost as fast as he'd come in.

'There's a new kid,' I heard him say.

'Where?' said another voice out in the corridor.

'In the TV room.'

A head popped around the door. I turned and looked, but the head disappeared, followed by an audible giggle.

'Wilkins, why aren't you changed out of your school uniform?' said Mr Mears.

'Sorry, sir,' said the boy.

'Well, don't just stand there looking gormless, go up and get changed!'

'Yes, sir.'

When everybody was seated in the dining room, Mr Mears introduced me and all of a sudden about 15 pairs of eyes were on me. I'd been through this before, several times, but the nasty feeling it evoked never faded. Some of the older boys gave me a kind of 'sizing up' look.

There were five dining tables, with three of the tables seating four boys at each, with the remaining two tables seating two boys and one member of staff at each. I was sitting with Mr Mears and another boy about my age. Glancing round, I could see most of the boys looked about 14, 15 or close to 16 years old, with perhaps a couple who were slightly younger. Most people left shortly after their 16th birthday, once they had a job to go to and their social worker had made the relevant living arrangements for them. I was (at just shy of 14) still one of the youngest there.

Some things never change.

Mr Mears introduced me to Chris Hutchinson, who was sitting opposite me. A little on the tubby side, he seemed relatively 'normal' in the grand scheme of things and was friendly with a pleasant demeanour. The food was nourishing and pretty good quality and the dessert was unexpectedly good. Dinner seemed pleasant enough with the boys chatting among each other, or with the staff member at their table, where there was one. After dinner everybody headed for the television room or the lounge, while two boys stayed behind to do the washing and drying, this being on a rota of two different boys each week.

The first evening wasn't too bad. I sat in the TV room with Mr Mears and several other boys, some of them asking my name and making general conversation with the usual questions: 'Where are you from?', 'How old are you?', 'What do you think of it so far?' Then they proceeded to give me their opinion about Danesbury School, the other boys and staff and the kind of things that generally went on there. But most of the older boys chose to weigh me up and figure me out from a distance with the occasional glance. The evening passed with relative ease and without incident, then bedtime arrived. I was in one of the main dormitories with three other boys. We all changed into our pyjamas, got washed, brushed our teeth, and then got into bed. When everyone was in bed, Mr Mears came round and closed all the doors.

'Goodnight, you lot,' he said, closing our dormitory door.

'Goodnight, sir,' answered the boys in my dorm in unison.

There was some hushed chit-chat from the other three boys in my dorm, with the occasional question thrown my way, but I soon fell asleep in my more modern single bed.

I don't know how long I'd been asleep when I was woken by what felt like warm water being poured over my head. When I tried to open my eyes, it jetted into my face. Although it was quite dark, it didn't take long for the moonlight coming in through the window to reveal that it was not warm water being poured onto my head and into my face, it was in fact one of the bigger boys pissing on me. The bastards couldn't even let me settle in for one night.

I jumped out of bed and away from the stream of piss and ran out to the bathroom, leaving the bigger boy and his two stupid friends laughing and giggling away to themselves. This bigger boy and his two minions were from the dorm next to mine. They'd come in to welcome me to the school with some sort of sick initiation process, only I didn't have any say in it. I washed my hair and returned to my piss-soaked bed. By now, the other boys had returned to their dorm. I stripped the sheets off and turned the mattress over, then folded my towel over three times to act as a pillow as the real pillow was soaking wet too. So, was this how it was going to be every single night? Pissed-on heads and who knows what other goings-on? Time would tell. For now I was sure their stupid antics were over, so I tried to fall asleep again.

The next morning we were woken by Mr Mears, who noticed my bedding and pillow on the floor.

'What's all this?' he said, pointing.

'It's wet,' I said.

'Wet, how did they get wet? Did you wet the bed?' he asked.

Kids who wet the bed in these places were not unusual, even in their early teens.

'No, somebody decided to use my head as a toilet during the night,' I told him, slightly surprised at my own words. However, two things were going on right then: I was growing in confidence, and I was well and truly pissed off.

'Who?'

'I don't know,' I said.

And that was the truth. Even if I did know, over the years I'd learned that grassing on other boys in places like this would bring me a whole load of trouble.

'Matthews, who was it?' he said, turning to one of my dorm mates.

'I don't know, sir, it was nobody in here,' he replied.

Mr Mears was angry at what had happened. He stormed out into the corridor and started yelling.

'Right, you lot! I'm going to give the culprit one chance to come forward, and one chance only, or everybody will be punished. Who pissed on Nigel during the night?'

'*Who*?' shouted one boy.

'The new boy.'

Nobody answered.

'I'm waiting.'

Still nobody answered.

'Right, have it your way, but somebody's going to have to pay for a new mattress and pillow and I think you can all guess who that's going to be. Final chance to come forward, there's no need for everyone to suffer.'

Nothing.

'Right, no pocket money for any of you for a month!'

'Oh, sir …' came the remonstrations and grumbles from the boys.

'Well, do you think mattresses grow on bloody trees? Now, get washed and dressed and downstairs for breakfast,' he ordered.

Then he came back to me: 'Scoop those up and follow me,' he said.

I grabbed the bedclothes and followed him down to the laundry room, where I dumped them in a large laundry basket before heading back upstairs to get washed and dressed.

Downstairs in the dining room some of the older boys were giving me filthy looks as if it was my fault they had just lost their pocket money for the next four weeks. After breakfast we headed out onto the large concrete playground and waited for school to start. This was where all the boys from the three houses, and the girls from their building, got together and hung out, talking in small groups, while a few of the boys kicked a football between two makeshift goals, one goal being a brick side wall to a storeroom, while the other one (about 60 feet away) was between two horizontal white lines painted on the wall of the gym. The housemasters from the three houses would supervise, along with two or three of the teaching staff, who came in during school hours for the sole purpose of attempting to educate the ineducable.

One of the staff members blew his whistle and everybody went and formed lines in front of the gym. There were four lines, girls at the front, and three lines of boys behind them; each house had its own colour jumper as part of the school uniform. My house (Greys) wore navy-blue jumpers. We lined up in the order in which we first arrived at the school – the person who had been at the school the longest was at the far left and the newest boy (in this case, me) was at the far right. Everybody else from the other houses kept looking round to check out the new kid. The longest-serving resident from each house would count everybody in their line and, when asked by the teacher at the front, he/she would say how many were in his/her house and how many were AWOL (Absent Without Official Leave). Then, we'd all stream off to our set classes according to individual timetables.

My first class of the day was Maths. There were about 16 boys from the three separate houses; the girls did all their classes separately. It wasn't long before the class was disrupted by a delinquent who thought it would be funny to throw a sodden wet fistful of bunched-up toilet roll at the blackboard while the teacher had his back to the class. This idiot had soaked a quarter-roll of toilet paper in water and brought it back from his toilet break, then waited for his opportunity. The paper splattered against the blackboard, startling the teacher, who spun around.

'Right, who threw that? Come on, who did it?'

Nobody said anything, but there were a few muted giggles.

'Right, you're all on detention! Thirty minutes after school.'

'But, sir,' said one boy.

'Oh, sir, that's not fair!' protested another.

'You know the rules, if the perpetrator doesn't own up, everybody gets punished.'

There were grumbles as well as a few more giggles. I knew straight away that these idiots would never learn, not even the hard way.

'Davidson, get up here and clean this board,' added the teacher.

'But, sir, it wasn't me!'

'I don't bloody care! Just get up here and clean it up … If I have to ask you again you'll be staying behind for an hour.'

The boy huffed and reluctantly made his way to the blackboard and started scraping the soggy toilet paper off and into the bin. And this was pretty much how it went in most of the classes on most of the days. Those delinquent boys and girls respected nothing, valued nothing and cared for nothing or nobody – for them, it was easier to destroy than to create.

So, after school, on my first day, I had to stay behind and write lines with one other boy from my house and a bunch of boys from the other two houses. This meant that when I did get back to the house, 30 minutes late, I had to explain why I'd been in detention after school. As it was only my first day, the housemaster, Mr Mears, cut me some slack.

After dinner some of the boys came into the TV room, where I was sitting and started making general conversation.

'Do you like The Beat?' asked one boy.

'Come on, Adam! Leave him alone, he's new,' said another.

'I'm only messing about,' said Adam, giving me a friendly shove on the shoulder.

Adam Pearce was one of the bigger boys. Fifteen years old, he had been at Danesbury for nearly two years. He was definitely one of the top dogs around there. The current craze at Danesbury was for a boy to ask another if he liked The Beat, as in the English 2 Tone Ska band. If you said yes, the boy would punch you. Everybody thought this was highly amusing, but after several dead arms I imagined that it would start to wear a little thin. Pretty much all the boys at Danesbury were into music and football. The music scene at the school seemed to be divided up into two main camps: Ska and New Romantic, with a few boys and girls who were not really fussed and liked just about anything and everything.

Football was also huge, with the majority being supporters of the London clubs Spurs, Arsenal, Chelsea and West Ham, with a few lower division sides thrown in. Although I'd never really been into football up to this point, apart from showing an interest in Liverpool with my friend Perry, back in Grange, I found myself favouring Arsenal on the count that Highbury was only a few miles away from where my mum lived and a boy whom I befriended was a Gooner. So far in life I hadn't found any social circle that I felt comfortable in, not even close, and from what I'd seen at Danesbury so far, I wasn't about to find one here. I would continue to remain a loner, alienating myself from the other boys, and for the most part keeping myself to myself.

The evening came and went, and bedtime arrived. I was more than a little anxious that there might be a repeat of the pissing antics from the night before. Fortunately, there wasn't, but something else did happen. About half an hour after lights out, when the night staff had settled in the staff bedroom, three older boys from the dorm next door came into my dorm and headed straight for my bed. It was nothing to do with me; it just so happened that my bed was in the corner, next to the window, and they needed to clamber over it to get out of that window. Because we were on the first floor, they would climb out of the window, heave themselves up onto the flat roof, run across it and climb down on the other side. They would then run off down into the town centre (about a 10-minute walk), break into a newsagent's to steal a tube or two of Evo-Stik and some packets of crisps. Afterwards they would tip out the crisps and squirt some of the glue into the pack then inhale the fumes to get a buzz, otherwise known as 'glue sniffing'.

Other times they would break into a chemist's to steal a bottle of Zoff (a seriously strong cleaning solvent), which they would pour onto their jacket sleeves to sniff for the buzz. I wondered what kind of damage all this glue and solvent sniffing was doing to their brain cells, as I overheard them bragging about their nocturnal runaway antics, not that this lot had much in the way of brain cells to damage.

Once in a while they would also break into a pub to help themselves to free beer or steal a car and go for a joyride. In all instances, they were usually caught by the police, kept in the cells overnight and then driven back to school the following day to await their magistrate's court appearance on charges of burglary, theft, TDA (a former term for auto theft), to name a few.

Police cars turning up left, right and centre and social workers picking boys up to take them to attend magistrate's court for crimes they had committed while absconding from Danesbury or at home on weekend leave were all par for the course. Although most of the boys got swept along in all this crap, I never submitted to peer pressure, which only made things worse for me.

Chapter 29

Fight Club

My 14th birthday came and went, pretty much unnoticed, just as the previous year at Pelham House. The only thing birthdays meant to me these days was that I was a year closer to adulthood and therefore a year closer to being released from the so-called 'care' system I was involuntarily embroiled in. I wasn't even allowed to go home for my birthday, although it was on a Saturday. They didn't let anybody home during the first three months after arriving at Danesbury, they considered it a settling-in period and figured a home visit would be detrimental. However, my mum did make the effort to hop on a train to come and see me that Saturday. It was quite an easy journey for her, compared to Pelham House. Five quick stops on the Northern Line from Kentish Town to Old Street, then a 45-minute overground journey to Hertford Town, followed by a 15-minute walk through town and up the hill.

She came with Jonathan and stayed for about two hours. I showed her around and we talked, but we didn't really have a two-way conversation. I would talk and my mum would not really listen, then she would talk about some irrelevant kitchen-sink drama going on in her life that didn't interest me in the least. Now that I was 14 I was starting to voice my opinions more strongly, and before too long Mum and me had stopped seeing eye-to-eye altogether. Now I wasn't going to listen to all her futile nonsense or crazy ideas anymore.

Every month it was something different: 'I'm going to start breeding cats' or 'I'm going into fish breeding' or 'I'm going to get into breeding guinea pigs in a big way'. No business plan, nothing. She'd just head on out to the pet shop and blow her fortnightly widow's allowance on two guinea pigs and a cage, plonk them down in the back garden and that was it. And if she wasn't going on about her next 'big' idea, she'd be complaining about this one or that one because they had more money than her – usually the wealthy people she was cleaning for, with their 'fancy bloody degrees'. She'd even started to complain non-stop about Anthony (now 19 years old, still in his bedsit with his girlfriend and working as a painter and decorator) and how he didn't come to see her as often, and when he did, he didn't give her money. I was still annoying her with my constant requests to go home to live with her again, but as usual, she was still refusing. The idea of living at home, even with the inevitable bickering and arguing that would follow, was still better than being stuck at Danesbury, where I was surrounded by illiterate, uneducated, delinquent morons who thrived on fighting, destruction, smoking, sniffing glue and other disgusting behaviour, criminal activities and mayhem.

When my mum and Jonathan left two hours later I felt mentally exhausted and severely depressed, as if someone had dumped on me. It was actually a relief when they left, but it would take until the next day before my resulting depression would lift.

The weeks rolled along and I was alienating myself from the other boys more and more, just as I had in the past. I'd tried to mix in, but I had absolutely nothing in common with any of them. There were one or two boys who were the exception, with whom I would hang around from time to time, but generally I preferred to be with the staff. I just wasn't like the other boys and I didn't want to be like them either. There were about six day staff, who rotated in pairs from one week to the next, plus a part-time young woman who worked some evenings and weekends. Over the months I'd got to know them all. Some of them were quite cruel and spiteful and loved to humiliate. Often they dished out brutality and hardship for no good reason and didn't seem to give a toss about the boys they were supposed to be caring for. While purportedly providing care for us they meted out abuse. To them, we were all an expendable demographic. Mr Mears and the part-time woman were the exception.

Mr Mears seemed genuine, while the part-time woman, Miss Smith (or 'Eleanor', as I would come to call her when none of the other staff members was within earshot), was incredible. Eleanor was in her late twenties and I developed a serious crush on her. She was beautiful, slim with long blonde hair and mesmerising green eyes. Even though she was a vegetarian hippy, she didn't dress as if she was on her way back from a CND march, she wore smart hippy clothes and had an element of class about her. Eleanor didn't mind me calling her by her first name and she had plenty of time for me and was always ready to listen to my problems. We got on well and I even fantasised that she really liked me too and one day, when I got out of there, we would get married and live together.

Mr Mears was about 36 years old. He didn't have any children of his own, but he was married and I often met his wife, Julie, for he was the live-in housemaster, which meant she lived there too. Like Eleanor, Mr Mears also had plenty of time for me and I enjoyed our conversations. I liked Eleanor and Mr Mears so much I started to show an interest in their lives outside Danesbury, what they liked and what they were interested in. Whenever we talked I would learn something new with every conversation.

I understood from quite an early age that we have one mouth and two ears for a reason and later in life I would read a quote by the Dalai Lama, who once said, 'When you talk, you are only repeating what you already know; but when you listen, you may learn something new.'

Like the previous places I'd been in, there was a lot of bullying and before too long I was introduced to 'Fight Club' against my will. This was a pastime that two of the older boys would indulge in. They would pick two of the younger boys, 13 or 14, and send one of their minions to bring them to the living room, where they would then make them fight for their entertainment, all very primitive. Up until then, I'd been excluded from this club, possibly because I was new, but they now felt that my initiation was due. Like in the movie of the same name that came several years later, the first time you went into Fight Club, you had to fight. But being the pacifist that I was, I refused outright and tried to leave the room, but was stopped by two minions.

'Get back in here, you've got to fight,' said Dixon, founder of the Fight Club.

'No, I don't,' I insisted.

The small crowd, knowing the rules, laughed.

'Yeah, you do,' said Dixon.

'Well, I'm not going to.'

'So you're saying that Marsden is tougher than you?' he said.

Timothy Marsden was a few months older than me and had been there about a year. A little shit with a foul tongue, he ran around acting all big and tough, but usually he only beat on boys who were smaller than him.

'No, I'm not saying that, I'm just saying I'm not going to fight him just because you tell me to.'

This comment got some jeers and grunts from the other boys.

'You just don't get it, do you, Cooper? Thing is, if you don't fight him, I'll fight *you*. That's just how it works,' he said.

'Not for me it doesn't,' I told him, trying to force my way past the two minions.

I got as far as grabbing the door handle, when Dixon grabbed me by the hair and pulled me back into the room. Before I knew what had happened he had landed about five successive hard punches to my face. They stung like hell and left me dazed and disoriented, but I was conscious enough to be aware of the boys leaving the room and chuckling away to themselves. I pulled myself together and could taste the blood in my mouth. My nose and mouth were bleeding badly, so I headed out into the corridor towards the washrooms on the ground floor. That's when Eleanor saw me.

'Oh my God, what happened to you?' she said.

'I'm OK, I just need to get cleaned up,' I explained.

I wasn't about to say who it was; I was now well and truly accustomed to the rules of these places. But she could see through the blood and tears and knew something else was wrong. She followed me into the washrooms and helped me with my bleeding face.

'Oh dear, just look at you!' she exclaimed, dabbing away at the blood from my split lip with wet paper hand towels. She continued dabbing and dealing with my bloody nose with the odd sympathetic comment.

I think it is fair to say that Eleanor knew a lot more about my life than I did about hers. Although I'd asked her many questions about her life, I had told her my entire life story and how I came to be at Danesbury. When I'd told her, there were tears in her eyes and I could see that she desperately wanted to help me, but what could she do? She knew I should not be in such a place, and had told me so, but her hands were tied.

There was no doubt that Eleanor had a soft spot for me. After she cleaned me up she went on the warpath, determined to find out who the culprits were. I'd never seen her so mad before and it was good to know that she truly cared and was fighting in my corner.

A few weeks later it was business as usual with Fight Club, but because of the incident with me, Fight Club nights were only on when Eleanor was not on duty. I was dragged into the makeshift Fight Club room on several occasions and, as usual, I refused to fight and took a beating from Dixon or some of his bigger minions, which usually resulted in a bloody nose, black eye, fat lip or even sore ribs if one of them decided to kick me while I was down. Eventually, they knew I was not a sport and gave up summoning me to the Fight Club room. But, outside Fight Club, I was still one of the main targets of bullying, name-calling and teasing, not only from the older boys in my house, but boys from the other two houses also during school hours.

I continued to keep myself to myself and eventually I got my head down and started to read novels, which proved to be a good form of sanctuary. As the saying goes, 'A book a day keeps reality away'. I devoured *The Rats* by James Herbert, then three Stephen King novels back to back: *Carrie*, *Salem's Lot*, then *Firestarter*. It was great! Reading a novel meant I could be somebody else, at least for an hour a day for seven days before becoming another character in another novel, and when there were no books, I always had the moon to fall back on.

I was about six months into my stay at Danesbury and things were not going well at all. The bullying had escalated and there were only two boys in the entire school who would have anything to do with me. Sure, I'd alienated myself, again, but for good reason:

I just wanted to be left alone to get through what was probably going to be my last care home before making my way out into the big world alone. But the other boys didn't let up, the bullying and name-calling and all sorts of other vile crap continued, while some of the staff got their kicks from meting out abuse and generally making life as difficult as humanly possible. One of their favourite petty torments was to wait until you were just about to go to school, then shout you back to tell you that your bed was not made correctly. I'd be escorted up to my dorm to find my bed had been stripped and all the sheets and blankets had been tossed onto the floor. I'd have to spend ten minutes making it all over again. The fact that I'd made my bed with military precision with 'hospital corners' didn't matter. The bed was perfect, this was just their way of making me late for school. Why? So I'd be held back for detention after school for being late. Then, when I got back to my house 30 minutes late, the same person, who'd deliberately messed my bed up that morning, could clout me around the head several times before setting me a ton of house-cleaning duties, which would take up my entire evening. And, if I complained about it, it would all be repeated the next day. In time, I turned 'smiling and looking happy and grateful for my punishment' into a fine fucking art – a difficult thing to do when you are boiling over with rage and frustration.

I was sick and tired of being bullied, abused and called every disgusting name under the sun – who the hell were they, anyway? And on top of all this, I was hardly getting an education during school hours – it was a joke. So, one evening after school I ran away, which was far easier to do than any other place I'd found myself in. For one, this school wasn't in the middle of nowhere; it was on the edge of a large town with a railway station. It was about seven in the evening and most of the boys were either in the TV room or the recreation room. The two members of staff on duty that evening, Mr Glover and his fiancée, Miss Haines, were busy in the office talking about their upcoming wedding. I grabbed my coat and sneaked out the kitchen door, across the football pitch and through a gap in the hedge to avoid being spotted, which I inevitably would have been, had I tried to leave via the main gate. It would be perhaps an hour before anyone realised I was gone and by then I'd be almost home, I figured. I headed down the hill and across town to the railway station.

Fifteen minutes later I was on a train to Old Street, London. Naturally I didn't have any money so my skills of avoiding ticket inspectors and ducking through barriers were once again called upon. I got to Old Street and changed for the Tube to Kentish Town without a hiccup. There was a 50:50 chance of there being a ticket inspector at Kentish Town as I'd been through there before. At the top of the high escalator was a small ticket booth where an inspector would sit and, as you walked through, you had to pass your ticket through a small hatch. Most passengers, especially during rush hour, would simply drop their ticket on this side of the hatch and not bother to slide it through. In anticipation of this I hatched a plan. I found an out-of-date discarded ticket on the platform and intended to place the ticket this side of the small hatch as I passed through and then, accidentally-on-purpose, drop it on the floor. The ticket inspector would have to come out of his small cubicle to retrieve the ticket, probably shouting after me at the same time, by which time I'd be long gone.

Passing the ticket booth at Kentish Town ended up being easier than I'd anticipated. It seemed I'd worried for nothing, as there was no inspector inside, which was not unusual during quieter times outside the rush hour.

I walked down Kentish Town Road towards my house. When I rang the bell, Jonathan answered. He looked surprised to see me, but not half as surprised as my mum when I waltzed into the living room. I don't know why, but I'd got it into my head that she'd be pleased to see me, that she'd be happy I'd found my way home, but no.

'What the bloody hell are you doing here?' she said.

'I don't like it there, it's horrible and I want to come home,' I explained.

'Oh, 'eck! Come and sit down. Are you hungry?'

'No,' I said, longing instead for her undivided attention while I explained my reasons for not wanting to be at Danesbury anymore.

'Sit down. Let me just go to the toilet and then you can tell me all about it.'

She headed downstairs to the toilet, leaving Jonathan and me in the living room. The television was on, but I was not interested in watching it. I waited for my mum to return so I could state my case and plead with her to let me stay at home.

'OK, what's going on?' she wanted to know.

'I hate it there, everyone's horrible to me all the time and I keep getting beaten up by the bigger boys.'

'Oh dear, what happened to your eye?' she said.

'Somebody punched me,' I said, surprised she didn't ask me about it the second I set foot in the living room. Hell, it was obvious enough!

So I proceeded to tell her about all the bullying and beatings I was taking from the other boys and the cruel and unusual punishments that certain members of staff dealt out for things that weren't even my fault. I went on and on, and I told her about all the horrible things that were happening to me there and that I wasn't even getting an education. But then my pleading and begging was interrupted by the doorbell. Mum got up to answer it and 30 seconds later she came back into the living room, two uniformed police officers right behind her.

'I'm sorry, son, but you'll have to go back, you can't stay here,' she said.

I couldn't believe it – she didn't really go to the toilet, she'd called the police using the downstairs phone – a total betrayal by my own mother.

'Come on, let's be going,' said one of the officers.

'But, Mum, *please*, I don't want to go back …'

'Come on, let's go! Don't make it difficult for yourself, you've got to go back to your school,' said the other officer, stepping closer.

'Look, you can come home for the weekend again soon, OK?' said my mother.

'But I want to stay here now,' I insisted.

'Come on, let's go,' said one of the officers, leaning down and taking my arm.

I stood up and momentarily lost balance due to my shaking legs.

'Don't worry, we'll get him back safely,' said the officer, escorting me out of the living room.

'Thanks a lot, I'm sorry I had to call you out,' said Mum.

She closed the door behind us without saying another word. One of the officers put me in the back of the police car then jumped in the front seat while his colleague started up the engine. The car pulled away and the officers were silent. About a mile up the road the officer in the passenger seat spoke.

'Pull in here,' he said, 'in there,' he continued, pointing.

The driver turned off the main road and into an abandoned piece of land with some demolished old warehouses and piles of railway sleepers and the odd length of rusty steel railway track.

'Just stop here,' he said.

Suddenly I was very scared. There was no reason for the officers to stop here. The officer in the passenger seat got out of the car and opened my rear door.

'Get out,' he told me.

'Why?' I said.

'Don't fuckin' answer me back, just get out!' he said, reaching in and dragging me out by the hair.

His colleague got out too and came around to my side of the car. Before I knew what had happened he'd smacked me around the head really hard.

'We've got better things to do than drive little runaway cunts like you back to whatever fuckin' home you came from!'

Petrified of these two big men in their intimidating uniforms I didn't say anything, but I was aware that a little urine had escaped my bladder and I was shaking.

'Do we look like a fucking taxi service?' said the other one. '*Well?*' he persisted.

'No,' I said, crying.

Then he punched me in the stomach, winding me badly. I fell to the floor, holding my midriff and scarcely able to breathe – adults can hit really hard. It reminded me of when I was thrown from that rope swing, years ago. I struggled for breath, but it didn't want to come.

'Get up, you little cunt, and get back in that car before I give you something to *really* cry about!'

Then my breath came; I inhaled deeply, tears flooding my face. Petrified beyond belief, it was a real struggle to maintain control of my bladder. One of the officers grabbed me by the hair, shoved me into the back of the car and slammed the door. They both got back in the front, the driver started up the engine and then the car pulled out of the wasteland and back onto the main road.

'I don't want to hear a fuckin' peep from you all the way back, OK?'

But I didn't answer; I was just too scared.

Mr Glover took me inside Greys House and the first thing he did was whack me around the head. By now it was 10.45 p.m. and all the other boys were in bed.

'Right, get up those bloody stairs and get to bed and don't make a bloody sound! If you run away again, you'd better make sure you don't get caught or your life won't be worth living, do you understand?'

'Yes, sir.'

The next morning we were woken up, as usual, only this morning things were going to be a little different for me.

'OK, everybody up,' said Mr Glover, entering my dorm. 'You can stay in your pyjamas and slippers,' he told me, giving me an angry look.

The other boys in my dorm just looked at me. So I got washed and brushed my teeth, then went and sat on my bed while the others got dressed.

Mr Glover came back in and saw me. 'What are you sitting there for? Get downstairs for breakfast!' he said.

I was confused, but would soon learn that runaways had all their clothes taken away and had to wear pyjamas and slippers for anything up to a month to prevent them from running away again. And it worked too; I imagined I'd look like an escaped mental patient and somebody would call the police if I were seen heading across town towards the railway station in my PJs. Mr Glover told me I'd have to wear my pyjamas and slippers for two weeks before I could have my clothes back. I had to wear them to school, to the gym, to breakfast, dinner and tea, everywhere. It was so humiliating, having to stand in line out on the schoolyard with everybody else staring and laughing at me. Just as well it was now summer or I'd be freezing my arse off!

If I thought that was the end of my punishment, then I thought wrong. After lunch I was told to go over to the main building to see the headmaster before going to class. So I knocked on his office door.

'Come,' said a deep voice.

I opened the door and entered.

'I'm rather disappointed in you, young man. You've wasted police time, you've wasted our time and you've upset your mother,' he told me. 'Now, we don't tolerate boys or girls running away from Danesbury and anybody who does must be punished. Now, do you understand?'

'Yes, sir.'

'Good,' he said, grabbing his cane from the corner. 'OK, bend over that desk.'

I knew the routine so I did as he said, but I didn't pull my pyjamas down and he didn't ask me to. Not that the thin PJs offered much in the way of protection and I didn't have any underpants on underneath either. He drew his cane back and whacked my backside six times. The pain brought tears to my eyes and I winced with each stroke.

'OK, stand up,' he told me.

I did so, my backside fizzing in pain.

'Now, hold out your hands, palms up …'

I hadn't expected to be caned on the palms too – I was sure the caning on my backside would have been enough, not to mention the fact that I'd have to wear my pyjamas and slippers for the next two weeks.

'Come on, come *on*! I don't have all day and you've a class to get to.'

I held out both my hands and squeezed my eyes tight in anticipation. The whipping sound as his cane came down through the air and the cracking sound it made on my right hand and the sharp pain were instantaneous. I flinched and closed up my hand. Before I had a chance to open my eyes to survey my palm he'd brought his cane down on my other palm. Then he sent me on my way, both palms on fire and stinging with agony, which made holding pens and pencils most uncomfortable that afternoon. But the punishment didn't stop there for after dinner that evening I was told that I was on washing-up duty.

'But it's not my turn,' I protested.

'It is now, you can take over from Dixon and Pearce,' said Mr Glover.

In the kitchen a pile of pots, pans and crockery was building up into a monumental heap. Usually there were two boys who did this chore, one washed while the other dried, and even that took long enough when doing it by hand. But when you had to wash and dry manually, on your own, after 15 boys and two members of staff – well, it's hardly a two-minute job.

'Well, get a move on, they're not going to wash themselves,' said Mr Glover.

'But who's going to help me?'

'*Help*? Nobody's going to help! Maybe you should think about that next time you plan to run away.'

I took the top plate off the huge pile and went to dunk it in the deep sink full of water and almost scalded my hand in the process because it was so hot. So I went to mix some cold water in to bring the temperature down, but, as I reached for the cold tap, Mr Glover shouted, 'Don't you *dare* add any cold water, just get on and start washing!'

'But, sir, the water's too hot.'

'I don't care, get your hands in there and wash!'

The sadistic bastard had filled the deep stainless steel sink to the brim with hot water to make my life even harder and more painful than it already was.

Typical! Punishment wasn't enough, he had to make it as difficult as possible with yet another of those petty tortures that he found so amusing. I had to dig deep inside my soul again to find that little nugget that gave me the will to survive, then I plunged my hands into the almost-scalding water and got to work. It was so hot I could only keep my hands in the water for a brief second to dip the plates, but Glover insisted that I scrub them underwater. My hands were turning red with the heat and the cane marks on my palms burned with increasing pain because of it. I tried to travel to the moon in my head, but the hot water kept dragging me back down to earth. After about 15 minutes the water temperature started to drop to a more manageable level. Efficient as I was, it still took me over an hour to complete the task, which included wiping down all the dining-room tables and sweeping and mopping the floors afterwards.

Of course, this made me late for school and my first teacher was not sympathetic either. He told me to come back and see him for detention for 30 minutes after school, when I would have to scrub graffiti off the toilet walls with some chemicals he'd prepared and hot soapy water – no gloves for protection here either. The cleaning chemicals were getting into my sore palms and burning like fire. This made me late back to my house, where Glover was waiting to dish out still more punishment for being late in from school.

'I don't care and I don't want to hear it. This is what happens when you run away, Cooper,' he said in response to my explanation.

After dinner, and after I'd done all the washing, drying, wiping, sweeping and mopping, he escorted me to the cleaning cupboard and presented me with a bucket, sponge and chamois leather. He made me wash and dry all the ground-floor windows to Greys House as punishment for being back late from school, which took me the best part of 90 minutes. And for the final punishment he would not let me sit in the TV room to watch *The Professionals*. Instead, I was sent to bed early, in the pyjamas I was already wearing.

And this is how it went on for the rest of the week, with four days of relentless punishment: washing, drying, wiping, sweeping, mopping. Detention after school for being late for school because I was busy being punished, then more punishment and chores after school for being late back from school due to being punished for being punished. No TV, early to bed, and if that wasn't enough, runaways were not allowed home for three months either. The whole system was designed to break you, to force you to submit to their will – it was all about fear and control.

On the final day of my punishment, Eleanor arrived on duty, and just in the nick of time for I needed to see a friendly face. I was so embarrassed that she had to see me in my pyjamas early in the evening, but she understood and had the decency not to mention it. I wasn't on washing-up duty anymore and, as a consequence, the knock-on effect of all my other punishments subsided. I still had to wear my pyjamas and slippers for another week, though. It was just after nine in the evening and all the boys were in the TV room, watching a programme while I was in the recreation room, reading. When I heard Eleanor and Mr Mears talking, I got up to go to the toilet and I thought I heard my name being mentioned in a low voice, so I edged my way a little closer to the office door, which was ajar, and listened carefully.

'Nigel shouldn't even be here; it's an approved school that's set up to deal with a different kind of problem entirely. The poor boy's sister and father died when he was only seven and his mum couldn't cope. What's happened to Nigel isn't his fault, he's a victim of circumstance and shouldn't have to suffer like this,' said Eleanor.

'I understand what you're saying and don't think I haven't noticed that he's not like the rest because I have,' said Mr Mears.

'So what can we do about it?' she persisted.

'Unfortunately, nothing – it's down to his social worker, not us.'

'It's a damn shame! Did you know his social worker tried to find him foster parents but there were none available? That's why he ended up in hellholes like this,' she added.

'Eleanor, I know you're a passionate woman, but you can't talk like that around here. Our hands are tied and we just have to make the best of it,' he said.

'I have to witness violence and abuse every time I come to work and it's really starting to get to me …'

'Eleanor, you can't get attached like this, try and keep some sort of emotional distance.'

'I can't do that, Sam, I'm human – unlike some of the savages working here.'

'Eleanor, that's *enough*!'

'I'm sorry, I just …'

It felt so good to hear Eleanor fighting in my corner, and Mr Mears understanding.

The week passed and Saturday arrived. I got my clothes back and who better to bring them to me at waking-up time than Eleanor herself, with a big beaming smile on her face? Most of the boys had gone home for the weekend and there were just three of us left: me, Chris Hutchinson and Justin Clarkson. Great! No big bully boys, and best of all, Eleanor was on duty all weekend.

It was the first break I'd had since I'd arrived there, and what a break it was. No sign of Glover or his equally despicable wife-to-be, Miss Haines, just a small skeleton staff. That afternoon Eleanor took the three of us to town and after that, as a surprise, she took us back to her flat and made us sandwiches and drinks. It was amazing and I felt normal for the first time in, well, a long time. Eleanor's flat smacked of hippy – an acoustic guitar in the corner, a CND sign here, a peace sign there and other psychedelic artwork and rainbow-coloured objects – but it was cosy and full to the brim with love. The only thing, or rather, things, that put a slight downer on the afternoon was the fact that I had to share her company with Hutchinson and Clarkson, but every now and then, she gave me a lovely smile, something I didn't see her do with the other two boys.

Sunday went the same way, just me, the other two and Eleanor. But as the cliché goes, all good things must come to an end. At 5.30 p.m. the other boys poured in from their weekend leave, and the more that arrived, the noisier it became. The serene mood, the soothing feeling of love and kindness, transitioned into a boisterous racket of angry delinquent testosterone. It was like a neutron bomb landing in the middle of a beautiful green meadow full of God's magnificent creatures as they grazed and basked in the love of his son. But now I had a wonderful new memory to replay whenever I went to the moon. I'd been touched by Eleanor's love and she'd invited me into her flat and her life. I longed for her part-time shifts to come around just so we could grab a few moments together to talk about the nice things that went on outside Danesbury. But then something happened and my world crumbled into a million tiny pieces.

A few more months had passed, it was a weekend and I was still not allowed home. Eleanor had come on duty and she called me into the office.

'Nigel, I'm afraid I've got some bad news,' she said.

I was worried; I'd never seen that look on Eleanor's face before. I knew this wasn't going to be good, but I could never have prepared myself for what she was about to say.

'I'm afraid I'm leaving.'

'What, I don't understand, why?'

'Personal reasons … I just can't do this anymore.'

She didn't have to say any more, I should have seen it coming. How a kind, loving, compassionate, peace-promoting, animal-loving vegetarian lady like Eleanor could be expected to carry on working in a place like this, witnessing the brutality and abuse, well, if I'm honest, I don't know how she stuck it for as long as she did. With hindsight, Eleanor simply didn't fit. But this was no time to be selfish. I had to take my own feelings out of the equation and appreciate the time she had given me – the love, the compassion, the understanding – the 'hope'.

'I … I understand,' I said, looking deep into her eyes, and I truly did.

She leaned forward, pulled me close and gave me a big hug, not just a brief 'goodbye' hug but a hug that lasted a good minute, a hug that would charge me with her love and keep me going for a while. Then she kissed me on the forehead and then my cheek, the edge of her lips touching the edge of mine.

'I'm not leaving for another month so we'll still see each other and talk lots more.'

'I know.'

The rest of 1980 ambled along with some hard-hitting newsworthy events on the way: the Iranian Embassy Siege had bolstered The Iron Lady's reputation, the Pac-Man video game came out, some of the boys and girls started bringing Rubik's Cubes back from their weekend leave, a new virus called AIDS had been identified and at the end of the year, on 8 December, John Lennon was shot dead. But for me, and a handful of other boys and girls at the school, the most significant news event happened right under our noses one Monday afternoon in December. A 15-year-old boy called Carl Fisher had climbed out onto the roof of the main building and was threatening to jump off onto the concrete playground below. The main building was two storeys high, but the added part of the roof put him three storeys up. Although he wasn't a victim of bullying, some of the staff had targeted him for cruel and unusual punishments and petty torments. Over time this had taken its toll and he became severely depressed. The woodwork teacher and two of the housemasters were trying to talk him down. A small crowd of us gathered round to see what was going on. Carl was shouting all sorts of abuse at the staff, calling them every name under the sun.

'You're all bastards and you don't care about us!' he yelled.

'Carl, come down so we can talk about this,' said the wood-work teacher.

One of the teachers came over to us and told us to leave.

'Right, you lot, there's nothing to see here, get back to your houses right now!' he said.

We turned to walk away. I'd only got five steps when I heard the woodwork teacher shout.

'Carl, *no!*'

I turned, just in time to see him hit the ground. I flinched at the disturbing sound it made as he impacted against the concrete. There was a dull thud as his body hit the concrete and the crack of his skull echoed across the playground.

He was dead before the ambulance arrived.

Chapter 30

And So The Bullying Ceased

I spent the Christmas week at home with Mum and Jonathan, but I had nothing to feel cheerful about – I was still reeling from having had a front row seat to Carl's suicide.

By now I knew that my being allowed to leave Danesbury to go home to live was not going to happen. This was also confirmed by my consultant psychiatrist, Dr Janet Harper, who had reservations about my leaving Danesbury and going home full time. So, after a not-so-nice Christmas break at home, I made my own way back to Danesbury on the train.

March soon arrived, bringing with it my 15th birthday, which, as before, went pretty much unnoticed as far as the staff and other children were concerned. However, my mother and Mrs Clements sent me a card and a gift. I was now at Danesbury's legal age to smoke cigarettes if I so chose. Pretty much every single boy and girl there who was 15 or over smoked, but it was not something that appealed to me, and somehow this isolated me even more. I didn't conform to the other boys' musical tastes or dress sense and now I didn't smoke either. To them I must have seemed like some kind of freak and I ended up getting even more stick than ever before.

Meanwhile, the military planning that would lead to the Falklands War was building, ships were deployed and the possibility of war was on the news on a daily basis. It was during this time that it was suggested that I leave the school three days a week to do work experience at a pub and restaurant a few miles away. I was really excited about it, mainly because I'd be away from Danesbury. However, it wasn't quite what I expected. I'd built up a picture of a French Cordon Bleu master chef teaching me all sorts of weird and wonderful cooking techniques, but instead I got to peel potatoes, do the washing up and mop the floor at the end of the day and generally be bossed around and told to do all sorts of menial jobs around the kitchen. But at least for a short time I was away.

The weeks continued to amble along and I was still on the frontline of relentless bullying and beatings, but then in April I got a pleasant surprise. Mr Mears called me into his office to tell me that Mrs Clements was coming to see me in two days' time.

I was so pleased and I could hardly wait. Of course, the next day and a half dragged, but then the big day came and Mrs Clements arrived just after lunch. Mr Mears came over to class to fetch me. I couldn't wait to see her.

'Hello, Nigel,' she said, all smiles.

There was another lady I'd never seen before standing with her.

'Hello,' I said.

We hugged briefly.

'You can use the TV room, I'll be in the office if you need me,' said Mr Mears, leaving us to it.

'Nigel, I'd like you to meet Mrs Huminski,' she said. 'She's going to be your new social worker.'

'Hello, Nigel,' she said, in a strong Canadian accent.

'Hello,' I said, shaking her hand.

Although her name didn't suggest it, Mrs Huminski was Canadian. She was younger than Mrs Clements, in her early thirties, with beautiful, long straight blonde hair. Like Mrs Clements, she had a gentle demeanour about her and 30 minutes into our three-way conversation it became obvious that she was a genuinely caring person. I warmed to her and her lovely accent instantly, which pleased Mrs Clements. Mrs Huminski was based at the Social Services office in Kentish Town, near where Mum lived, so she would be able to help me during the remainder of my stay at Danesbury and help me get set up when I left.

'You've really filled out,' Mrs Clements noted, 'I can't believe how you've grown since I last saw you.' Naturally she was pleased that I no longer looked malnourished and three years younger than my actual age. 'You look like a young man now.'

'Thank you,' I muttered, looking down at my shoes to hide my red face.

Mrs Clements and Mrs Huminski only stayed for about an hour as Mrs Clements had a long journey back up north.

'It's been lovely seeing you again and you're looking really well,' she said.

I was thankful that she'd turned up during one of those rare instances when I didn't have a bruise of some sort or another on my face. I didn't like the idea of Mrs Clements knowing how much I was suffering, especially during what was now almost certainly going to be the last time I ever saw her. In our final meeting together I didn't tell her about any of the horrors at Danesbury, there would have been nothing she could have done anyway and it would just upset her. Perhaps I'd dump all that on Mrs Huminski at some point, or maybe I'd simply ride it out now until my 16th birthday, then I'd be out of there anyway.

'OK, Nigel, you take care of yourself and feel free to write to me any time.'

'OK, I will,' I said, feeling choked.

I hugged her for one last time.

'Goodbye, Nigel, it's been great meeting you,' said Mrs Huminski, extending her hand. 'I'll see you again soon, OK?'

'When?' I asked, a little too keenly, shaking her hand and at the same time taking in her lovely perfume.

'Soon,' she said.

They both smiled and then headed off to Mr Mears' office to tell him they were leaving. I spent the afternoon daydreaming in class, thinking about my new social worker, Mrs Huminski. I hoped and prayed she would be able to help set me up with some sort of life when I reached 16, as I certainly didn't have anybody else to help me when I was set free into the big wide world.

May arrived and Bob Marley's death was all over the news. One of the girls, a huge fan, was devastated and started to cry in the playground when she found out. A few of the boys began teasing her for crying until her friend, Tracy 'gutter mouth' Wentworth, punched one of the boys in the face, giving him a nose bleed.

'Christ, Tracy, we're only messin' about!' said another boy, studying his friend's bloodied face.

'Just fuck off, Wakeman!' said Tracy, holding her crying friend.

'She broke my nose,' said Bloody Nose Boy.

'Yeah, and I'll fuckin' break your balls if you don't fuck off, you little cunt!' said Tracy, escorting her sobbing friend away.

'What a nut job!' mumbled Wakeman.

At this Tracy turned around. 'Fuck off, you little cunt!' she said, helping her friend back into the girls' house.

I found it odd that Tracy, who was petite and by far the shortest person at Danesbury, called everybody a little cunt. Tracy 'gutter mouth' Wentworth was a Rude Girl/Skinhead and just as hard as the boys around there; she fought like one too. This wasn't the first time she'd drawn blood from a boy, and it wouldn't be the last. Whenever she had one of her volatile mood swings and beat the crap out of somebody, the staff and other boys were always in hysterics as they witnessed little Tracy fly into some boy with clenched fists, like a maniac. I steered well clear.

A few other events of note occurred in 1981, and something happened to me that would change the way the other boys viewed and treated me in the future. It was all down to something Mrs Clements had said about my appearance and how I'd grown up, filled out and become a young man.

There was this kid called Timothy Marsden, a nasty little shit who'd been giving me constant hassle ever since I refused to fight him in Fight Club – I guess he'd got it into his head that he was tougher than me. The fact that he was just too thick to see that I was a pacifist and hand-to-hand combat did not interest me didn't deter him from constantly trying to pick a fight. I always ignored him, but he just kept on prodding and poking, like a fool antagonising a rattlesnake with a stick. Every time Timothy walked past me in the dorms, corridor or the school class, he would bump into me on purpose, knocking me to one side. He spat at me, called me names and even tested the water with a punch to my stomach every now and then, yet I continued to ignore him in the hope that he would eventually give up. But Marsden was never going to do that, he would always be there, trying to get a rise out of me and, every now and then, punching me.

Well, the day finally came when I'd had a gutful of Marsden and every other boy in the place. I'd been beaten up four times that week by bigger boys and had taken more than I care to mention. I was in the downstairs washrooms cleaning my boots in preparation for a football game the next afternoon when Marsden came in and started up again.

'Come on, Cooper,' he said, shoving me in the shoulder.

'Just go away, Marsden, I'm trying to clean my boots,' I said.

'Don't fuckin' call me Marsden,' he said.

He grabbed the boot out of my hand and threw it across the room.

'Come on, wanker, what ya waiting for?'

I looked up at him. He held his fists up in front, like a boxer. But I just shook my head and picked up my other boot to clean that one instead. This time Marsden was more determined than ever. He grabbed my other boot and hit me on the head with it, hard. That was it; I had a thing about being hit on the head with football boots. Memories of all those boys who had whacked me on the head came flooding back. He was the straw that broke the camel's back.

I'd seen Marsden beat up a few kids in the past so I knew he could handle himself and I wasn't even confident I could beat him, but I was so wound up, he'd brought me to boiling point and beyond. In an instant I leapt up and forward, driving my head into his chest. I kept my forward motion going until his back collided with the tiled wall then I grabbed his balls and squeezed with all my might. Marsden screamed in agony and, while he was trying to figure out how I'd got the better of him, I released my grip, grabbed both his ears and head-butted him in the nose. Now he was in pain at both ends and he didn't know whether to hold his balls or his splattered and bloody nose. I was so angry I didn't stop; I pushed him to the floor, straddled him and rained punches down on his face until I was physically exhausted.

Eventually I got off him and went to the sink to wash his blood off my hands, though some of it was mine, as I'd split the skin on my right-hand knuckles on his teeth. I looked at him in the mirror while I dried my hands on some paper towels. Adrenaline was coursing through my veins and my heart beating so hard it felt like somebody was punching my chest from the inside. I held out my hands to look at the damage to my knuckles – they were shaking uncontrollably.

Meanwhile, Marsden was lying on the floor, hardly moving, just groaning in pain, cupping his face with his hands. I left him there and went to the television room to try to calm down. Then I sat there, trying to hide the fact that I was shaking and my heart was pounding. When no one was looking I took a few deep breaths and tried to calm myself down. I was looking at the TV, but I didn't know what the picture was as my mind was not in the room. About three minutes had passed when another boy came charging into the TV room.

'Sir, sir, come quick, there's something wrong with Marsden!' he said.

Mr Glover got up to follow, as did some of the other boys.

'Stay,' he said.

The other boys did as they were told and sat down. Panic set in as I started to go over the consequences of what I'd done. A minute later, Mr Glover ran into the office and picked up the phone.

'Ambulance, please,' he said.

He gave the address, hung up the phone and came into the TV room and made a beeline for my chair.

'Get up!' he said, grabbing me by the hair and dragging me out of there and into his office.

The other boys in the TV room looked on in shock, not having a clue what was going on.

In the office, Mr Glover whacked me across the head several times with his big meaty hand. I put up my arms to defend myself, but he simply grabbed them and continued to whack me repeatedly.

'Now, let's see how you fuckin' like it!'

WHACK, WHACK, WHACK!

I couldn't believe it, after all the times I'd had the crap beaten out of me by older boys and he never did anything about it. Whenever I got beaten up, whenever I had black eyes, a bloody nose or a split lip, he never asked who did it, he just told me to go and get cleaned up. Yet I beat up just one other kid and there he was, laying into me, like all the other boys owned the franchise on bullying and beatings and I didn't. Eventually he stopped and threw me back onto the spare office chair so hard I flew straight over the edge of it and cracked the back of my head on the corner of a steel filing cabinet. I put my hands up to the back of my head and when I removed them it looked as though I was wearing a pair of claret gloves, blood all over my palms.

'Great, that's all I bloody need!' said Glover, on seeing the blood pouring from my head. 'Get up and sit down,' he ordered me.

He opened one of the office desk drawers and took out a box of tissues and removed a thick wad of them.

'Lean forward,' he instructed me.

He fumbled about, parting my hair and then pushed the wad of tissues hard against my bleeding wound.

'Hold that there, tight,' he said, then he went to attend to Marsden, who was still on the washroom floor.

The ambulance arrived and two paramedics came in through the main door.

'Down here!' shouted Glover, noticing them at the entrance from the end of the corridor.

After about a minute one of the paramedics ran back out to the ambulance and came back with a stretcher. As he passed the office he could see me holding my head, with blood-stained tissue.

'Are you injured too?'

'Yes.'

'OK, sit tight, I'll be back in a minute.'

He took the stretcher to the washroom and returned to look at my head. It can't have been that bad and didn't need stitches. He patched me up and wrapped a bandage around my head to hold the dressing in place. Then he returned to the washrooms. Moments later he and his colleague, followed by Mr Glover, carried Marsden out on the stretcher.

By now the boys in the TV room had found the courage to venture out into the hallway and got a close-up view of Marsden and his busted-up, bloodied face as Mr Glover held the door open for the two paramedics. It actually looked far worse than it was. I heard one of the paramedics say something about his nose needing some attention in A&E.

A few of the boys looked round the corner into the office at me. They knew I had something to do with it and before the evening was out every boy and girl at Danesbury would know that I'd battered Timothy Marsden half to death and that he'd been taken away to hospital. There had been hundreds of fights at Danesbury and, when serious enough, kids were taken to the local hospital as a consequence.

Mr Glover didn't even wait until school hours before taking me over to the headmaster's office to be caned. He'd phoned over to the main building and explained what had happened, what I'd done, and that he was bringing me over.

Later in life I'd read that under corporal punishment law you could only strike a boy between four and six times on the backside, with trousers on. They hardly adhered to those laws in the various children's homes and approved schools I found myself in. The head made me drop my trousers, and underpants, and bend over his desk. I stopped counting at 12 as the pain was too much. Eventually he stopped.

'Now, pull your pants up and get out of my sight!' he told me.

I think he was furious to be pulled from his cosy living quarters and his wife at the end of the main building. As I pulled my underpants and trousers up, my backside was on fire, stinging and throbbing, sending a whole multitude of painful messages to my brain. It was like nothing I'd ever experienced before. For some reason, the headmaster was going for some sort of corporal punishment record, and I think he just achieved it. I could hardly walk to keep up with Mr Glover as he escorted me back to Greys but the pain was worth it because none of the other boys, even the older ones, gave me any shit anymore. Generally, whenever there were seriously violent outbursts and people were badly hurt and hospitalised, the police were never involved (and didn't want to be). The hospital staff just got on with fixing up yet 'another damn delinquent from *that home* up the hill'.

Everyone just kind of left me alone in my world after that.

Chapter 31

Home on Trial

Soon after my uncharacteristic violent outburst in the washroom, something quite unexpected happened. My new Canadian social worker, Mrs Huminski, had somehow, against all the odds, convinced my mum that I should go home on trial. She'd found this 'special' school about three miles from Mum's house called The Arendelle Centre, which was close to Chalk Farm Tube station.

Mrs Huminski had arranged for me to go and spend the day at this day school to see how I got on. She picked me up at Danesbury early on a Monday morning and we arrived at the school in north London at 10.30 a.m.

The Arendelle Centre was a large four-storey Victorian property. In the basement was a recreation/music room, the ground floor had a large teaching room, the first floor housed the dining room, the second floor had two more teaching rooms and there were some offices on the top floor. There were three girls and five boys, aged from 15 to 17. Mrs Huminski left me in the capable hands of the staff and told me she would be back to collect me at 2.30 p.m.

It seemed fine – I chatted with the staff and was shown around and introduced to the others during the course of the morning. I had lunch with them and in the afternoon I hung out in the music room with another boy, Gary, who was 16 years old. A heavy metal nut, he was really into Iron Maiden and had just bought their second album, *Killers*, and kept telling me how great it was. Gary could play guitar a little and knew a few riffs so he plugged the house Stratocaster copy into a battered-up Peavey amp and started playing Deep Purple's 'Smoke On The Water'.

'Can you play the drums?' he asked.

'I've never tried,' I said.

'Go on, sit down, have a go,' he told me, nodding towards a red Pearl drum kit.

So I sat down, picked up the sticks that were balancing across the snare drum, thumped the bass pedal a few times with my right foot and tested the water by hitting the snare and three toms with the sticks.

'Let me show you,' he offered, putting the guitar on its stand.

I hopped off the throne and handed him the sticks.

'Do this,' he said, knocking out a basic beat.

I watched his foot on the bass drum pedal and took note of what his hands were doing; it looked simple enough. So I sat down and tried what he had shown me. And I took to it like a duck to water. Although I didn't know much about music making back then, I was playing a fairly simple 4/4 beat using the bass drum and snare drum with my right foot and left hand while tapping out quaver notes on the closed hi-hat, which I kept closed with my left foot. I continued to play while Gary strapped on his guitar and started to strum 'Smoke On The Water' in time with my drumbeat.

Wow, this is amazing! I thought.

I really got into it, listening to his guitar and playing in perfect time. Before long I was opening and closing the hi-hats and putting in a few fills using the toms. I knew the song really well as I had previously bought an older Deep Purple album called *Machine Head*. One of the teachers came into the room, having heard us from out in the corridor.

'Wow, that's really good!' he said, nodding in time to our Deep Purple cover.

It was brilliant. Gary and I spent the next hour or so jamming away – he'd play various rock songs that he knew (most of which I'd heard before) and I played the drums. I was in my element and felt human for the first time in a very, very long while as I interacted with Gary. The staff, three men and two women, all seemed really nice and I couldn't wait to be living at home again and to get started there at my new day school. Already I had a new friend, Gary, who also lived in Kentish Town.

Mrs Huminski arrived on time and drove me back to Danesbury. During the journey back she asked me what I thought of the new day school, where I'd have to attend between the hours of 9 a.m. and 4.30 p.m., Monday to Friday.

'It's great,' I said.

I then proceeded to tell her about my day at the Arendelle Centre.

I was only back at Danesbury for two weeks before Mrs Huminski came to take me home. I remember the day well. It was mid-morning and I was waiting around with my belongings. I didn't say goodbye to any of the kids as they were all at school, and didn't care to anyway, I just wanted to get the hell out of there. My home trial was designed to be a stepping-stone and then she would help find me my own place to live. For now I would be sharing the large bedroom in the basement with my younger brother, Jonathan. I was so relieved and so happy, my miserable life of brutal children's homes and approved schools finally at an end.

But it didn't stay that way for long.

I'd tried my best to settle at home with Mum and Jonathan, but we just argued all the time and didn't see eye-to-eye about anything.

I didn't see a whole lot of Anthony as he lived elsewhere and I wasn't fussed anyway because we hardly had a *close* relationship. I was growing up and felt like I was on a different wavelength to my mum and we simply could not converse on any level; I refused to go down to hers and she was certainly not capable of coming up to mine. As for the Arendelle Centre, well, that wasn't working out either. Apart from Gary, it soon became apparent that the three girls and the other four boys were delinquents who spent all day misbehaving.

I couldn't stand being surrounded by them for a moment longer so I started to truant. I'd spend my days in the library reading books on all manner of subjects – I wasn't getting any education at the Arendelle Centre and the library was nice and warm and I never bothered the librarians. I was only a few months away from my 16th birthday so maybe the staff at the library assumed I'd already left school and so they weren't concerned about my being there so often for they never called the authorities. But word got back to my social worker from the Arendelle Centre that I hadn't been attending regularly.

At first I'd take one day off each week, which soon turned into two, then three, then I stopped going altogether. On the home front, things were fast coming apart at the seams. Mum and I argued more than ever and Jonathan and I were not on the same wavelength – he annoyed me, which led to me annoying him, which became a vicious circle. There was nothing my social worker could do to help fix the situation. It all seemed like a lost cause. So, after a few short months, my home trial came to an end and I was carted off back to Danesbury. However, my 16th birthday was fast approaching so I knew I wouldn't have to endure the place for too long; soon I'd be free.

Chapter 32

Goodbye, Sister Moon

My final few months at Danesbury went without a hitch; most of the boys still had the memory of what I'd done to poor Timothy Marsden, who was now fine and actually became a good friend during those last few months. I'd heard of similar friendships developing out of violence.

The rules were that you could leave Danesbury when you were 16, so long as you had a job to start and somewhere to live. I knew I was going to leave as close to my 16th birthday as possible so I started to prepare myself for leaving, with a seriously questionable education, no qualifications and no prospects. I didn't even get a chance to sit my CSEs as I wanted to get out of there as soon as possible – I'd just have to fill in all the educational gaps at some point in the future.

A few weeks before my birthday, my social worker, Mrs Huminski, informed me that she was going on maternity leave. She introduced me to my new social worker, Mr Gerald Waterman, who promised to do whatever he could for me once I left Danesbury. He told me he could help me get a bedsit or a flat share in London, and he was true to his word. Mr Waterman was a strange little man who'd suffered from polio in the past – his physique reflected this. I felt sorry for him, but I admired how he worked as a social worker and still made the best of life.

My 16th birthday was on a Monday, and I had been allowed home the weekend immediately preceding it. On my way home that Friday afternoon I'd bought a copy of the *London Evening Standard* from the man selling newspapers outside Kentish Town Tube station, with the sole intention of looking for a job. I spent that night looking through the jobs section. There wasn't much in there that I was qualified to do, but one job did seem like a possibility.

Claude's Hair Salon in Swiss Cottage was advertising for a general help. So, first thing the next morning, I phoned to enquire about the job. I spoke to Claude himself, who asked me if I could pop along to see him for an informal interview at lunchtime.

'Yes,' I said.

'Good, I'll see you at 12.30 then,' he said, hanging up the phone.

I was so excited; I knew if I could nail this job I would not have to return to Danesbury on the Sunday night. Even though I was not 16 until the Monday, I was confident I'd be OK. Worst case scenario I'd just say I felt ill and could not return that night, then the next day I'd be 16 anyway, and hopefully, with a job to start. Also, in case I did manage to get a job over the course of the weekend I'd packed all the clothes and items that I cared about and had brought everything home with me on the Friday. The only clothes and other bits I'd left behind were things I didn't really want anyway.

I got the bus to Swiss Cottage and arrived promptly at Claude's Hair Salon.

'Hello, I'm here to be interviewed for the job,' I said.

'Ah, come in, I'm Claude,' he said.

Claude was an olive-skinned, well-groomed Frenchman in his thirties. He was pleasant enough as he told me about the duties I'd have to carry out while working with him. The salon was quite small and it was just Claude and an assistant who worked there, but his last assistant, a young girl, had left the previous weekend so Claude was having to do everything himself, including washing hair and sweeping up. He was desperate for somebody to start straight away.

'Can you start on Monday?' he asked.

'Yes,' I said, smiling from ear to ear.

I left the salon and headed back home to tell my mum the good news. She seemed genuinely pleased for me.

'That's wonderful, Nigel. I'm really pleased for you. All we need now is for Mr Waterman to find you a nice bedsit and you'll be all set,' she said.

I didn't really want to become a barber and I didn't exactly relish living in a bedsit either, but beggars can't be choosers so I would have to work with it until I could figure things out for myself. I'd just come off the back of eight years of relentless abuse of every conceivable kind and my feet hadn't touched the ground in all that time.

The rest of Saturday and Sunday went really well and at 5.30 p.m. on the Sunday afternoon I was due back at Danesbury. I phoned to tell them I would not be returning.

'Hello,' said Mr Wyndham, the History teacher/house help. I recognised his voice straight away.

'Hello, Mr Wyndham, it's Nigel Cooper,' I said.

Although Mr Wyndham typically helped out in Harris House, he'd taught me History for long enough and so he knew me by name.

'Hello, Nigel,' he said.

'I'm just calling to say I'm not coming back tonight. I'm 16 tomorrow and I have a job to start at a hairdressing salon in Swiss Cottage,' I said.

'Oh, OK, Nigel – well, we wish you the best.'

'Thank you.'

'OK then, goodbye,' he said.

And that was it. I was surprised it was so easy. He didn't ask me any questions about my job or anything. I guess I was just another kid less for them to deal with.

Monday came and I hopped on the bus to start my new job assisting Claude, the barber. The first thing he asked me to do when I turned up at 9 a.m. sharp was to make him a cup of tea. Then he showed me where the industrial-size bottles of shampoo were and told me to top up all the shampoo bottles. A few customers started to amble in after that. Claude asked the first man if it was OK if he showed his new assistant how to wash hair, and let me have a go; he agreed. When I'd finished, Claude handed me a towel to wrap around the gentleman's head. While taking up his adjustable seat in front of the mirror the customer told me I had done a good job. After Claude cut his hair, he instructed me to sweep up the trimmings and dispose of them in the bin in the corner.

After three hours of sweeping up hair, refilling shampoo bottles, cleaning sinks and mirrors, taking customers' coats and making cups of tea for Claude, I'd had enough. I left just after lunch and told him that I was sorry but working as a barber's assistant wasn't for me. He understood and offered to pay me for my morning's work, but I didn't take it because I felt guilty that I was leaving him without an assistant.

I just felt that I had a creative side that had been sitting dormant all my life, but was now itching to get out. I'd always had a unique and unorthodox way of thinking and I felt that I had entrepreneurial aspirations too.

So I grabbed my coat, said goodbye to Claude and headed around the corner and crossed the road at the traffic lights. There was a wooden bench at the edge of a small patch of green. I headed over to it and sat down for a moment. Then I sat there, reflecting on my life to date, and wondered what the future held for me.

I looked up at the large trees, the gentle spring wind rustling through their branches and leaves. As I scanned the horizon and the sky, I noticed the moon. I don't recall ever seeing the moon in the sky during the day, especially when the sun was shining too, but there it was, just hanging above the horizon, auspicious. It was so clear I could make out the large basins and other markings on its surface. Transported back there for one final vacation, I closed my eyes, took up my comfy chair on its surface and held my little blue dolly, Lynda's dolly, again. I gazed down at the blue earth below, then looked at dolly and her blue Mackintosh vinyl coat, then I opened my eyes and I was back on earth, sitting on the bench. As I stood up, I glanced at the moon and realised that I wouldn't have to go back there anymore. My eight years of hell were over and now, as the saying goes, the world was my oyster. I looked up at the moon one final time and waved goodbye.

As I walked away from that bench I didn't really know what the future held for me, but then again, who does?

Acknowledgements

I'd like to say a massive thank you to Sara Cywinski and the team at Ebury/Penguin Random House for their kindness, professionalism and wisdom, especially Sara for all her hard editorial work and for suggesting the many improvements that tightened up the story.

I'd also like to thank the fastidious copyeditor, Jane Donovan, for her tremendous work, attention to detail and editorial suggestions. I know it is not a copyeditor's job to give praise and compliments, so whenever I found one written in a comment box in the manuscript, I was overwhelmed by the words – they meant a lot to me. Thank you.

Thanks definitely have to go to my agent, Jon Elek at United Agents, for all his hard work, attention to detail and priceless advice. Thanks also go to Jon's assistant, Millie Hoskins, for picking up my manuscript in the first place and being so enthusiastic about it – without you this book would not have happened.

Last – but never the least – I must thank my unofficial reader, Louise Wessman, who spent countless hours reading the manuscript throughout the various stages of writing. Again, I have incurred a debt by exploiting your time and critique skills. Also, for supporting me emotionally on this painful and difficult journey as I relived my childhood. Thank you.

About the Author

Nigel Cooper is a British author of contemporary fiction, crime and horror. He found his voice as the editor of his own magazine, which he founded in 2004 and ran for seven years before becoming a full-time author of fiction in November 2011. Prior to this he studied screenwriting in London and ran a successful video production company. He has a wealth of experience as a freelance journalist, writing articles, reviews and stories for numerous magazines and newspapers. Nigel also has a degree in classical piano performance and loves nothing more than to sit and play Chopin Nocturnes when he isn't writing. Nigel lives and writes in Cambridgeshire, England.

For more info about the author visit: www.nigelcooperauthor.co.uk